In the Company of Men

IN THE COMPANY OF MEN

Inside the Lives of Male Prostitutes

Michael D. Smith and Christian Grov

Sex, Love, and Psychology
Judy Kuriansky, Series Editor

 PRAEGER

AN IMPRINT OF ABC-CLIO, LLC
Santa Barbara, California • Denver, Colorado • Oxford, England

Copyright 2011 by Michael D. Smith and Christian Grov

All rights reserved. No part of this publication may be reproduced, stored in a retrieval system, or transmitted, in any form or by any means, electronic, mechanical, photocopying, recording, or otherwise, except for the inclusion of brief quotations in a review, without prior permission in writing from the publisher.

Library of Congress Cataloging-in-Publication Data

Smith, Michael D. (Michael David), 1965–
   In the company of men : inside the lives of male prostitutes / Michael D. Smith and Christian Grov.
      p. cm. — (Sex, love, and psychology)
   Includes bibliographical references and index.
   ISBN 978–0–313–38438–7 (hard copy : alk. paper) — ISBN 978–0–313–38439–4 (ebook)
   1. Male prostitution—United States. 2. Male prostitutes—United States. I. Title.
   HQ119.4.U6S65   2011
   306.74′30973—dc22   2011000782

ISBN: 978–0–313–38438–7
EISBN: 978–0–313–38439–4

15 14 13 12 11   1 2 3 4 5

This book is also available on the World Wide Web as an eBook.
Visit www.abc-clio.com for details.

Praeger
An Imprint of ABC-CLIO, LLC

ABC-CLIO, LLC
130 Cremona Drive, P.O. Box 1911
Santa Barbara, California 93116-1911

This book is printed on acid-free paper (∞)

Manufactured in the United States of America

*So many people have helped us with this project that
we could not possibly thank them all here.
However, we would like to give special thanks to our mentors,
Dr. David Seal with the Center for AIDS Intervention Research (CAIR)
at the Medical College of Wisconsin and Dr. Jeffrey Parsons and
the research team at the Center for HIV/AIDS Educational Studies and
Training (CHEST). We also express gratitude
to our undergraduate research assistants at Susquehanna University
(Sam, Joanna, the two Katies, Tim, Jackie, Pat, Peter, and Nick)
and Brooklyn College (Rohima and Tai Asia). Last, a special thanks
to our husbands, Scott and Carl, without whose forbearance and
support none of this would have been possible.*

*To Martin,
the* College Boys, *and all of the guys and girls in the sex work business,
we express our many humble thanks for allowing us to come
into your lives and for being so generous
and open with your amazing experiences.*

CONTENTS

SERIES FOREWORD

At first, when reading *In the Company of Men*, I was drawn into the authors' tale like a fascinating novel. I thought, "This is not only a great story, with fascinating characters and insight into a whole new world, but it will make a great movie!" Indeed, the authors describe the business owner "Martin" and present captivating narratives of his male escort service workers in such detail, you can "see" the rooms they lived and worked in, "hear" their conversations, and "feel" their emotions.

What a great movie this book makes.

But reading on, I am also drawn into the book for professional purposes, as it is a fascinating academic exploration of the world of male escorts. The authors, both members of the Society for the Scientific Study of Sexuality and other professional organizations and faculty members of universities, give us professional insight into the psychological needs and motives of the men— who are very real, not fictional! Health professionals are made privy not only to the inner lives of the people in this world and the types of men who make this choice, but to historical perspectives and to academic research (such as that about the nature of decision making) as well as the specifics of how the escort business works, with clear tables (e.g., about the places, demographics of the escorts, types of sex acts) and creative figures that describe the socio-logical, psychological, and entrepreneurial structures.

The authors, Michael Smith and Christian Grov, both teachers and research-ers, certainly have the expertise to tell this tale. Smith, a clinical psychologist and associate professor of psychology at Susquehanna University, studies male prostitution, identity development, risk behavior, and HIV/AIDS prevention in young men. Co-author Grov, assistant professor in the Department of Health and Nutrition Sciences at the Brooklyn College of the City University of New York and a faculty affiliate with the Center for HIV/AIDS Educational Studies and Training in New York, researches sexual health, HIV/AIDS, and gay and bisexual men.

As I read this book, I was reminded of my first exposure to a type of this male escort world when covering stories about sexuality for a Fox television show, *A Current Affair*. Well-known were the "hostess clubs" where men went to be entertained by women, who served them drinks and lit their cigarettes. I was fascinated to be taken to equivalent "host clubs" where young attractive men would light female clients' cigarettes, pour their drinks, dance with them, and flatter them in talk. The female clientele were either older women who sometimes, I was told, gave the young men Rolex watches and expensive suits. The other customers were young hostesses, tired of serving men and wanting to turn the tables and be served by them! I was privileged to be given an inside look at the time; a producer took me through a door and down a stairway, the walls lined with photos of young men so you could preview your pick. Downstairs in a large room, young men circled the few female clients. A few got up to dance. Others would lean over and light a woman's cigarette. These establishments were part of the Japanese "pink trade"—a term for anything-goes sex. Though once secretive, they now have become commercial and openly available for visitors and tourists.

Of course, escort services are now freely advertised on cable TV stations, clearly seen when flipping channels even from a news show to a comedy series. And of course, prostitution has been "the oldest profession." Then, too, recently there have been many sex scandals with American politicians and celebrities. So this book is timely, as the authors delineate various types and levels of "sex for money" and take us into this world well worth learning about.

Throughout their compelling storytelling, the authors engage us in facing powerful psychosocial questions and issues about the nature of our culture and sexuality itself. As such, this book is a must-read for all health professionals at all levels who want to understand a unique part of our sexual culture and of men's lives and choices.

Any number of Hollywood producers—or documentarians—should also read this book and make the movie.

Dr. Judy Kuriansky

Chapter One

AN ACCIDENTAL AFFAIR

OVERVIEW

This book tells a story about modern male prostitution; as such it is a story about sex work based on the Internet. This is not a particularly new theme—nor the only book that talks about guys and girls working the electronic corner like some cyber Sunset Boulevard; but it does present the lived experiences of men selling their sex, told largely from their own perspectives and often in their own words. Unlike many other published reports, we did not speak with men working the real concrete streets of an American city, men who would typically be called *hustlers*. In academia, this is often described as "street-based" sex work. Instead, we talked with a group which is often harder for researchers to find and even more difficult to access. We talked with escorts or "call boys" if you will, who were employed by a male escort agency located in a small mid-Atlantic city of the United States. Although in writing this book we have pulled information from available research on male sex work, we choose to emphasize the lives of a particular group of men in order to ground our analysis in a particular place and at a particular time. We want you to learn more about today's male prostitutes from the escorts themselves—we want them to share their own stories directly with you. As prostitution is still socially stigmatized and represents a crime throughout most of the United States, the names of the people with whom we spoke and of the agency itself have all been changed.

It took us a while to convince the agency's owner and manager, Martin, that our project would not threaten his staff or business. Early on he seemed to accept that we were not law enforcement, but this did not mean he would allow strangers to become overly familiar with the intimate workings of what represented a semi-legal operation at best. We had contacted him late in the fall of 2003 just as the weather became chilly and damp. A regular email exchange followed as Martin checked our backgrounds and confirmed that we were legitimate researchers whose main interest in his business was one of professional curiosity. As it turns out, Martin was a very friendly man who soon invited us out to lunch at a local Mexican restaurant, mariachi band and all. Once convinced of our intentions, Martin opened up and described his business, staff, and the work they did. He had canvassed his escorts about their willingness to be interviewed; they were almost universally interested. By the early spring of 2004, we had approval and funding for the project. We were thus ready to begin. Martin helped us to edit our interviews, allowed us to recruit participants from among his employees, and said that we could come and go from the agency as we wished—we would have full access to the agency as long as we maintained its confidentiality and did not disrupt the functioning of its business. We worked with his agency for the next several years, eventually speaking with more than 90 percent of the escorts.

The Agency

Our interviews began at Martin's home—the social and business hub for his male escort agency, which we will call *College Boys*. The house was close to the downtown area in a working-class neighborhood of an ethnically diverse and relatively poor section of the city. The city was an attractive business location besides being Martin's home town. Although not one of the larger East Coast metropoli, it was located within a two-hour drive of four of the major Northeast corridor cities. Businessmen and government officials frequently came through staying for a few days at a time, and *College Boys* catered to their interests. The house was convenient to the airport and to the strip of hotels and motels travelers often used. Near a freeway interchange, the agency could send escorts out to clients quickly and clients or staff could reach the agency easily, without much chance of getting lost. Local men also hired the *College Boys* escorts; most of these customers were in relationships and looking for something different or new and most of them were married and wanted a male-on-male encounter of which their wives would never learn. Martin wondered if sometimes the wives knew about their husbands hiring a male escort, even though they might never fully admit this knowledge to themselves.

Martin's home, the left half of an old rambling duplex, had three floors and a basement. Although the basement was predominantly Martin's personal living space, it also was a social area in which escorts often interacted with him on an informal basis or where they could just do laundry. It also served as a private locale where Martin and his staff could discretely discuss business or personal matters out of earshot from anyone else in the house. The house reminded us more of a college fraternity than a brothel: youthful antics were everywhere, people were always around, and one never was quite sure of who would saunter in or what was going to happen next. The house hummed with energy, and buzzed with activity. Martin relished being the center of it all, holding court as a benign and somewhat forgetful monarch (he would say "queen bee"). All of the boys liked him. He was generous to a fault and very fair, but held high expectations that were rarely compromised. About eight years older than most of the escorts who were in their younger 20s, Martin was the cool big brother, understanding and fun, but someone the escorts respected. He naturally attracted people to him and this personal gift was a core factor in the success of his business—handsome, young men responded to him with loyalty and affection. They would literally do anything for him. Clients trusted him, confident that their privacy would be protected and their wishes accommodated. Martin's house allowed it to all come together. It certainly did not hurt that most everyone was making a lot of money.

Built sometime in the years prior to World War II, the house showed its age with peeling paint. The front porch creaked as you walked up to the leaded glass door. Stepping through a small entryway, one could see that the house followed a modified hall and parlor design—once inside, a short hall-way took you up wide stairs where an open arch to the left opened into the first of three rooms running in a line to the rear of the house. Public areas occupied the first floor where three rooms served distinct functions: all of the rooms serving more than one need depending upon who was around and upon the time of day. However, to one degree or another, all of the first-floor rooms were used to receive and entertain clients prior to and after appointments—for escorts, their friends, and family members to socialize and to conduct agency-related business. On weekend nights, men would return from the local clubs or late appointments and crash on one of its empty sofas.

The onetime parlor at the front of the house was primarily used as an office, equipped with two desks, each with a computer. Heavy drapes covered the front windows for privacy, although small narrow windows set high on the side wall allowed some daylight to enter. The manager used one desk for con-ducting agency-related business whereas the escorts predominantly used the second workstation for personal business and entertainment, checked their email, or talked with friends online. An old couch was positioned across from Martin's desk, usually holding one or two boys chatting and joking with their boss. Originally designed to be the dining area, the middle room's functions varied throughout the day. It held a large television complete with gaming station and DVD player. Two threadbare couches and an overstuffed chair took up most of the wall space. From noon until midnight, the room operated as the main social center for the house; here the escorts would lounge on the couches, play video games, and watch movies. Their friends and clients frequently joined them. Martin, his desk located near the archway that divided the front and middle rooms, could survey activity in either and join in when he wished.

A kitchen was the third room at the rear of the house. It led out to an open back stoop and small parking area used by the staff. People often gathered around the center island, which served as a bar late in the night when parties spontaneously erupted as escorts returned from calls or just came to the house accompanied by their friends. During the day, the kitchen was quieter. Sometimes, people would go there to talk or pass through on the way downstairs to Martin's more private basement space. A back stairway leading up to the second floor also attracted some traffic, but it was winding and small—only used frequently by the men living upstairs. Martin kept the refrigerator stocked with drinks and snacks. More nourishing food sometimes found its way into the kitchen among the pizza boxes, TV dinners, and bags of junk food. Occasionally, one of the regular clients would cook a meal for the escorts or bring take-out to eat with them, while watching movies and enjoying the salacious attention of handsome young men good-naturedly trying to drum up some business.

The two upper floors contained five bedrooms and one bathroom. Five of Martin's escorts occupied four of the bedrooms and lived full-time at the house. The front bedroom on the second floor, a spacious affair with a grand bay window, was occupied by a couple—Tommy and Nick—who were both athletic-tanned dancers, educated, and in great demand by well-paying clients. Given the constant level of "comings and goings," privacy was often hard to find at *College Boys*. Martin respected the personal space of escorts living at the agency; he did not expect them to see clients in their rooms, but treated each person's living space as their own. They could stay for as long or short a time as they wished, with some using the building as temporary housing between apartments and others for a longer-term residence. One escort, not getting along with his parents, lived at the house during the summers and other breaks from college. Although Martin did not charge rent for the four bedrooms, those residing at the agency occasionally gave him money for food and utilities. As will be discussed later in more detail, escorts not assisting financially were thought of as "using" Martin by the others. This caused some tension among the escorts and was a source of gossip and bickering behind Martin's back. But Martin did not let on even if he ever noticed.

Martin's fifth bedroom was exclusively used to entertain clients. This type of space is known in the escort business as an "incall" facility—as opposed to seeing clients at their homes or hotels, known as doing an "outcall." The room was well-apportioned and near the head of the stairs and bathroom. Towels and cotton bathrobes were kept there; sheets and blankets were washed after each client call. A dresser was placed diagonally in the far corner at the foot of the soft queen-sized bed, piled with comfortable pillows. The old dresser held a small television/DVD unit; several pornographic films sat in a stack next to it. Various flavors and consistencies of sexual lubricants had been arranged on a mirrored tray near the television as well as a basket of different types and sizes of condoms. Dildos, vibrators, handcuffs, and other sex toys discretely awaited use in the top right-hand drawer. Martin expected his clients and escorts to consistently practice safer sex, requiring all of his employees to use condoms. Similar to other studies examining the sexual risk behavior of indoor escorts (e.g., Estep, Waldorf, & Marotta, 1992; Vanwesenbeeck, 2001), our research at *College Boys* strongly suggested Martin's escorts almost always protected their health and that of their clients (Smith & Seal, 2007).

Martin's Story

We interviewed Martin first; it would be the initial conversation of several held with him over the years. Martin closed the door of the incall room where we were to talk, crossed the room, and then lounged in the upholstered chair next to the tastefully-draped window. Bright sunlight peered around the layered curtains. He must have known that we were going to ask about how he started the business and was ready to talk about it. Martin smiled at our obvious curiosity. He then became serious, moving his leg down from the padded arm so that he could lean forward and face the bed where the tape recorder's microphone perched expectantly. Always charming and a very good storyteller, Martin spoke about the beginning of his own sex work and the creation of his escort agency. The story he related was one we would hear in several different variations from the men working at *College Boys*.

After high school, Martin had worked his way into a corporate training position for a locally headquartered firm. The company had a number of locations spread across several states. Then in his early twenties, Martin had a mortgage and a car payment; he felt successful. Being closeted with a girlfriend and more self-conscious about his appearance in those days, Martin had occasionally hired male escorts when he wanted to have sex with another man:

> I actually hired escorts when I was pretty young [compared to most customers] because I had put on a significant amount of weight; I was closeted. I didn't want people to know I was gay. I didn't go to gay bars. I didn't know anybody. I wasn't

out at all, so the way that I dealt with that was to hire escorts. That's how I discovered the world of escorting.

Martin felt successful in his job. He worked at the firm for several years, eventually buying a car and home. Just as his life was getting started, Martin hit unexpected financial hard times. He became unemployed when the company downsized and laid off almost everyone in the staff development department.

Having lost his home with the layoff, though not without options, Martin soon found work managing a hotel and bar; it provided him with a place to stay and some income. However, the job did not last and Martin was soon out of work once again. The unemployment checks could not cover all his bills and the cash-strapped situation gave him an idea. He remembered hiring escorts and the good money they made, money he had paid them. Having slimmed down and now more open about his sexuality, at least with his friends, Martin decided to secretly try escorting for himself. Through this decision, Martin expressed a theme of coping with unmet or blocked economic goals that was ubiquitous among the escorts we interviewed. It seemed to be a key situational precondition for men starting to consider prostitution as a viable form of employment. The desirability of sex work as an income opportunity increased as one's financial situation grew increasingly discrepant from important material goals. This presupposed that an individual already had some familiarity with the monetary possibilities sex work could provide, which Martin already had due to his past role as a client. When in financial straights, Martin considered his options with this potential in mind:

> At that time I had lost a significant amount of weight. I was in pretty good shape. I had hair [laughing as he rubbed his hand across a balding scalp]. So I thought that I could make money escorting. I advertised in the [gay newspaper] and I advertised online which was virtually a free ad. [As a result,] I found quite a few local clients.

Although Martin earned some money working as an escort, he soon discovered that many potential clients preferred to hire men in their late teens or early twenties. Martin, then about 25, was what he classified as "too old" with the "wrong" type of body to be as marketable as he would have liked. Youth and good looks were the coin of the realm in escorting then, as they certainly are now. Looking for additional opportunities, he got the idea to start an escort agency from a random conversation he had with another escort in a similar bind. This individual told Martin, "that if he ever had the opportunity to have five or six 18-year-old boys he thought he could make a fortune." Martin still smiled three years after that chance conversation; the concept for *College Boys* had been born.

Being ambitious and with personal experience as an escort bolstering his self-confidence, Martin decided to see if he could find some guys for whom he would arrange advertising, set up appointments, provide transportation, and screen potential clients in return for a cut of their hourly fee. He possessed a definite business model in his mind, much as any entrepreneur might. But whom would he hire, and how? An opportunity soon presented itself. Having become bolder and more outgoing since his days in the closet, Martin approached a good-looking young man who was working late at a convenience store. He asked if the man would like to work as a male stripper. To Martin's surprise, Aaron agreed; one thing led to another and the *College Boys* agency was open for business. Aaron, a masculine and personable young blond man with a girlfriend, turned out to be a highly successful escort, especially once he learned to manage having sex with male clients. Martin told the story this way:

> I stumbled upon a kid one night, I was actually coming from an appointment with a client; the kid was working as a grocery clerk, stock boy. It was Aaron; that was my first employee. I gave him my number. I didn't have a business card or anything like that, nothing. I told him that I wanted see if he would be interested in working with me. The way that I promoted him was as a stripper for men. Whatever he felt comfortable with beyond that was up to him, anticipating he wouldn't do much more than maybe get serviced [receiving oral sex from a client]. Within a short period of time I think I did like one or two doubles with him [going out to see clients together]. He did just about everything including bottoming [acting as the receptive partner in anal sex] because that's just what we did at the beginning. Through him, he had a friend, [who became] my second person. It was a friend of his who was, I guess, bisexual, and then I had two people. So there were three of us.

The agency grew and prospered. During the two years between that time and when we conducted our first *College Boys* interviews, Martin had developed a staff of about 30 escorts and was working with scores of clients per month. He was now running a successful Internet-based enterprise; Martin became an e-entrepreneur and intentionally so. It was not an accident that he chose the online environment in which to primarily advertise and establish his business. By the time we began our research, more than 90 percent of Martin's business came from his website and online banners. Martin maintained a discrete ad in the local Yellow Pages under "escort services" and he and the escorts always passed out business cards when they went out to local gay clubs or when one of the escorts performed in public as a male stripper. Distributing business cards also allowed Martin to recruit new escorts from the young men who patronized these clubs should anyone catch his eye as a promising candidate. However, like much of the gay-oriented erotic industry, more and more of his business occurred online with less and less conducted in more traditional outlets.

Demand—The Clients' Point of View

Despite changes in the sexual marketplace created by widespread development of Internet-based commerce, the basics of supply and demand for male
sex work seem to have changed little since ancient times. Typically, more
mature and older men seek the social and erotic company of attractive younger men, exchanging their experience and money for youth and sexual virility.
We had only one opportunity to interview a client for our study. Richard had
been hiring young men with the agency almost since the beginning and had
struck up a friendship with Martin. In his early 40s, an amateur web designer,
and a full-time musician, Richard was contracted to create and maintain the
College Boys website once the agency went online early in its existence.
Richard discussed a conversation he had with the first escort that he ever
hired:

> He [the escort] really viewed what he did as a ministry. He saw that people had a
> need and everyone's need was different. Some just wanted sex. Maybe they were
> married and were trying to express a part of themselves that they couldn't in their
> marriage. Others were looking for companionship. Others were trying to explore
> some of their fantasies that they could not in their relationship. So he looked upon
> what he did as providing a safe way for clients to do that, to do those things or to
> experience whatever they needed to experience. And the way he was talking about
> it was something that I could really relate to. Obviously it fulfilled what I was look-
> ing for at the time. I quite often wonder if I had met someone else and it hadn't
> gone as well, would I ever have hired a second time?

Richard went on to discuss that over the years his own views of why clients
hired escorts and how escorts could uphold their end of the transaction had
grown to closely mirror those of this young man. He related that the best
escorts met the client's expectations, "If you're paying for something you
should get what you're paying for. I think there are those escorts who are very
sensitive to meeting the client's needs and then there are those who are more
sensitive to just getting the buck out of the pie." The best escorts could communicate with clients and meet their emotional as well as their sexual needs.

In these comments, Richard discusses several themes that the escorts themselves raised and that have been debated in other research studies (e.g., Morse,
Simon, Balson, & Osofsky, 1992). First, men hire escorts in order to accomplish goals that they would not otherwise be able to achieve. Some men married to women and ostensibly heterosexual in the rest of their lives might
desire to have sex with another man. Not willing to run the risk of exposure
by going to a gay club, running a personal ad, chatting on a gay website, or
hanging out in a gay-oriented adult book store, park, or bathroom, this individual could hire an escort. Such a client could compartmentalize homosexual
experiences within the anonymity of his interaction with a prostitute,

knowing that the man he hired had real incentives to keep their meetings private and that the relationship with the male sex worker would not intrude into other areas of the client's life. It was a business transaction, time-limited and very discrete. Martin estimated that 60 percent of agency clients were men married to women.

Martin also noted that an additional 30 percent of his clients were men in long-term relationships with other men, perhaps highlighting the issue of sexual variety that Richard also touched upon in his comments. Recent research has shown some men express strong preferences for variety in their sex lives either in terms of sexual activities, different partners, or a combination of both (Peplau, 2003). In hiring male sex workers, it is not only men in relationships with women who can increase their sexual repertoire; anyone could experience activities their regular partner might not wish to perform, enjoy sexual activity with additional sex partners outside a primary relationship, or expand their horizons in ways they might not have previously attempted (e.g., in terms of sexual variations such as sadomasochism). This variety could be accomplished without threatening the emotional integrity of a primary relationship because the paid sexual situation was neither initiated by nor contained within a context of personal intimacy, but via a commercial transaction. No emotional investment on the client's part, or with the paid sexual partner for that matter, would be required. As long as one's primary partner was not negatively impacted by the encounter with a male sex worker (directly or indirectly), then hiring another man could satisfy important needs while preserving other areas of the client's life intact—all for a reasonable fee.

This is not to say that clients do not report hiring sex workers for emotional or relational reasons, Richard actually notes that many clients do exactly that. Often, such non-physical needs interweave with sexual activities during an appointment with an escort. There may also be times when clients hire only for emotional or relational goals. Even though these "social" appointments may be less common than calls where some degree of sexual activity occurs, they do take place as one escort, Nick, described in almost adoring terms:

> There's a little old man; he's so cute, I have never seen him take his clothes off. I've seen him seriously 20 or 30 times and I've never seen him take his clothes off. This little old guy—all he wants to do, he just wants to sit there, put his head on my lap, and watch TV for like an hour and tell me about his week. Like that's all he wants to do. I just love him.

Most escorts enjoyed these types of calls very much and in some cases, friendships grew between clients and the men they hired. As when hiring for sexual needs, the customer who seeks relational services from an escort is better able to insure that he will receive the attention he wants from an individual whom he will find desirable. He does not run the risk of rejection. The client has a man who will listen to him and talk for an appointed amount of time. He can remain more in control of the social and emotional aspects of this situation than would normally be possible in a non-commercial interaction. The escort is obliged to provide this experience by virtue of his employment, and some male escorts specialize in it. For the customer, the illusion is that of socializing with an emotionally available and attractive man who will focus only on the client; the boundaries and pace of that interaction are dictated through the relational power of the client's role as patron.

The role of employer created another advantage that Richard discussed in his interview. He talked about a time in his life when he was not interested in a relationship, but still wanted male companionship. He did not feel confident going out to gay bars where he could meet other men, or in meeting men online. Richard found that hiring escorts got him exactly what he sought with less effort than would otherwise be possible:

> I wasn't into the game playing online. I found that to be rather repulsive, you know the lying and the bullshitting and all that. So hiring an escort was very appealing to me because it was what it was. There was no game plan. I wouldn't have to worry about hurting another person's feelings if it were a one night stand or anything like that. Plus, the bottom line, you could hire what you're interested in. Online, you have to go through the thing of getting a picture. You have to wonder, "Do you like it? Is this really the person or was it ten years ago?" You don't have to deal with any of that when hiring an escort. I hired someone I was attracted to and was able to do the things I found interesting. I didn't have to worry what the other person was wanting out of the relationship because they were there to fulfill what I desired. That's why I hired, and that's what I got.

Not only could a client get exactly when he wanted, when he wanted, the client was able to satisfy his needs immediately and without risk of rejection or entanglement. If one had the money, sex and company could be had without perceived effort or emotional cost—hiring a male escort represented a safe, expedient, and satisfying transaction to meet important needs that would otherwise have been quite difficult to accomplish. Such needs have apparently always existed through recorded Western history, and some men have been willing to provide them in exchange for a fee (Dorais, 2005; Dover 1989).

Supply—The Structure of American Male Prostitution

Venues prior to the Internet

Researchers in the years before Internet-based commerce recorded several different venues for male sex work and a number of "levels" in terms of perceived quality and desirability among which sex workers assorted themselves, marketed their services, and established prices. Their findings suggested that

Table 1.1
Elements of Male Sex Work

Venue of Sex Work	Services Provided	Work Commitment
Hustlers	*Massage-Body Work*	*Incidental*
Streets, Subway Platforms	Professional or amateur	Not sex work identified
Parks, Beaches	Can be erotic in nature	Chance encounters
Many solicit online now	Little overt sexual activity	Not actively seeking work
Bar Hustlers	*Limited Sexual Activity*	*Part-Time*
Gay Bars & Clubs	Restrictions in activity	Identifies as sex worker
Bathhouses	Main activity is oral sex	A few clients/week
Many solicit online now	Often no kissing or anal sex	Usually has other job
Escorts	*Unlimited Sexual Activity*	*Full-Time*
Independent	Few limits on activity	May identify professionally
Agency-Based	Involves anal intercourse	Has many clients
Online Ads	Safer sex still the norm	Often main income source
Kept Boys	*Relational Services*	*Career*
Patron(s) support	Conversation, emotional	Identifies as professional
Paid boyfriend	support, paid dates/trips, or	Main source of income
Typically do not advertise	other social activities	Longer-term involvement

the lowest rung of this hierarchy was occupied by men soliciting clients directly off the street or in public parks and rest rooms—the hustlers. In one of the first social-scientific studies of male sex workers in the United States, Butts (1947) noted that these young men were often homeless and transient. He would take them to local restaurants, give them a hot meal, and listen to their stories. They appreciated being able to eat and talk about their lives with someone who seemed interested in them as people and not only as sexual objects. Hustlers working the street are often heavily involved with drugs and alcohol (El-Bassel, Schilling, Gilbert, Faruque, Irwin, & Edlin, 2000; Morse, Simon, Baus, Balson, & Osofsky, 1992), likely to be under-aged and runaway youth (Leichtentritt & Arad, 2005; Price, Scanlon, & Janus, 1984), and exchange sex for survival needs (Coleman, 1989; Newman, Rhodes, & Weiss, 1998). Teenaged juvenile delinquents were often recorded as working the streets for extra money, with strict codes of conduct governing what they would and would not do with other men and equally strict punishments when these rules were violated (Allen, 1980).

Next in the old hierarchy were men who worked the gay clubs and bathhouses. Known as "bar hustlers," this group of men had the resources to gain entry into such establishments, could present themselves well to potential clients, and thus commanded better fees. Proprietors and bar hustlers often had informal arrangements regarding the rules of the house, any cut of the hustler's fee owed to the establishment, and which clients should receive special attention. Such indoor venues were considered to be safer and more desirable than working the street, with protection from the weather and less likelihood of random victimization or police harassment. When an arrangement existed between the house and a sex worker, he could be even more assured of regular business and perhaps, even a safe location to entertain his customers. Bar and bathhouse hustlers were a mainstay of the gay subculture for decades (perhaps centuries), though worked at the sufferance of what could be mercurial relationships with the proprietors upon which their trade depended.

Close to the top of the pre-Internet ladder were the call boys; they were the true escorts who either worked independently or through an agency. Many had graduated from the lower levels of sex work through careful planning, husbanding of resources, or ongoing support from regular customers. Some began their careers as escorts without working their way up the ladder. These men likely possessed more social capital in terms of an education, knowledge of middle- or upper-class culture, and greater linguistic fluency. Such skills allowed the escort to socialize with clients appropriately, hold a conversation about recent events, and know proper etiquette in a public setting. Men at this level of the profession may have originated from the upper classes themselves, or gained experience with such norms through opportunities afforded by clients and other mentors. An escort would have a "call list" of clients who had his telephone number and would call to set up an appointment. Thus, the escort was not as dependent on a constant stream of new customers and could develop more personal relationships with them. Clients using call boys were often more affluent, with more to lose if their use of their services became known. They also might want more of a "boyfriend experience" with an escort taking him out to eat, for a show, on short trips or wanting to talk about current events and other more cultural topics. Escorts could, and still do, charge more for their services and often spend a significant portion of an appointment socializing rather than in sexual activity—significant differences from the work of hustlers.

When working for an agency, the escort provided a portion of his fee to a manager in exchange for marketing, incall, and scheduling services. Many escorts preferred working for agencies, especially when less familiar with the business, because an agency could pre-screen clients, knew which customers to trust and what they typically wanted on an appointment. Agency affiliation offered a sense of location and place that in many ways legitimized the escort's activities as true employment. However, *College Boys* escorts frequently discussed trade-offs inherent to working as an independent escort versus working for Martin. Working for an agency may also have its downside for an individual escort. He would have less control over which clients he took and might have been mismatched with a particular client in the agency's attempt to send someone out to a call even though that person may not have been exactly what the client wanted (Smith, Grov, & Seal, 2008). Not surprisingly given the choices they had made, most were quite satisfied to have Martin arrange appointments and do the "leg work" instead of assuming these responsibilities for themselves.

Kept boys occupied the highest rank of the ladder, acting as pseudo-boyfriends for only one or a very few patrons—wealthier clients who supported the sex worker in exchange for a more extended and frequent relationship with him. Kept boys often lived with their "sugar daddies" who provided housing, cars, clothes, tuition, and sometimes, even a regular paycheck. Some boys had their "daddies" pay rent instead of living in. Men working at this level never had to solicit for new customers (unless the relationship with their patron fell apart); their world was more akin to that of a well-ensconced mistress than that of a street worker. They looked down on other sex workers as "prostitutes" and may not have even considered themselves to be in the business, but to have an arrangement, or an understanding, with their affluent older men to the mutual benefit of both parties. In our own interviews with the *College Boys* escorts, kept boys were often disparaged as "pets" who sacrificed personal integrity and independence for money and a cushy life.

Online Venues

With the widespread penetration of the Internet in the 1990s and the migration of men seeking sexual encounters from other men into its chat-rooms and electronic bulletin boards, sex workers found themselves using e-media to solicit clients at an increasing pace. By the early twenty-first century, researchers had noted a significant shift from street and bar solicitation to escorts advertising their services online (Parsons, Bimbi, & Halkitis, 2001). Instead of putting themselves at risk and outside by working the parks, strolls, and sidewalks, street hustlers were increasingly visiting chatrooms and identifying themselves as available for hire. Bar and bathhouse hustlers also began to advertise online. These men, often with fewer resources, could access computers in coffee houses and libraries for little or no cost. Personal ads and chatrooms could be used for free. Although street and bar hustlers have not disappeared from American cities, they have become less numerous as more effective and comfortable marketing venues became possible. They could enjoy some of the benefits previously available only to escorts in terms of working from home and the ability to pre-screen clients. They also could reach more potential customers. Furthermore, by advertising and participating in electronic forums catering to men seeking sex from other men, they increased customers' ability to find them.

Sexual commercialization of the Internet has also changed how independent escorts and agencies conducted their businesses. Instead of relying solely on print advertising, escorts now targeted their marketing efforts toward those venues where they had the best chance of coming into contact with customers; the same chatrooms and e-bulletin boards were now being used by men who might have previously worked the streets. Entrepreneurs, noting the potential demand, set up classified ad websites where escorts could pay a fee to advertise—complete with pictures, descriptions, and listings of services and fees. Entire marketplaces for male prostitutes appeared on the Internet. Thousands of ads are posted in them at any given time, neatly organized by city and cross-indexed such that potential clients could search for particular activities, physical attributes, and price points. Free versus paid advertising websites have created new strata among male prostitutes such that those marketing themselves in the open access domains are often considered "lower class" or "less professional" than men paying for ads on male escort websites. Men advertising in the open access, no-fee venues typically charge less for their services than men do on the paid websites, sometimes half as much of the more expensive fees. They may be viewed as transient or incidental sex workers looking to make a "quick buck"; men who might not work on a regular basis or who might be less reliable.

The Internet has impacted the clientele of male prostitutes as well. Men who might not have wanted to go to a bar or cruise the street for a hustler could now search for sex on demand with another man from the safety and anonymity of their own homes or cell phones. They could see what they might be getting before even meeting the sex worker, and could talk with him via Internet chat in order to confirm that their interests and financial expectations were compatible. It is likely that this has led to an increased demand for male sex work just as the number of men who might consider earning income in this way has also expanded. The overall marketplace has grown significantly. It has entered parts of the United States outside of the major urban centers, areas that might not have known male prostitution in the past. Clients have even established their own escort rating and customer satisfaction websites where posted reviews note whether the sex worker met expectations in terms of looks, personality, and activities. Prices are reported and personal accounts are compared. Favorably reviewed escorts receive much more business. Escorts themselves respond to negative reviews, hoping to miti-gate the damage done to their professional reputations. Thousands of reviews are posted each year from men hiring escorts throughout the world. Martin was quite aware of the Internet's impact upon his business, especially from clients posting online reviews of his escorts. Each morning, Martin checked the cus-tomer satisfaction website and would use positive reviews of escorts in his own advertising, e.g., "John has many good reviews—check him out."

Services Provided

Broadly speaking, the services which male sex workers sell to customers can be separated into sexual and non-sexual (what we will call relational) catego-ries, and into physical and relational labor. Although later sections of this book will address these areas in more detail, it would be useful to introduce them here in order to provide some general outlines for the types of labor male sex workers sell to their clients. The term "sex worker" may actually be too general in this regard, as some men do not engage in sexual activity with clients (or at least not with all of their clients), even though strong erotic undertones often weave through these interactions. As will be discussed, sex work varies by the degree of physical contact and erotic involvement between the worker and his clients; the same sex worker can vary this involvement from time to time or from client to client depending upon personal preferences or financial needs.

Physical labor involves using one's body for an economic purpose. In sex work, physical labor signifies the commercialization of the erotic body whether or not sexual activity actually occurs between consumer and provider. Thus, nude dancing and pornography are considered forms of sex work even though neither the dancer nor the actor engages in sexual behavior with the person paying for their products. The situation itself is erotic, and possesses inherent value for someone seeking out this type of experience. A key difference among these types of jobs and the type of sex work primarily discussed in this book is that prostitution and escorting involve the presence of provider and consumer in the same environment for one-on-one interactions. As we will see, not all of these interactions involve sexual activity, but they all represent some form of sexualized context or behavior, and some element of implied or overt eroticism which yields commercial value.

Men providing *massage* and *bodywork* exemplify a gray zone between a legal personal service and a sexualized encounter forbidden by law in most of the United States. Bodywork represents a general category of techniques that all involve physical contact between a provider and client with the purpose of improving the client's well-being and health, or with the intent of addressing physical or emotional complaints. Some consider it a branch of complimentary and alternative medicine (CAM). CAM has increasingly gained in popularity over the past several decades (there is even a National Center for Complimentary and Alternative Medicine, NCCAM, within the U.S. National Institutes of Health). Massage is included under the CAM umbrella, as would be acupuncture, energy work, respiration therapy, and various forms of yoga. Most states require some type of professional certification for an individual to advertize themselves as a "masseur," and in fact, one could safely assume that most bodywork conducted in the United States does not involve an erotic component.

We will consider bodywork which includes some level of eroticization for purposes of our analysis of male sex work. Bodyworkers advertising online for clients frequently present themselves as providing a massage, but do not label themselves as certified or professionally trained. In such cases, advertisements often include the word "experienced" to indicate that the provider may have given massages in a specific style (e.g., "experienced in sports massage") without having received formal education in that method. Also likely are other men who identify themselves as having professional credentials—bodyworkers who list the styles in which they have gained advanced proficiency and can legally offer as massage to paying clients as part of a legitimate fiduciary transaction.

What these two groups of men share in common is the inclusion of an erotic component in their advertising and their services. Masseurs will identify themselves as providing "erotic" or "nude" massage to indicate that the masseur will work on the client's genitalia and other erogenous zones and/or that the masseur will not be clothed while providing massage to the client. "Mutual touching" is a term used to indicate that a client may feel free to touch the nude body of the masseur or perhaps, even engage in masturbation and/or fellatio with him. In an erotic massage, the terms "happy ending" and "release" signify that the masseur will bring the client to orgasm (typically via masturbation, though perhaps through oral sex), but that the masseur may not himself achieve orgasm with the client. Thus, experiences with erotic massage could run the whole gamut from a mutually nude encounter that does not include sexual activity to one that involves some level of genital contact and sexual satisfaction for the client. Often, sex workers advertise as providing massages in order to evade censorship or law enforcement action even though they might not actually do much bodywork with their clients.

Thus, the next level of service provided by male sex workers would be explicit sexual activity without the inclusion of a therapeutic bodywork component, or that which would occur before, during, or after a massage or other forms of bodywork. Many sex workers limit their activities to those deemed less personally and physically intrusive. Kissing and anal sex are both frequently curtailed activities; clients often comment in their reviews on the lack of escorts who will kiss, especially in an open-mouthed fashion. Many *College Boys* escorts considered kissing "too personal" an activity; one that felt too uncomfortable in a work situation and which violated emotional boundaries they did not want to cross with customers. Anal sex was often viewed similarly, although here issues of power, dominance, and trust also entered into the equation. Anal sex implied a more engaged relationship with the client, or one which left the sex worker more vulnerable (especially in the receiving or "bottom" position). Thus, it too was often limited and this can frequently be seen in the online advertisements of many sex workers. Men identifying themselves as heterosexual are especially likely to limit their activities with clients, allowing themselves to be "serviced" by a client or to assume the insertive ("top") position in anal sex but not more. Men working with fewer predetermined limits usually advertize themselves as such, sometimes using the term "full service" to indicate that they will engage in most any activity and defining whether they prefer to be insertive, receptive, or both (also known as "versatile") with respect to anal sex. This is not to say that "full service" sex workers engage in unprotected intercourse with clients—although some male sex workers will advertise or imply being open to sex without condoms (e.g., "All fantasies fulfilled," "no limits," "uninhibited"). Most men, however, will state "safe sex only" in their advertising.

Sex for pay would be legally defined as prostitution, though few men selling their sex would self-identify themselves as a prostitute. In fact, none of the *College Boys* we interviewed spontaneously described themselves in such a manner. Instead, they most frequently used the term "escort" to label their sex work. Some men, often when joking around or discussing more explicit aspects of their jobs would call themselves "hookers" (a term more frequently used to describe female street prostitutes), reflecting a common undercurrent in Western gay culture for men to cross-identify with feminine gender roles when discussing sex, dress, or behavior (Bailey & Zucker, 1995; Pillard, 1991). However, when seriously discussing their work all of the *College Boys* we interviewed quite clearly defined themselves as offering more than just sex for sale, and often went to great lengths describing the differences between *escorts* and *prostitutes*.

For them, escorting involved the provision of *relational services* to the client in terms of conversation, emotional support, and non-sexual activity; the escorts perceived these services to be absent from prostitution, representing a key point of departure from being "just" a hustler or hooker. Escorts go out with clients to dinner or a movie, take trips with them, spend the night, cuddle at home on the client's couch; they are paid temporary boyfriends who meet the client's interpersonal as well as sexual needs. Kissing, affection, holding hands, and other such tokens of emotional intimacy could occur during such interactions. Thus, escorts sell what has been termed a *boyfriend experience* (also known as a BFE) to their customer, a fantasy for which the client is happy to pay. Kept boys would provide such an experience on a more or less full-time basis. As we will see later in the book, escorts frequently appraised this relational component as being the service clients valued most and one which helped escorts adjust to the stigma and stress of having sex for pay.

Work Commitment

Male sex workers also differed among themselves in terms of their occupational commitment to the job. Such commitment can be gauged through the number of hours worked with clients and the degree to which sex work became an aspect of a man's occupational identity. As in other forms of work, one can often select the degree of involvement with a particular job ranging

from moonlighting once in a while for some extra income to making a significant personal commitment by developing a career in that field. With the
Internet, it has become increasingly easy for young men to work occasionally
and/or intermittently through selling their sexual services to earn extra cash.
Although incidental sex work in the United States was reported in the
1940s by Butts (1947), typically with men who were looking to supplement
their income and already had a regular means of support, the widespread
availability of the Internet in almost every American home has certainly
brought the awareness of such an opportunity to many more individuals than
would have previously been the case.

A young man "lounging" in an Internet chatroom might see another person
offering or discussing sexual services for pay and could "private message" that
person to talk about it with him. Likewise, such a person could be engaged in
other conversations and have someone message him asking if the young man
would like to be paid for some sexual act (typically to receive fellatio from the
paying customer). Such events seem to occur with relative frequency and, as
will be seen in later chapters, represented one way in which Martin searched
for new escorts. Even if someone prior to the Internet had been aware of making extra money by selling sexual services, they may not have known how or
where to bring about that opportunity. Such an individual also might not have
wanted to work a stroll or park given that these areas were typically in less
desirable or safe parts of town and individuals loitering there were often identified as homosexuals, harassed by the police, or victimized by a more criminal
or delinquent element. In previous years, such informational, psychological,
and physical barriers likely prevented many people who might have
worked incidentally as prostitutes from doing so. Most of these barriers have
been removed by the anonymity and interpersonal distance afforded via
the Internet.

Some men make a conscious decision to engage in sex work more regularly.
Their increased commitment to sex work is represented by working part- or
even full-time as a sex worker and in some way acknowledging their work as
such. Here, the individual probably identifies himself as an "escort" or "rent
boy" and begins to incorporate this occupational affiliation within his sense
of personal identity. People in his social network may be informed of the work
and he may be in contact with other sex workers. The part- or full-time male
escort often devotes a significant amount of time and effort to his occupation.
He depends upon it more for his livelihood and for achieving financial and
individual goals. Even working part-time could accomplish worthwhile goals.
During his interview Rick told us, "I could make an extra three or four hundred bucks real quick to go home with. So basically I only did it so that I could
pay for college and then work less and still have money to do what I wanted."
Some men chose to work part-time because they were going to school or had

other jobs, seeing sex work as a way to augment their income and maximize the amount of money they could earn during the time they were not involved with other occupationally related tasks. As we will see, men supporting themselves as escorts could often attain desired lifestyles with a shorter work-week and less burdensome labor than afforded by other types of employment.

CONCLUSION—THE REST OF THE STORY

Between the words of this introduction to American male prostitution is a more complete story waiting to be told. We continue in the next chapter with a history of male sex work that emphasizes how social scientists have tried to explain it over the past one hundred years. In the later chapters, the book turns to the thoughts and experiences of the male escorts themselves. We discuss how they get into the business, how escorting impacts their relationships, and the nature of their work. We expand upon the needs and experiences of clients, the men who helped make the *College Boys* agency viable, to show how escorts tailored their services to match customer interests. In the appendices, you will find a table showing the demographic characteristics of the escorts and a listing of all the people involved with the agency along with some personal information about each one. These appendices will be useful background information as you read about Martin and his staff. Thus, the rest of this book will provide a deeper and more thorough analysis of the ideas broached in our opening chapter, settling *College Boys* into place among its peers and allowing you to come backstage with us into a fraternity of young escorts making their way down the wild electronic highway.

work research, such a disposition is likely a result of the two aforementioned biases: (1) social and political pressure to avoid controversial research and (2) prevailing sex-negative sentiments creating an atmosphere where researchers felt "obligated" to narrow their studies on those who seem at highest risk of HIV and STI transmission, substance abuse, and mental health problems. Certainly, this does not discount other factors that may also play into the overrepresentation of street-based samples of sex workers. For example, it might also be due to subject availability and ease of recruitment (street-based sex workers congregate in specific places at specific times), a lack of researcher knowledge of the diversity of sex work venues, or lack of researcher access to those other venues.

In defense of the abundance of research incorporating street-based samples, we argue that this focus makes sense from a public health perspective in the U.S. socio-political climate. Why spend valuable research dollars and time doing work with populations who are not at higher risk for HIV transmission, are not homeless, and/or who do not have drug or mental health problems? What can society gain by studying relatively well-to-do, educated sex workers who are involved in the field to maintain a middle class lifestyle, supplement their income, or pay for personal luxuries? Is it threatening to think that those involved in sex work could be similar to most adults in the United States? Is it safer to think of sex workers purely as lower class, marginal individuals, who "are not like the rest of us"? Even though this book cannot answer all these questions, the lack of research in this arena raises important questions about what insights could be gained from research involving men who do not work on the street. We explore some of these possibilities in the next section.

A Sex-Positive Shift in Research

Admittedly, the public health perspective is a lens researchers can use to prioritize their research foci, but there is a tremendous amount to be learned when viewing sex work through other lenses, be they sociological, anthropological, or psychological. For example, Sanders (2005) applied the idea of "emotional labor" to female sex workers. Emotional labor is a type of work, unlike physical labor, whereby certain occupations require the expenditure of emotions as a facet of the work experience (Hochschild, 1983). For example, health care workers often convey compassion and empathy with their patients. In her study, Sanders found female sex workers are actively engaged in several forms of emotional labor in addition to physical labor (i.e., physically having sex).

Another researcher, Vanwesenbeeck (2005) studied the impact of sex work and emotional labor on "burnout" among female sex workers. She compared her sample of sex workers to others who involve emotions as part of their labor experience—nurses. Surprisingly, Vanwesenbeeck found that burnout was not as much associated with engaging in sex work, but rather with the conditions that surround sex work, such as stigma/negative social reactions around being a sex worker, and lack of a worker-supportive environment. While this was not the conclusion Vanwesenbeeck drew, could it be these "poor" conditions surrounding sex work are actually the factors that contribute to some of the negative outcomes other researchers have identified among sex workers (such as substance abuse)? And, by improving such poor working conditions, can we create safer and more supportive environments for sex workers, thereby reducing some of the negative outcomes other researchers have observed in some samples of sex workers? A 2009 study published in the *American Journal of Public Health* would suggest so. Lippman et al. (2009) sought to determine the association of social environmental factors with condom use and sexually transmitted infections (STIs) among 420 male and female sex workers participating in an STI/HIV prevention study in Corumbá, Brazil. They found that increased social cohesion was inversely associated with unprotected sex among women, and there was a marginal association among men. Women's increased participation in social networks was associated with a *decrease* in unprotected sex, as was men's access to and management of social and material resources. Social-environmental factors were not associated with STIs. Their study concluded that the social context within which populations negotiate sexual behaviors is associated with condom use. In total, the perspectives put forth by Sanders (2005), Vanwesenbeeck (2005), and Lippman et al. (2009) provide a smorgasbord of ways to re-think sex work. Such ideas would likely not emerge if sex work is only viewed from a deficit (cause-cure) model.

Thus far, we have discussed an accumulation of factors that have inhibited viewing sex work from perspectives outside a public health model. Although limited, there has been increasing interest in sex work from a more sex-positive perspective. This trend has occurred both for male and female sex workers and has emerged both within research and via grassroots organizations. Much of this work has challenged status quo and has started to alter the trajectory of sex work research.

In 1999 and 2000, Jeffrey Parsons and other researchers at the Center for HIV/AIDS Educational Studies and Training (CHEST) conducted a study called *The Classified Project*—a qualitative and quantitative investigation of Internet-based male escorts. Findings from this study have run counter to many of the popular beliefs about this population. For instance and as already briefly mentioned, they found that a majority of the sex workers interviewed use condoms with their clients. Moreover, they found that sex workers often use their interactions with clients as an opportunity to *educate* clients about sex and HIV (Parsons, Koken, & Bimbi, 2004).

Others have noted how stigma and stigma management play central roles in the lives of sex workers (Padilla et al., 2008). Mark Padilla and his co-authors noted that Latino sex workers face multiple types of stigma including fear of disclosing same-sex sexual behavior and disclosing sex work. They noted that the techniques sex workers use to manage stigma (i.e., to save face) imposed, "severe constraints on men's sexual risk disclosure, and potentially elevated their own and their female partners' vulnerability to HIV infection" (p. 380). Many other researchers have noted the impact that stigma surrounding sex work has in a host of negative snowballing effects among sex workers (Calhoun, 1992; Infante, Sosa-Rubi, & Cuadra, 2009; Koken, Bimbi, Parsons, & Halkitis, 2004; Kurtz, Surratt, Kiley, & Inciardi, 2005; Vanwesenbeeck, 2001, 2005). Given this observation, we wonder whether or not some of the negative findings about sex workers (e.g., substance abuse, HIV risk) result from the impact of stigma on people engaged in prostitution? Would efforts to address social stigma around sex work mitigate some of these observed negative outcomes? Furthermore, it is notable that the discourse around stigma in the lives of sex workers has emerged only recently, within the last decade or so, suggesting something of a paradigm shift in how the lives of sex workers are understood. In tandem with this shift has been the growth of the Internet, which has dramatically changed access and exposure to sex workers and sex work advocacy. This is discussed further in the next section.

Sex Work in the Age of the Internet

Outside the academic sector, there has been some movement in changing social and political views of sex work. This shift has been concurrent with emerging sex-positive research that contextualizes the downsides of sexuality within its many healthy and affirming aspects. And while this slow change has come in many forms, one dominant driving force behind it has been the Internet. Although some researchers have highlighted a digital divide between various socioeconomic groups (i.e., unequal access to the Internet), others have argued this divide is rapidly closing, particularly within industrialized nations such as the United States (Kalichman, Weinhardt, Benotsch, & Cherry, 2002; Kind, Wallace, & Moon, 2008; Wagner, Bundorf, Singer, & Baker, 2005; Watson, Bell, Kvedar, & Grant, 2008). As such, the Internet has become a powerful tool for activities ranging from information seeking and online shopping, to dating and finding partners to engage in nontraditional forms of sexual behavior (Lever, Grov, Royce, & Gillespie, 2008). Given the Internet's growing role in the lives of many individuals, we now focus on the ways in which the general public's increasing use of the Internet has contributed to changing views on sex work. We will highlight how changes have come about via a self-reinforcing cycle where escorting may be perceived as more favorable online than on the street, thus more individuals escort online. Subsequent increases in the online visibility of escorts provide opportunities for others to come in contact with sex work as observers or participants. As a result, we posit that such an emerging pattern has inadvertently created and, in some cases, shifted discourse around the topic. In addition, the Internet has been used in more direct and purposeful ways with respect to sex work, such as the development of websites by and for escorts whose principal purpose is to advocate, politicize, and protect sex workers (physically through "teaching" them how to stay safe with clients, and legally through lobbying and political organizing).

Sex Work Is "Safer" and "Easier" Online—A Portal to Entering Sex Work

Certainly not all individuals use the Internet, but a growing body of research suggests it is one of the most common media gay and bisexual men use to meet their sex partners, let alone for other purposes such as online shopping. A 2006 meta-analysis found that 40 percent of men who have sex with men used the Internet to find sex partners (Liau, Millett, & Marks, 2006). Meanwhile a 2007 study of gay and bisexual men in New York City and Los Angeles found 54 percent of men met a recent sex partner from the Internet (Grov, Parsons, & Bimbi, 2007). These two studies highlight how gay and bisexual men use the Internet specifically for meeting sex partners, while a much larger proportion may use the Internet for pornography and other sex-related behaviors that do not necessarily entail searching for sex with a physical partner.

Given the amount of time that men who have sex with men spend online seeking potential sex partners, the Internet may be an ideal medium for an escort to advertise himself and for clients to find an escort from the convenience and privacy of their own homes. Many men-seeking-men websites, whose primary purpose may not be to facilitate escorting transactions, will allow escorts to advertise themselves in their profiles. Escorts and clients can electronically negotiate prices and behaviors, which may make it easier for both parties to identify a partner who will suit their particular needs, and budget.

With the convenience of a "click," it has become relatively simple for an escort to more easily enter and exit the profession of escorting. For instance, individuals can now enter longer-term commitments in escorting by buying a re-occurring monthly membership on rentboy.com, or enter short-term endeavors such as posting an advertisement for sex work on the men-seeking-men section of an online bulletin board or classifieds website in hope of finding a single encounter that will add revenue on a more casual basis.

Meanwhile, escorts and clients may consider engaging in sex work via the Internet as safer compared to meeting clients on the street, in bars, or other public venues. Escorts and clients can maintain electronic chains of corre-spondence (via email or instant message), in addition to mutually agreed-upon meeting locations, times, and potential phone contacts by which to reach each other. This degree of such a communication is less likely to occur when picking someone up off the street or other public venue. In addition, there is some research suggesting that online escorts are paid more than street-based escorts (Mimiaga et al., 2009), providing additional incentives to escort online.

In all, the Internet has apparently facilitated the ease by which men can enter escorting, and for clients to find escorts. Although it is likely that a minority of men engages in sex work or purchases sex, the abundance of escorting online has exposed many men, who may have not otherwise come in contact with sex work, to the breadth or possibility of commercial sexual behavior. Repeated exposure to sex workers online, even casually, may contribute to the behavior being viewed as more normalized and socially acceptable.

Internet Users Regularly Come in Contact with Sex Workers

The Internet is a portal linking individuals with similar interests, particu-larly those with marginalized sexual interests (Lever et al., 2008). This may include connecting rural gay, lesbian, and bisexual individuals (i.e., from areas that lack a visible gay community) as well as individuals with similar sexual interests, ranging from more conventional pursuits (e.g., finding a date) to those that are less normative (e.g., sadism and masochism, fetish behavior). It has also created an environment where individuals who may not have oth-erwise been exposed to sex work could encounter it on a more casual basis. As mentioned, many men-for-men dating and "hook up" websites now enable users to list themselves as escorts in their profiles. Some websites charge nominal fees to list oneself, whereas others allow users to simply add "escort" to the list of interests they may "check off" in their profile. In addition, there are now a growing number of websites specifically devoted to marketing one-self as an escort (e.g., rentboy.com, men4rentnow.com).

The Internet exposes men (be they sex workers, clients, or potential clients) to other sex workers. For example, a man, during his casual online endeavors in the "regular" men-seeking-men section of a website, might chat with and view profiles of individuals advertising themselves as escorts. This would be in contrast to intentionally visiting a website devoted to escorting and would represent a casual contact with sex work. Further, such an individual may also see banner advertisements on this "regular" men-seeking-men website that would link him to escorting websites. As a result, this man, who may have never thought of escorting—neither being one nor paying one—may now easily encounter escorts' profiles. Similarly, the same man may encounter someone who offers to pay him for sex (i.e., propositioned by a potential client). Even though he may have never thought of paying someone else for sex (or lacked the courage to "hire" an escort in a more traditional ways such as calling ads in the back of sex magazines or hiring someone off the street), the same man may anonymously approach an escort online. And as a result, he might now utilize the Internet as a medium to purchase sex. In total, this increased exposure of escorting online can facilitate conversations between non-escorts and escorts. It can make people aware of their own potential sexual capital or the ability to purchase sex from others in ways that may not have otherwise occurred to them. Meanwhile, the number of escorts online in the "regular" sex-seeking sections of websites could help to normalize the behavior, conveying a sense of social acceptability at least in an online community.

Internet Pornography Portrays Sex Work

In addition to exposing individuals to "actual" sex workers and opportunities to either be a sex worker or hire one, Internet pornography is a flurry with imagery portraying sex work. Websites such as twinksforcash.com and gay4cash.com are entirely themed around getting men to engage in sex for money on camera. Sex scenes typically involve negotiating a financial transaction whereby a man will engage in certain sex acts with another man (or solo) for a negotiated price. This price is often overtly negotiated as part of the scene, and money is handed to the actor at the close of the scene. While we have used examples from gay pornography, such imagery is common in straight pornography (e.g., teensforcash.com, slutload.com, bangbus.com). Whether the transaction is real or fictitious, such pornography is viewed by thousands daily. Much as men may come into contact with sex workers when they are browsing for a sex partner, they may also encounter sex work when browsing for pornography (but not necessarily when they were looking for a sexual encounter with a real partner). This, too, has likely contributed to shifting social views on the social acceptability of sex work. In addition, the plethora of Internet pornography themed around paying for sex may also be an example of the widespread interest in sex work. After all, if there were not a financial market for such pornography, websites selling this content would not stay in business.

Sex Worker Advocacy Has Blossomed Online

The Internet has facilitated discourse among escorts and among clients; escorts can now easily contact each other, discussing experiences in the field and providing feedback on suitable and unsuitable clients. Meanwhile, there are numerous websites whereby clients can post reviews of escorts (e.g., daddysreviews.com). Such reviews allow clients to more thoroughly search for an escort that will suit their needs. The electronic escort review process can also keep escorts "in check," as those with bad reviews may be forced to change their behavior/attitude or suffer the consequences of lost business. These client- and escort-driven processes have created online communities for escorts and clients alike. Meanwhile, given that such websites are often available to the public (without any form of membership requirements), it also creates an electronic environment and archives that non-escorts and non-clients (i.e., the general public) can learn more about sex work. As a result, such websites have become a virtual opportunity for the general public to learn about escorting, something that would be otherwise invisible without the Internet.

In addition to websites devoted to connecting clients and escorts, the Internet has also been used as a tool for advocacy. Clients and escorts have organized themselves on the Internet, with some websites specifically devoted to e-training escorts on how to be safe with clients (e.g., hookonline.org). Other websites are devoted to providing escorts and clients with political and legal support/advocacy. For example, the Sex Workers Project (sexworkersproject.org), Adult Industry Medical Health Care Foundation (aim-med.org), the Prostitute's Education Network (bayswan.org), Hips (hips.org), and the Sex Workers Outreach Project (swopusa.org), all have a substantial online presence. Each of these organizations is devoted to protecting sex workers through increased access to health care, empowerment, and political activism. In addition to creating online dialogues between sex workers and clients, such websites lay the foundation for sex worker advocacy in the "real" world. Thus, although these websites can serve as a virtual locale for the general public (in addition to clients and escorts) to learn about escorting, they also provide the foundation for instituting social change.

CONCLUSION

The Internet has exposed more individuals to the wider world of sex work. This includes sex workers, potential sex workers, clients, potential clients, and the general public. Although it is impossible to estimate how much the Internet has impacted the field of sex work, in addition to impacting social views around the behavior, the accumulation of the ways sex work has propagated online has contributed to new social perceptions around the behavior. Furthermore, such a shift may be particularly evident within gay and bisexual communities (compared with the general population) who seem to frequently use the Internet for sex-related purposes. And while many of the examples we have used are based in the United States, world-wide access to the Internet, in addition to the world-wide growth in Internet technologies, facilitates the translation of ideas globally. Even though sex work is far from normalized or socially acceptable, historical events—ranging from more positive views of homosexuality and increasing "sex positive" academic research, to grassroots organization of sex work online and consistent exposure to sex workers online—have slowly built a foundation for change in prevailing social and political views around sex work and sexuality more generally. It is evident that the Internet will continue to play a central role in this transition, and historical events suggest a gradual shift to more favorable views around sexuality and sex work in the future given that sex work in some form is now legal in many countries of the developed world and that calls for enlarging this space have become more numerous in recent years.

Chapter Three
JOINING THE CLUB

OVERVIEW

"Why would men want to be escorts?" Invariably, this is the first question we get asked when talking to someone about our research. We have been asked by friends and family, by colleagues where we teach, and by other social scientists. Their comments typically seem motivated by curiosity of the different and unknown, yet also mixed with inherent disapproval and distaste. However, they always seem to be intrigued. One might say that the whole scientific study of prostitution and its various forms began with fascination about why people do it and apprehension about its morality. This chapter addresses factors associated with the decision of young men to work as escorts, taking into account their own points of view, life histories, and circumstances. We present an analysis of the components that enter into such a decision and then organize these elements within a theoretical framework.

APPROACHING THE QUESTION

In terms of satisfying this curiosity, it would be far simpler if there were just one answer to the question of "Why do they do it?" However, given that we are devoting a whole chapter to this question (with some spill over into other sections of this book), one can already tell that there are no simple answers and no easy ways to deal with the moral discomfort felt by the public and often shared by sex workers themselves. In examining these issues, previous research suggests that we should be able to derive a "menu" of motivations, traits, and backgrounds related to how and why young men enter prostitution. We could then sub-divide sex workers into clusters of individuals expressing similar sets of characteristics. Doing so could lead to identifying "types" of young men more likely to begin escorting given a particular set of situational conditions. It would produce a method for understanding how these different "types" of men interacted with various situations in terms of initiating sex work; both internal and external influences would be considered in developing a more complete understanding of why particular individuals market their sexual services.

Even though we will introduce types, it is worth mentioning that no one person will fully fit into a particular categorical "box." Social scientists have learned through experience to be wary of the accuracy or consistency of sorting individuals into discrete categories. Human behavior is complex and determined by multiple interacting factors. Too often, the cause of behavior is assumed to lie inside an individual. However, causes for behavior area also likely to be found in their surroundings; it seems to be through the interaction of internal and external factors that most behavior emerges (e.g., Blass, 1984; Mischel & Shoda, 1995; Pervin, 2001). It is an observation that would appear especially true for more complex forms of behavior such as deciding whether or not to escort. Thus, it appears that as soon as one creates a method for grouping people into neat sets of mutually exclusive checklists, the number of people failing to match any one category seems to become the majority. We doubt that trying to categorize male escorts based on factors related to their initiation of sex work is going to violate this pitfall of social science research. Thus, we are not going to take our typology as the final word, and we are not going to start with creating groups of escorts. We need to be a little more careful in reaching broad conclusions and thus begin our examination closer to the source with equal consideration given to an individual's life circumstances, as well as to their personal characteristics.

Taking this need for scientific humility into consideration, our research explored the question of why men decided to go into sex work by starting with the view that the surest approach may be the simplest . . . to ask the escorts directly. We felt a need to be especially cautious with a "back to basics" approach given the current underdeveloped state of the research literature regarding male prostitution. Of the few studies in this domain, fewer still have delved deeply into personal and situational factors around men entering sex work. Despite some notable exceptions, very little has been published on why men begin sex work—almost none about U.S. male prostitutes.

Previous Research Findings

In examining male sex work in the developing world, Padilla's (2007) research in the Dominican Republic describes how some men who previously might have worked in agriculture or other local industries shifted into providing sexual services for American and European tourists. This affords Dominican men (most of whom self-identify as heterosexual) the opportunity to access a much higher level of income than they would otherwise be able to achieve. These men report that they preserve their masculine identities by assuming the more "male" and insertive roles with their clients, although Padilla notes how many of these workers also form longer-term friendships with clients who will visit the young man's home, send gifts and money when not on the island, and offer repeat business upon returning to the Dominican Republic. Primary motivation for these sex workers appears to be a context of limited economic options and the opportunity for gain presented by male tourists seeking sex with other men. The exchange mostly occurs in the context of culturally consistent gender roles relative to the worker and thus can be accepted because it allows him to preserve his masculine identity.

The interplay of culture and economic opportunity also finds expression among male sex workers studied in developed countries. Research conducted by Minichiello and his colleagues in Australia (2000) and Shaver and her colleagues (2005) in Canada suggests that many indoor male sex workers in their samples viewed prostitution more professionally and had a higher degree of control over their working conditions than had been previously assumed in studies only examining men working on the streets. Legalization, either fully or in-part, of prostitution in these countries may have contributed to this type of attitude. Further, their research suggested that men were staying in the business for what the authors called "relatively long periods of time"—they were typically not transient sex workers or individuals experiencing overtly negative life circumstances. They had made a career choice based on their personal situation and understanding of the risks and benefits involved. As such, men in the Minichiello research expressed relatively low levels of work-related stress, unsafe sexual behavior with clients, and rates of drug and alcohol use. Many of their findings are consistent with other studies of male sex workers in the developed world (e.g., Bimbi & Parsons, 2005; Parker, 2005; Smith & Seal, 2007).

As we have outlined in Chapter Two, instead of focusing on personal or contextual motivations for entering sex work, most investigations of male prostitution in the United States have focused upon public health concerns like HIV risk behavior (Bimbi, 2007; Morse, Simon, Osofsky, Balson, & Gaumer, 1991) or on at-risk individuals experiencing problems such as homelessness (Estep, Waldorf, & Marotta, 1992), delinquency (Reiss, 1961; Allen, 1980), and heavy drug use (Morse, Simon, Baus, Balson, & Osofsky, 1992; Rietmeijer, Wolitski, Fishbein, Corby, & Cohn, 1998). These are all downside elements. Most U.S. researchers have, therefore, apparently approached male sex work as a risk to the community and the individuals who engage in it as somehow deviant, criminal, or mentally challenged. Taking a more neutral position, our interviews focused more on the "how" and "why" rather than on the "should" and "should not" inevitably associated with prostitution. Even though we present results from a single data set, there is much to be learned and potentially applied to those for whom our particular data may not represent (e.g., independent Internet-based escorts—male and female). In addition, we will compare and contrast our findings with those of other researchers to craft a more holistic understanding of this topic.

What the *College Boys* Had to Say

The *College Boys* interviews provided a wealth of new leads about not only the factors involved in starting to work as a male escort, but also regarding the thought processes that combined these elements together. When men had a chance to speak for themselves, they provided a rich and extensive set of narratives about what got them into the sex business. We are not saying that anyone possesses a complete understanding as to why they do something, but we did discover that going to the men themselves was perhaps the most reasonable way to begin, and may have been the most informative for understanding how they began to market their sexual services. As will be shown through data collected in our interviews, men are influenced by a number of factors when deciding whether or not to become escorts, some of them situational and some based on internal characteristics such as personality, preference, and individual history.

Elements of the Decision

Three common themes emerged from our interviews with the escorts working at *College Boys*. First, men who worked for the agency wanted to earn money and they saw escorting as a particularly lucrative opportunity to do so. Economic motivations were central to men's consideration of whether or not to engage in prostitution—sex work was all about making money for them; it was a job. Second, most escorts reported that they were introduced to the idea of their involvement in sex work through friends affiliated with the agency. Men had already known of sex work and prostitution, but typically did not consider it for themselves until the topic came up in a conversation—and usually when interacting with someone they trusted. As Keith, a *College Boys* escort related, "[My friend] Evan introduced me to Martin. I came over here kind of to survey things like and then I started working." Because Keith trusted Evan, he was willing to meet Martin and see what the agency was about for himself.

Such *social facilitation* functioned bidirectionally. As we saw in Martin's description of how he hired the first several escorts, having his first employee,

Aaron, provide a point of entry to other men. It allowed Martin to expand his workforce and increase business potential without having to be the only one recruiting new hires. Furthermore, new employees had a trusted friend's word that Martin would be a reliable employer and that there were good opportunities to make money through *College Boys*. Some form of social facilitation occurred with nearly all of the men Martin eventually hired, and is a common theme in other studies that discuss entry into prostitution—having contact with someone on the "inside" provided a means, justification, and gateway into the business. Secondly, *taking the initiative* was a common element in many narratives. As we will see, the *College Boys* escorts frequently learned about the job through their social network when important financial goals were on their minds. These men were able to earn income when they believed that they had the means to do it successfully and when their own doubts and hesitations about sex work were overcome by personal or conditional factors. Thus, motivation for income co-occurred with an unconventional employment opportunity to initiate a decision-making process that led to escorting.

Economic Goals—"It's All About the Money"

Sex work such as escorting is not usually the first income-generating opportunity that comes to mind when men consider how to earn a living. Given the strong cultural stigma associated with sex work (especially with respect to men selling sexual services), stereotypes about the job, and limited knowledge of how to participate in the industry, few men pursue this avenue of employment. Most men in general would certainly consider sex work as undesirable employment, at least initially, and for the great majority this option would not ever be a viable one. Due to these considerations, most people would need more motivation to seriously consider entering sex work (Earls & David, 1989). We surmised that such motivation could be provided by one's economic need: A relative difference between an individual's economic reality and their financial requirements and goals. The larger this discrepancy, the more impetus a man would possess to consider less conventional means of gaining income. When combined with previous knowledge of the business or some personal contact with it (such as through a friend), this motivation could facilitate a decision to begin escorting.

Based on our interviews and reading of the literature, two broad types of financial situations provide pre-conditions for sex work. First, as in Martin's case, men expressing a motivation to *pay for basic expenses* in a situation where they were experiencing limited resources. For these men, escorting was a way to pay their monthly bills (e.g., rent, tuition, car payment) and to maintain a standard of living. This situation is the one most commonly presented in previous research from the developed world with male sex workers (Vanwesenbeeck, 2001), even though there has been a distinct trend in more recent literature to broaden the scope of motivations to include additional possibilities such as curiosity or entre-preneurship (Koken, Bimbi, Parsons, & Halkitis, 2004). When motivations are discussed at all, a "survival" motive often represents the only avenue discussed as a point of entry into sex work. This has tended to encourage a discourse focusing on economically deprived sex workers commoditized by customers with greater financial and social privilege. Individuals with more financial resources and more social authority, in terms of access to the system and its material benefits, provide a small portion of those resources to less advantaged individuals whose only re-source is their body—in this case, the sexualized body (Weitzer, 2005).

An underlying assumption in this literature often seems to be "Why else would a man market sexual services?" except to meet basic need. Studies con-ducted with men working in street-based venues frequently present this point of view with authors discussing "survival" or "exchange" sex to provide food, shelter, or drugs for male prostitutes (e.g., Morse et al., 1992; Rietmeijer et al., 1998). Research in this domain tends to deemphasize an individual's personal agency in making the decision to enter sex work, but rather focuses on over-whelming situational or personal characteristics (such as poverty, disempower-ment, mental illness, or drug addiction) that constrict free will and significantly restrict the man's options to an ostensibly undesirable outcome, i.e., prostitution. An underlying assumption seems to be that were other income possibilities available, a man would not freely choose sex work to earn a living . . . only when all other options are blocked would a man choose to do so.

We do not dispute that many male prostitutes might indeed work to obtain the requirements of life. We do suggest that there is likely to be a continuum of personal agency in their entry into the business; and we fully recognize that many men and boys may be trafficked and exploited against their will (Dennis, 2008). However, to assume that *all* men enter sex work involuntarily or under dire circumstances would be to treat the issue with too broad a brush-stroke. If we consider cases where a given male sex worker was not being coerced, we suggest that certain individuals might perceive their work as a necessity and others might see it as one option among several. The degree of personal agency probably corresponds to a man's circumstances (e.g., home-lessness), functioning (mental health and/or drug issues), resources (education, finances, and social network), and history (e.g., teen runaway) interacting with the environment in which he finds himself. Street-based workers are more likely to fall into a "necessity" category whereas the large majority of escorts in our research would classify themselves into a "voluntary" category in terms of their ability to freely choose entry into prostitution—even though both groups might use their sex work income as their primary source for food and shelter.

Elements of a daily needs motivation were clearly evident among escorts working at *College Boys*, especially for those men who lived at the agency, but the men did not express a sense of disempowerment. Even though economics motivated men to work in the business, the *College Boys* escorts emphasized their free will in working for Martin. Thus, what differed in the stories that we collected from the conclusions of many other published accounts was a sense of personal control in terms of entering prostitution. The men we interviewed typically viewed escorting as one of a number of job opportunities in which they could engage and did not express a sense of being exploited by clients. If anything, the escorts sometimes expressed a view that they were exploiting their customers, and many felt uncomfortable about it. Marc expresses this view well when he struggles with the idea that escorting might take advantage of clients:

> I honestly just because of the way that I am, I feel like, I feel kind of like a dick for like taking money for that. But then I realize that I'm doing something for them in exchange. So I mean, I hope that's enough reason because I don't want to make money off weak people.

Contrary to what many studies have concluded about individuals engaging in prostitution, there was an element of *choice* expressed by the men in selecting escort work, rather than *necessity* in having to sell sex to survive. This difference almost certainly relates to the *College Boys* escorts' overall economic position. None were homeless; the large majority of escorts were employed in other lines of work or had recently been so, with many of those not working outside the agency attending college. Thus, the urgency of being fed, clothed, and housed was not the same as it would have been for men experiencing homelessness or chronic unemployment—i.e., men working on the street who have been the focus for much of the previous research. Regardless of the reason, many of the men working for *College Boys* did use their agency income to meet basic needs. A number of men relied exclusively on sex work as their main source of employment, either because they had been unemployed when they started or because sex work had proven so lucrative that they left their previous job to work full-time as an escort. Several escorts described their sex work as a *more* desirable way to earn a living than previous forms of employment:

> I'd go to work [at a restaurant], like I use to work Saturday night I'd go to work at 3 get out of there at like 11:30 or 12. I'd run my ass off they were so busy, and I'd make $150 bucks a night. When I work an hour I make like $150 bucks not even an hour like 20 minutes and I'd make $150 bucks in 20 minutes. (Tommy)

Some men, especially men currently in school, were only seeking part-time employment. Escorting represented a high-paying job in these cases, freeing them to pursue their studies or to just increase their leisure time relative to what would have required full-time employment in order to keep the same standard of living. Because they made more per hour, the men could work fewer hours to maintain a given standard of living:

> It's addictive, the money's good. You can escort and actually, not want to work a job, and escort three or four days a week. Three or four times a week. You can make $500 in four hours escorting in a whole entire week; there's people working 50 hours a week not making that. Over last summer for instance, I worked for *College Boys* on the weekends, made 400 bucks, and then not work all week long. In the summer I was off of school anyway. I didn't want to work. I wanted to be off. So for two days escorting I got 400 dollars and then got to have 5 full days off to do whatever I wanted to do. (Hector)

What all of these escorts shared was using sex work to help cover the expenses of everyday living. Some may have found themselves doing so out of necessity whereas others could enter sex work from a more entrepreneurial, if less conventional, mindset. What they all had in common was supporting themselves through the physical capital that their bodies provided and the social and sexual skills that allowed them to take advantage of the sexual marketplace.

A second group of men used income from escorting to augment basic needs, to go beyond maintenance expenses and to fulfill economic goals that they viewed as otherwise unattainable. These men used escort income to enhance their current financial situation and to reach for material objectives that they believed would have been difficult to attain through other means of employment, given the value of their labor in more conventional markets. By converting their social skills, youth, and bodies into actualized capital, these men could increase their earning power and realize a higher level of prosperity.

Men expressing this motivation often discussed being able to do things for other people that would not be possible with the conventional forms of work normally available to them. Joshua, a certified public accountant, put it this way:

> It was just when I started getting the extra money for the escorting I didn't have anybody else to spend it on. I didn't have a boyfriend, so I would do extravagant dinner parties for all my friends. I did them myself for about 5 years. And I always loved to just show up at friends' houses with a really nice bottle of wine or jewelry or something really nice. I love spoiling the people in my life . . . a lot.

Other men talked about being able to gain luxuries for themselves or better types of housing through the income they earned from escorting. A third group of individuals used their escort income as a financial windfall, leveraging the extra income into some type of investment that could provide even greater returns in the future. Men in this group reported using the money they earned from *College Boys* to pay for their education, provide down payments for real estate, act as seed money to start a business, or serve as investment capital to purchase equities for retirement.

Entering prostitution to augment one's standard of living or to provide money for investment or educational purposes is a key theme that tends to be ignored by much of the previous research, perhaps as much of this work has tended to focus on individuals in more dire financial straits. Very few researchers address how and why persons with the basics of life in hand decide to enter prostitution. The lack of discussion of this more advantaged group may reflect cultural stereotypes of who enters sex work and their motivations for doing so. Most research with prostitutes has been conducted with individuals working on the streets, people more likely to be in economic distress, homeless, and deeply vulnerable. But are these persons representative of most sex workers? They are probably not, at least in more economically developed countries where the Internet has increasingly supplanted the street, bar, bathhouse, and other venues for male sex workers to connect with their clients (Bimbi, 2007; Mimiaga, Reisner, Tinsley, Mayer, & Safren, 2009; Morrison & Whitehead, 2007; Parsons, Koken, & Bimbi, 2007).

Most earlier research samples were not characteristic of men with more personal resources who were using the Internet to market their services or who work for escort agencies like *College Boys*. In fact, the use of sex work income to raise one's standard of living, to provide gifts or support to others, to bring otherwise unattainable luxuries into their lives, and to provide money for longer-term investments may now reflect the normative economic pathway into sex work for men in the United States and similar societies, not the exception, at least as far as Internet-based sex work is concerned. The Internet has become a clearing-house for information about the possibility of male sex work and on how to enter the sexual marketplace should one be interested in doing so. Previously, this type of education might only be available to those having contact with street, hustler bar, or bathhouse culture; placing significant constraints on who entered male sex work.

With the dissemination of sex work information into a much broader swath of the population, one would reasonably expect that individuals entering the field would now have a greater variety of economic backgrounds—increasing the variance of the type of economic motivation for getting into the sex work business, the frequency with which one worked, and the services that were offered. Thus, instead of the "basic survival" motive being the more typical economic condition for entering sex work, this motive has become one of several more diverse pre-conditions. Thus, alongside survival sex, one now finds men expressing more entrepreneurial aspirations, the desire to increase the proportion of leisure time, and the use of sex work as a lucrative second job to enhance one's material lifestyle. These economic goals are as old as work itself yet their attainment through sex work might be relatively new, facilitated by information from the Internet that has informed a more general public about possibilities for gain through sex work and created a marketplace which easily and efficiently connects the provider with his customer. Men working online rarely charge less than $100 per hour for their services. Going rates in the larger U.S. metropolitan areas average $200–$250 per hour.[1] Men possessing particularly desirable characteristics (i.e., in terms of their physique or from having appeared in pornographic films) often command much higher prices and/or require multi-hour minimum appointments. Escorts working for *College Boys* charged $160 per hour, with the escort retaining $110 of the hourly fee plus any tips or gifts he received from the client. By comparison, the hourly fee for a prominent male escort agency in New York City was $300 during the period we conducted our interviews.

Social Facilitation

More than three-fourths of the men in our sample learned about an opportunity to work as an escort from someone they knew personally. Usually, this was a friend who worked for *College Boys* or was close with someone who did. Many of the escorts had visited the agency several times with their friend(s) before starting to work for Martin, being gradually introduced to the business, the agency's social norms, and the nature of sex work for an escort. Often, they would meet clients coming to the agency for an incall. They would talk with escorts before and after appointments, and they would get to know people at the agency on a social basis by watching movies, playing video games, and going out to nightclubs and restaurants together. Even when an escort had not learned of the agency through their personal social network, Martin brought them to the house to meet the potential new employee and have him socialize with the other escorts. What about this type of social facilitation led men to begin working for the business?

Although men possess a general awareness that sex work exists, it is likely that few spontaneously envision themselves as strippers or escorts. It is estimated that there are fewer male prostitutes than female (Dennis, 2008), with men engaged in sex work defying gender norms that typically cast females in these occupations—most people just do not think of men working as prostitutes or escorts. Having a friend introduce one to the possibility of working in prostitution provides a point of entry into the business that might not otherwise be available to most people. Social facilitation in this respect bridges one's economic needs and goals to their satisfaction via sex work—it informs

---

[1]We wish to note that this going rate is substantially less than what female Internet-based escorts typically charge. In essence, escorting may be one of the few professions where, at least in industrialized nations, men earn less than women.

the individual about a real possibility for making those ends meet that might not have previously been considered. A young man probably would not have made that connection himself given pre-existing stigma and gender norms surrounding sex work. This would be especially true to heterosexual men who might also need to work through their homophobia when providing services to male clients.

That the great majority of escorts working at *College Boys* were introduced to the agency by friends also suggests that the trust and positive regard with their friend helped the escort overcome initial hesitation to learn more about the agency and its employment opportunities. One escort described his experience:

> My friend Debbie said, oh I'll ask my friend Martin about making some money. I'm like, "Okay, you know go ask Martin." I didn't know who it was. That's when I had the first real initial contact with him. And Martin explained to me what was going to be going on and like what kind of clientele and everything that I could expect and what was expected and all that. And I wasn't comfortable with it at all, but a friend of mine that I had met years ago when I was 17 appeared in my life. Well I talked to him online. He had done escorting before and it's like right around the same time that Debbie had given me the proposition to do this for Martin. I was nervous and I told him, "Okay, if you go with me. I don't know what the deal is. I don't know anything about Martin or *College Boys*. I don't know anything, but come with me and I'll feel better and maybe you'll do it too. And it worked out." (Mike)

Psychological research on decision making shows that people consider information obtained from others who are seen as similar or as part of the same group (i.e., from friends or peers) to be the most influential in forming attitudes and social norms (Terry & Hogg, 1996). The potential escort would value the information more when it came from a friend, and be much less likely to discount it offhand. Further, through observation, an individual would see his friend earning money, attaining financial and material goals, and doing so in what many considered to be "easy work" compared to other forms of more traditional employment. Interaction with the friend would indirectly encourage the young man to see the advantages of escorting for himself, and have the opportunity to discuss *pros* and *cons* of the job with someone he knew and probably trusted.

Spending some time at the agency was a key element in encouraging men to work as escorts for many of the *College Boys* employees, though not all. From the potential escort's point of view, he could first make the assertion that he was simply accompanying his friend to somewhere fun and interesting. The house often seemed like it was a fraternity, with young men talking, surfing the Internet, watching movies, or playing video games. Martin treated all of the men as equals and made sure that new people were introduced and developed a positive impression. He took people out to eat and would regularly organize weekend nights at the local clubs and bars. Small groups of escorts would often do so on their own as well—and new people would be included in these outings if their friends were part of a group that was going somewhere. Psychologically, the more a potential hire came to identify with and like the other escorts, the more likely he would be to adopt their norms regarding sex work and consider it for himself.

By creating a social space through the agency, *College Boys* became less of a "brothel" and more of a place to hang out, to have fun, socialize, and even spend the night when the escorts came back too late or too drunk to go home. We also note that most service calls were conducted in clients' homes or hotel rooms and not in the agency's incall room. It was fun; violating nearly all of the culturally derived stereotypes of brothels as female-oriented, seedy, and dirty. Here was what otherwise looked to be a cool place to be, full of other young men with a permissive and affluent "big brother" who was nice to you, made you feel included, and insured that you had a good time. Indirectly, a potential escort could also "learn the ropes" of the job just from the natural conversations that occurred between the current employees with whom he was associating. He could hear about what they did, what was expected, and how much money they were earning. They talked to a new person about their lives and how escorting did or did not fit into them. Learning "how to" be an escort is further discussed in Chapter Five. There was always the inevitable joking and teasing about a newly introduced guy going on a call or "taking one for the team" himself, which may have been the first time a potential escort may have seriously or publically considered prostitution as an option.

From the agency's point of view having potential new hires spend time at the agency represented a winning situation all around. The manager could observe new men interact with other escorts and even with clients who came to the agency for an incall. Martin would notice how the new person socialized and what they said about their personal lives, looking for signs of stability, dependability, good social skills, and flexibility. He could come to know about their "partying" in terms of alcohol and drug use, and hear about their personal experiences with sex and relationships. Martin would often start to joke with and talk to new people about the possibility of becoming escorts mentioning that "if you ever wanted to," he could set them up with a client just to see if it would work out. Martin said:

> I look to make sure that they understand that their whole goal isn't about making money; it's about making the other person feel good. People that are genuinely interested in other people, sometimes you can just tell by the things that they say. If they're all about how much money they're going to make and how soon, if they are too focused on that, it doesn't seem like those people do as well as the people that are all about what the other person wants.

Many potential escorts had the chance to meet clients coming to the agency, talk to them, and see who they would be working with long before actually having appointments.

For Martin this allowed many new hires to already have a good deal of training before starting to work for *College Boys*. He knew what some clients and most of the other escorts thought of a possible new hire, especially in terms of his social facility and attitude. Martin also gained opportunities to observe the new person in a number of different situations and over a period of time. Should this person actually start to see clients, Martin knew that individual had already been brought up to speed about the culture of the agency and its requirements for customer service. Martin could then reinforce these requirements with the new escort and fill in any informational gaps, rather than having to start from the beginning with someone who would be completely unfamiliar with how the agency operated. Having potential new hires introduced to the agency by friends was an ideal situation for everyone concerned.

Taking the Initiative—Let's Do This

Once someone has been introduced to the personal possibility of sex work, they must consider whether or not to work in the business. The cultural stereotype regarding prostitution seems to be that relatively few people would sell their own sexual services, even if they perceived an opportunity to do so. It is likely that the common perception in the United States is that most people would be attracted to a job where they could earn more money per hour than would otherwise be possible, until they learned that they would have to engage in prostitution. In fact, most of the escorts we interviewed for our project reported the same set of hesitations and biases about escorting and prostitution. Economic need and material goals alone were not sufficient pre-conditions for them to start working in the sex industry. So what might be these other factors associated with men entering the business?

Perceived Personal Capital

As we presented earlier, certain people felt able to take advantage of a perceived income opportunity through the agency because they believed they possessed the necessary characteristics to do so; personal and physical qualities that could be marketed and sold to clients at a price that would make downsides of the job worthwhile. In learning about modern male prostitution, these men became aware that they had a type of capital of which they were previously unaware, capital that could be converted into cash income. Discovery of such potential in the context of learning about a market where their physical assets could be leveraged into money allowed men to connect material needs and goals to an employment opportunity with potentially high returns. It was an ideal "investment" situation that, although probably not acceptable to most people in the United States, could be realized by a few.

The most obvious type of personal capital for an escort would be that person's physical attributes, and this was the characteristic of which the escorts in our interviews were most aware at the onset of their sex work. Although wide variations in client tastes were recognized, consistent with research on general factors associated with male attractiveness (e.g., Grammer, Fink, Møller, & Thornhill, 2003), reported that most clients preferred escorts in their late teens or early twenties with a youthful appearance, lean athletic body, and a larger penis. Less body hair was typically desirable as well, perhaps as this may also be more indicative of youth. One study examining the Internet advertisements of about 1,300 male escorts showed these qualities to be those most emphasized in efforts to solicit business from clients (Pruitt, 2005).

Variations on this type existed (college jock, skater, the guy-next-door), but the basic physical attributes were typically similar across these different categories; differences had more to do with "packaging" than substance. More tangible variations from the standard type reflected client preferences for escorts of a certain ethnic or racial background, bulkier body builds (e.g., the "football player" build), or other characteristics (long versus short hair, tattoos, more body hair, etc.). Men whose physical attributes more closely matched client desires were in higher demand and Martin sought to hire them more frequently than others. The very name of his agency suggested that escorts of this type would be available, although he needed to have enough variety in his employees to satisfy clients with interests outside of the mainstream. The right staffing balance was hard to strike as the roster of escorts was always fluid.

Attitudes and Values

Although appearance was a key element in marketing oneself as an escort, it was not the only important characteristic that one should possess in order to work in the business. Other characteristics were considered to be equally, if not often more, important than an escort's physical attributes, especially as one gained more experience with what clients usually wanted from their hires. One of these attributes represented being "open minded" about sex, sexual partners, and morality in general. One needed to possess this type of attitude in order to seriously consider and then, actually begin work as an escort. Without it, the psychological barriers to having sex with people one normally would not consider as a partner and the moral prescriptions against prostitution may have been too high to surmount—especially before one had actually started to see clients. Open mindedness provided a psychological pathway that allowed someone to set aside or bypass conventional views of prostitution in order to begin working in the business, allowing men to have sexual partners who would never be considered as such in their personal lives, let alone charge them for social companionship and sex.

It is perhaps the moral dimension that holds most importance for first considering whether to work in the sexual services industry, before the actuality of sex with clients has occurred. Escorts most often discussed issues of values when talking about getting into the business and immediately afterward, less so once they had been working for a while. This suggests that many of the male escorts had initially doubted the personal and moral integrity of the job, but had found a way to manage this concern so that they could start to work. Reese discussed acclimating to sex with paying clients:

Interviewer: What were your thoughts when you first started escorting?

Reese: Wow I guess I'll give it a try and I was a little shook up the first time, the first couple times and I was drunk and using some kind of miscellaneous drugs but then after that it kind of clicked, it didn't bother me anymore.

Interviewer: You said you were shook up, what shook you up?

Reese: Just the whole thing I don't know.

Interviewer: Why did it shake you up? What about having sex with clients shook you up?

Reese: I guess I was like did I really just do this? And then I was worried about a lot of things, a lot of things went through my mind the first couple of times.

Interviewer: What did you worry about?

Reese: Oh I did this and I did that and I felt kind of gross, but after a little while that faded.

Or, as Andrew noted, many newer escorts often felt dirty or ashamed when having sex with clients for pay until they had gotten used to the job:

> I couldn't even get it up—I just felt dirty. I couldn't even get off because I couldn't get into it. Like when I first started, like there's like a wreck inside you. When you first start you get the shit calls. And when I first started I got the shitty calls: old people, dirty people, nasty people, people who paid you exactly what the fee was, didn't give you any tips whatever and those were the worst because they made you feel the worst about yourself.

Andrew began to adjust to the work when he met a client who had himself been an escort, suggesting to Andrew that he develop an alter ego while working to keep his work and personal lives separate.

As will be seen, very few escorts expressed an increase in moral concerns about sex work after they had been working for a while. Reese and Andrew both expressed the much more common experience of decreased moral and personal concerns as they gained more experience with the job. Escorts who did continue to hold serious moral reservations about prostitution did not work for long or were considering the need to end sex work in the near future. Thus, in most of our interviews, value/moral-related concerns were greatest at the start of an escort's career.

How did male escorts come to have a more open mindset toward the morality of prostitution when first considering whether or not to work for *College Boys*? There were several different avenues men used, and some exhibited more than one. First, many escorts had a *pragmatic* attitude toward this moral and legal question. They viewed sex work as a business transaction, "Escorting's just a job. It's something you go and you do. You get paid and you come home; so it doesn't really affect me in a negative way" (Rich). From this viewpoint, no harm was being done to anyone and thus, there was no moral problem with the activity. Because they perceived a lack of exploitation or damage, they did not consider their work in prostitution to be immoral even though it was illegal.

The law was not viewed as a moral imperative by these men, but as a barrier to a legitimate activity between consenting adults. People backing such laws were often seen as unreasonable, out-of-touch, antiquated, or right-wing—positions which defined the anti-prostitution laws and their backers as "others" relative to the escort who may have considered himself more liberated, realistic, and/or contemporary in his values or attitudes regarding sex work. Some of the men expressing this attitude viewed their sex work as enhancing the quality of the client's life. Mark said that:

> I don't ever think this job is wrong because we're here making people happy you know. The sex is just something that people tend to feel that they need and if being with somebody for that time makes their day, ok. It wasn't that big of a deal to do. Like you know I can find good in everybody. I can always find something attractive in someone even if they aren't great looking. You know for that hour I was there, that overnight that I was there, they felt like they were the only thing in my world and that they were mine. And it makes me feel good knowing that I was able to do that for them. A lot of times I wish that I could have a relationship with every single one of them. But unfortunately it's a business and it's like I need to make money.

In a similar vein, Daniel related:

> A couple of calls I've been on they just wanted to sit down and talk, just have a decent conversation. Most people are just lonely. They want someone there that can talk to them that they can relate to in some way just like a companion, a friend. I make conversation with people and get to know them. I may not ever see them again for the rest of my life but hey it made them feel better. I'm sure I made that person feel that somebody wanted to get to know them. (18, White gay male)

Mark, Daniel, and similar minded escorts saw themselves as fulfilling important psychological and physical needs for clients in a way that was emotionally satisfying for both the provider and customer alike. They gained a sense of being helpful, supportive, and compassionate while they were working.

A second approach was used by men who questioned the moral validity of prostitution, but who argued that more good than harm came from it. These individuals took what could be described as a *cost-benefit* perspective on the escorting profession. For men expressing this viewpoint, thinking about becoming a sex worker had some real downsides morally, legally, or psychologically. Some men wondered about the latent morality of having relations with people they did not know; many did not do so in their personal lives, especially escorts who were in relationships. Others were more concerned about the idea of charging money for having sex. However, these concerns were outweighed by the upsides of an income level that they would not otherwise be able to attain.

Positive views of escorting were reinforced in the social fabric of the agency; Martin and the escorts often discussed the "good" that their work did and the benefits that it provided to the escorts as well as to clients who appreciated the services they obtained from the young men they hired. Being among a group of like-minded individuals helped to create sex work-positive local norms while negative views of sex work were challenged and minimized. Within *College Boys*, escorting and prostitution were valued business activities; a narrative crafted by the men in this circle supported their work, its importance, and the gains that were to be found in it both for clients and escorts. New escorts could see that clients provided additional supportive feedback in terms of money, gifts, praise, and personal testimonial, which significantly reinforced this narrative as a powerful counterweight to an escort's personal morality, developed before his initiation into sex work with the agency.

Lastly, escorts sometimes asserted that "the ends justified the means" when balancing the chance to earn good money with personal values against prostitution. Men discussing this viewpoint did not contest that prostitution was somehow "wrong" in the moral or legal sense. Many expressed strong reservations about how sex work conflicted with their personal values or their sense of integrity—what they saw as longer-term core aspects of their identities. Mitigating these concerns were two elements: the *goals* one would achieve through sex work and the *duration* for which one would engage in prostitution to acquire those goals. As Allen put it:

> I've gotten used to the money now which sometimes that can be a downfall, you get used to having easy money like extra money other than a paycheck so when you don't have that money you don't know what to do. So at this point escorting helps me maintain the lifestyle I choose. The clothes I wear, the shoes I buy, the cell phone plan I have; things like that. I plan on escorting until I have my career. Once I'm set, then I'm not going to do it anymore. There's an expiration date.

Thus, the importance of a goal would allow the individual to set aside their concerns about the nature of their work so that the desired outcome could be attained. Achieving this end outweighed the moral considerations in the means used to do so, especially as prostitution provided income that frequently would not otherwise be attainable given the man's other employment prospects. The income from sex work would speed acquisition of the goal in ways that would not normally be possible.

Furthermore, men employing this mindset also tended to emphasize the transient nature of their involvement with sex work; most had an end date established for themselves (e.g., graduation from college) or a specific financial target (e.g., enough to make a down payment for a car). By emphasizing the time-limited nature of their involvement in prostitution, these men established mental boundaries around their behavior that minimized its impact on their identity and integrity. Sex work became a somewhat undesirable, yet efficient way to achieve an important goal within a pre-specified time period. It allowed the escort to reassure himself by saying, "this is something I'm doing temporarily" rather than requiring him to integrate sex work into his sense of occupational and perhaps, personal identity.

A SOCIAL-COGNITIVE EXPLANATION OF MEN ENTERING SEX WORK

Albert Bandura (1978) conceptualized a social-cognitive perspective to provide a theoretical framework for how behavior interacts with internal (i.e., cognition) and external (i.e., social situational) factors. A comprehensive viewpoint, this perspective suggests that all three elements interact reciprocally in a cyclical manner with one aspect reinforcing or altering the others. Thus, perceptions and expectations from the cognitive element of the model interact with environmental realities to determine which behavior occurs. Likewise, once behavior takes place, it produces changes in the situation which then become the raw material for the next sequence of perceptions that drive further expectancies and actions. Such a system is self-regulating and self-determining, with one's internal cognitive functioning an external behavior significantly dependent on what occurs in the immediate social situation, as seen in Figure 3.1.

As we have discussed, previous explanations for the entry of young men into sex work have focused on the deviance of the individual (i.e., the cognitive or internal element of the social cognitive model) or on an exploitive socioeconomic situation (i.e., the social element of the model). Although one cannot dispute that these two theories are able to explain some of the reasons why certain men might engage in prostitution, one might ask if they do so comprehensively—and especially for men who are more personally or economically empowered. One might consider these two viewpoints as potential

Figure 3.1.
Bandura's social-cognitive model

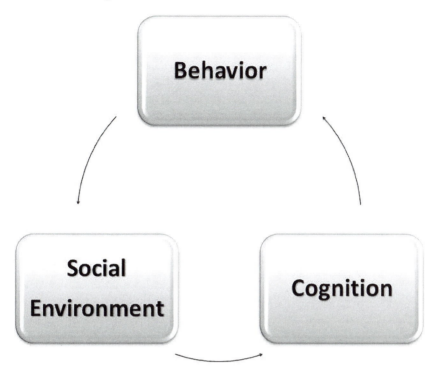

elements within a more robust social-cognitive framework that also introdu-ces other individual and environmental characteristics into the decision-making process. Furthermore, it may be that a deviance or exploitation model would not fit many men working in the business at all. We believe that this would be the case for most men working as escorts through the Internet—men who likely have their basic needs in hand or for whom escorting would be a desirable way to attain their goals. A social-cognitive perspective might be more adept in explaining their decision-making process more objectively and with greater emphasis on an individual's own perspective, rather than on preconceived notions of dysfunction or a more generalized social structure.

We have discussed how economic goals form an important foundation for entry into sex work. These considerations would be represented in the cognitive element of the model as they signify interpretations of one's circumstances. Per-ceptions of need and want generate behavioral options which experience has shown might provide satisfaction. Thus, for a man to consider work as an escort, he must have prostitution "appear" on his list of options when considering how to meet his economic needs. Social facilitation provides the key means for this to be the case, introducing many men to the idea that sex work could generate income.

Figure 3.2.
Social-cognitive elements for entry into sex work

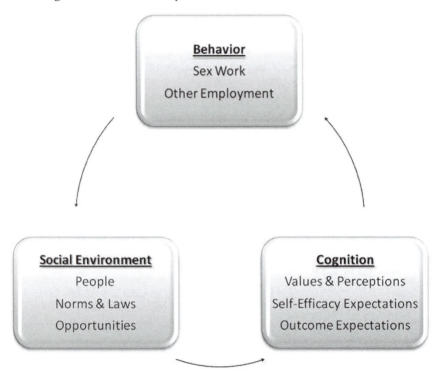

However, how does one actually choose which behavior to perform in order to attain a specific goal? There could be many possible routes toward meeting economic needs. How do we pick which route to pursue? Social-cognitive theory suggests that behavioral options are evaluated through the lens of *self-efficacy* beliefs—the expectation that a given behavior will achieve a desired goal in the current situation (Bandura, 1977). Thus, as shown in Figure 3.2, the cognitive element of the model considers the benefit from the behavioral option, the cost of engaging in that given action, and the estimated likelihood that the behavior will actually succeed in attaining the benefit. Behavioral options are simultaneously compared in this manner to determine which would be most likely to succeed in producing the largest payoff (net of anticipated "costs").

It is the estimated likelihood of success, the self-efficacy belief, for a given behavior that is particularly important—the behavior must be judged to result in a given goal and the individual must be confident that they could actually successfully engage in the behavior to be performed. Unless both expectations are present (the belief in the utility of the behavior and in one's ability to carry

Table 3.1
Possible Benefits and Costs of Escorting

Benefits	Costs
• Income	• Legal problems
• Higher hourly wage	• Values against prostitution
• Trips and perks	• Sex with undesired partners
• Friendship with manager	• Risk of violence and disease
• Friendships with other escorts	• Conflicts with identity
• Friendships with clients	• Unpredictable hours
• Favors from clients	• Unpredictable income
• Excitement	• Stigma from others
• Enhanced sense of attractiveness	• Relationship difficulties

it off), then the person will ignore that option and consider another possible action (Maddux, Norton, & Stoltenberg, 1986). The behavior where both elements are the strongest within a given situation relative to a certain need will be selected. These expectations are developed based on one's personal experiences with the behavior in question and from what one has been able to observe directly from others (via real life experiences watching other people) or indirectly through various media (via the printed word, movies, television, and the Internet). Self-efficacy beliefs are constantly updated as the individual has additional experiences.

One can see how social facilitation plays an especially crucial role in this formula—either in the direct manner of personal experience with people who themselves escort or via media such as the Internet. Firstly, a stigmatized and gendered behavior such as prostitution might not even appear on a young man's "behavioral menu" in a situation where economic needs are present. Learning of the possibility of earning income through sex work allows escorting to become one choice for meeting financial goals. Yet social facilitation also provides key self-efficacy information before that individual has actually engaged in prostitution for himself. He can observe and learn about the experiences of other people to form the beliefs about the effectiveness of prostitution in meeting his financial goals. As shown in Table 3.1, the costs and benefits that might enter into his decision-making process are better known and the likelihood that sex work will lead to goals can be evaluated. Social facilitation informs him of the possibility of a new income-generating opportunity, the degree to which that opportunity could meet his needs, and the likelihood that he would be able to successfully engage in that occupation to earn the income (as well as possible side benefits) he desires while minimizing other outcomes that he does not desire.

Our research suggests that men engaging in sex work likely have less commitment to traditional values regarding psychosexual norms or else the internal cognitive barriers (e.g., values) would be too high for most any degree of opportunity to surmount. Gay and bisexual men might already have less commitment to broad social values regarding sexuality and sex work (Cates & Markley, 1992) and find it acceptable to have sex with men in general (Allen, 1980; Earls & David, 1989), making them hold less negative views about escorting as elements of their sexuality and identity are already stigmatized through pervasive homophobic cultural norms. Additionally, and partially referring to a "deviance" perspective, heterosexual men might be more inclined toward sex work if they had engaged in other types of socially disapproved behavior in their past—such as having a history of delinquency or drug use. In fact, some of the earliest social-scientific studies of male sex work in the 1960s propose just this type of connection (e.g., Craft, 1966; Deisher, Eisner, & Sulzbacher, 1969; Reiss, 1961). A less conventional behavioral morality for heterosexual escorts is a connection borne out in our own research; six of eight heterosexual escorts working for *College Boys* reported some trouble with the law or a history of delinquency.

Thus, some decreased connection to traditional values and social norms does appear to facilitate entry into sex work, but not in the strict sense as proposed in earlier deviance models. Unconventionality in this sense would not be viewed as a "trait" but as a "mindset" derived from one's experiences and upbringing. Social facilitation may provide an alternate set of norms by which individuals can judge their behavior (considering anti-prostitution values and other internalized stigma as a cost of engaging in sex work) and decrease the downside of seeing clients. In an agency setting, or were one to have a friend or two also working in the business, one would find strong mutual support for these alternate values and perceptions and more easily be able to identify with a like-minded group of desirable individuals, rather than the norms held by "other" people in the larger society. Such a mindset would be encouraged if one already started from a somewhat "outside" position either by virtue of his sexual orientation or past behavioral history.

CONCLUSION

The need to make a living and desire to enhance one's lifestyle through higher paying work represent key motivational similarities between prostitution and other forms of employment. In fact, it is likely these internal factors provide the impetus for occupational behavior in most working men and women. Finding employment through one's social network would also be normative—an external similarity between escorting and non-sexual labor. Many people find jobs through friends and family, socially facilitated employment in professional circles via "networking" constitutes a time-honored practice. *College Boys* escorts possessed typical motivations toward wanting employment and typically encountered their work opportunity at the agency through some type of social network (actual or virtual) in very similar ways to how nearly anyone in the modern economy would find a job. What makes sex work different from other forms of employment are the moral and legal prohibitions regarding prostitution and, in the case of *College Boys*, homosexuality. A social-cognitive perspective explains negotiation of these prohibitions as mediated by attitudes and beliefs that negate such barriers. These internal cognitive constructs can be facilitated by certain personal factors (such as a homosexual identity or a non-normative moral framework) as well as external social relationships (with individuals who hold contracultural viewpoints). Usually a combination of both external and internal elements permit formation of new cognitive sets that would allow the occurrence of a previously untried behavior such as escorting. Thus, the decision to enter sex work can be explained using psychological models adapted to understand general decision-making. There is no need to create a "prostitution-specific" model as the elements of such a decision are found in everyday life and adhere to a regular process.

The only deviance that might be considered would be that an individual, either before or after working as an escort, would develop a set of values permitting him to engage in prostitution. In as much as non-sanctioned values could be considered "deviant," then that individual could be described in such a manner. However, the modern social and medical sciences no longer classify psychopathology along moralistic lines—no accepted diagnosis can be based upon values or morals that differ from cultural norms. Decreased commitment to prevailing psychosexual norms regarding sexuality and prostitution no longer represents a deviance in the traditional sense of that label, even if most people would object to such beliefs and behaviors. What we conclude is that the typical sex worker (at least those employed in an agency) needs to make a living, wants to enhance their material lifestyle, encounters an opportunity through their social network, and already possesses or subsequently develops cognitive structures that would permit him to engage in that occupational behavior himself.

Chapter Four

GETTING INTO THE GROOVE

OVERVIEW

In many "traditional" job settings, new employees receive training to orient them to the workplace environment. In so doing, employers provide achievement benchmarks for their employees, and employees often have a clear understanding of their roles and responsibilities. In many parts of the hospitality industry (hotel guest services workers, flight attendants, restaurant servers), employees are provided formal and extensive training on how to please clients while achieving the business' goals. In addition, employees informally gain many skills while on the job through their own occupational experiences. They observe their colleagues, taking note of work environment and culture, standards for attire, and other aspects of their new job. Employees also learn while engaging clients and customers; they learn how their own behavior may result in achievement or loss, and subsequently modify their approach to maximize achievement while minimizing negative outcomes. And, of course, employers often hire staff based on an individual's prior work experience/ training, preparedness, or skill set.

Although many formal opportunities exist for on-the-job training in "traditional" career paths, few such mechanisms are available in the sex work industry which is still quite fragmented given social stigma and its illegal status in most of the United States. Certainly, some sex workers have written memoirs about their experiences (Delacoste & Alexander, 1998; Good,

2007; Greta, 2004; Lewis, 2006; Oakley, 2007) from which one could learn about the business. There also are some books specifically designed toward training women how to be escorts (e.g., Brooks, 2006; Meretrix, 2001; Roberts, 2004, 2007), but there really are no "how to" guides or entrepreneurial textbooks for men on becoming a successful escort. It is unsurprising that not a single college, training institute, or business school in the United States offers degree or certificate programs in sex work.

As a caveat, we should mention that in recent years, grass-roots organizations and sex work advocates have convened to provide more formalized trainings; however, such events are infrequent (e.g., annually) and, one may have to travel hundreds of miles to attend such a training. For example, the Desire Alliance (desirealliance.org) hosted their 2010 conference in Las Vegas. In prior conferences, the Desire Alliance hosted workshops with topics ranging from "screening clients" and "self-marketing" to "personal privacy" and "working with disabled customers/clients." However, almost none of these resources were specifically oriented toward male sex workers. Thus, by-and-large a majority of sex workers appear to rely on informal mechanisms for learning the trade. This may include partnering with other escorts, affiliating oneself with an escort agency, or going it alone and learning the trade through trial-and-error. More support seems to exist for women than for men.

In this chapter, we describe how the men we interviewed learned to be escorts. First, we discuss formal and informal mentorship that occurred within the agency. This could include formal experiences (e.g., being "shown the ropes" by the agency manager) and informal experiences such as conversations with and observations of other escorts. Next, we describe self-taught methods that many escorts "picked up" while learning the trade. The experiences we describe often included drawing upon and adopting social skills learned throughout one's life and "trial-and-error" used with clients. Third, we describe how men altered their own attitudes and perceptions about their sex work, and how such changes were often needed for long-term resilience in this line of work. We describe some of the mental "tools" escorts used to cope with the emotional and physical aspects of their labor. And, finally, we describe how men incorporated escorting into their social networks to include their family, friends, and romantic partners. We note how sometimes this blending of personal and work life provided an important positive outlet for coping with sex work, but it more often than not resulted in negative reactions. As a result, escorts actively managed their disclosure of professional activities, and carefully considered how much detail to provide. In some cases, escorts created new social networks to manage the emotional labor of prostitution, surrounding themselves with individuals who were more understanding and less judgmental about their work.

Mentor and Mentee

Many of our participants described varying types of informal "on the job" training. This training typically took the form of a mentor-mentee relationship. Mentors could have included other more "seasoned" escorts, the agency manager, and even clients who were well known to the agency and to whom the manager would refer newer escorts.

Although as we previously discussed, the *College Boys* agency did have an "incall" facility such that they were able to see clients on-site, most clients preferred to have appointments in their homes or hotel rooms. Thus, to reach their clients, escorts either drove themselves or, more often, were driven to calls. Mentorship occurred to and from the appointment. The mentor was often the driver who was either another escort, Martin (the agency manager), or a friend of people at the agency. Some of the men we interviewed described that they learned how to best work with clients in this time leading up to and after seeing a client. Martin often used this commute time to engage in discussions with his employees, especially those who were newer to the business. During this time, he would tell escorts what to expect from a certain client (particularly if this was a repeat client for the agency), and give them pointers on how to develop rapport with clients while maintaining their own sense of dignity and personal safety.

Oftentimes, it was Martin who would initiate this conversation/training with newer escorts. However, many escorts appreciated this information and jumped on the opportunity to learn as much as possible. Brian described his conversation with Martin prior to seeing his very first client. "The first call I went on, I drove Martin out of his mind asking questions on what to do, what they [escorts] charge, what to ask, what not to say, what to say, you know, stuff like that. I just wanted the basics." After finishing a call and on the commute back, escorts often capitalized on this time by "debriefing" with their travel companion. In particular, escorts would often dialogue about their feelings around engaging in sex work, coping with the emotional impact of their labor. They may have described the session with a client and talked about both negative and positive aspects of the session. As escorts became more experienced, the manager was less likely to ride along (providing there was someone else to drive) and the mentee would then become, in his own time, the mentor for new hires at *College Boys*.

Although infrequent, sometimes clients would request more than one escort for a sexual encounter. Here, teaching and learning took place within the sexual situation itself and always involved another escort. To facilitate the process, the manager often would pair a new escort with an experienced one for "dual" calls. He would intentionally pair newer escorts with seasoned escorts on such calls so that they could gain experience from the longer-term employee; not only in terms of learning how to handle the sexual aspects of the call, but also with respect to providing new escorts with sound role models for providing good customer service, handling boundary-crossing client requests, and managing stigma or other negative emotions that might arise as a result of the work. Escorts expressed positive feelings about going on calls with one another, especially when they were new to the business, "It's both of us doing things together. And not some person we don't know; [you know,] someone we really have no attraction to" (Jerry).

We also found that Martin would take other direct steps to foster a newer escort's transition into the field. For example, he often would send new escorts to clients who were known well to the agency. Not only would the client gain access to a new escort (which the manager reported to be highly desirable among his customers), but Martin could also be assured that the client would be an active participant in the mentorship process, guiding the escort in how to be successful during appointments. In this circumstance, the agency manager made it clear to the client that this escort was new to the field. In response, clients would treat any of an escort's faux pas during a session with a higher level of empathy. In this regard, the client's role incorporated in vivo guidance and perhaps, learning through observation as the mentor was an active participant in the appointment. Martin would also benefit from receiving candid feedback about the new escort's work, providing information he could use to further train the new employee and determine his suitability for remaining with *College Boys*.

Escorts recognized and appreciated the manager's matching them with "seasoned" clients during their transition into escorting. Some specifically described feeling "protected" while they were still new to the field. Berto related that, "Martin would first start by sending me to people that he knew—regular clients. I knew he knew the people and that it made it easier for me." Berto went on to describe how seeing clients known to the agency while he was still new to escorting was beneficial not only because of the information he would receive from the manager about the client ahead of the encounter, but that he would also learn about the client from other escorts working at the agency:

> I could talk to some of the boys that had already seen him [the client], so it would be easier because I'd get to know the person [client] before I got to go see them. I just felt more comfortable because I knew somebody else had already gone to see him and nothing [bad] happened. It's always scary to see someone—especially for the first time—that no one's seen. You don't know what the person's really like or what they're really expecting. It's easier to go through a service [call with a known client] than to do it on my own.

It warrants mentioning that the different types of mentorship we have described often resulted from direct efforts that Martin intentionally fostered.

As indicated, Martin would (1) often ride along in the car with escorts on the way to and from calls, (2) pair newer escorts with seasoned ones on calls involving multiple escorts for a single client, and (3) assign newer escorts to clients that were well known to the agency. In these circumstances, the agency manager provided a powerful and important role in men's transitions into escorting. Such "leadership" might not occur in other agency-based settings and would not be available to men working independently. Because our research examined a single agency, we do not know if Martin's efforts represented his own personal style and previous experience as a corporate trainer, or whether such methods might be more widely used in the industry as a whole.

Further complicating the issue of employer-provided training, many male escort agencies now operate virtually: The agency hosts a website listing multiple escorts who work "for" the agency, but who have no direct physical interaction with agency management. To book an escort, clients call a single number or arrange an encounter via email through the agency. The agency then dispatches escorts to appointments—calling an escort and telling him where to go and when. In these circumstances, and in an effort to self-market and drum up maximum exposure to potential clients, escorts may list themselves with multiple online agencies in addition to their own independent advertisements (in the back of magazines or online). In this way, escorts would be unlikely to encounter each other on a regular basis as they would often be working alone, "telecommuting" if you will, with respect to their agency, which would function more like a booking service than a "bricks and mortar" establishment. Escorts might also be less likely to interact face-to-face with the agency manager, as (unlike *College Boys*) there may not be a physical space where escorts could gather, socialize, and share experiences with each other and their manager(s).

In essence, although the experiences of mentorship we have described were certainly important for the men we interviewed, and facets of the various types of mentorship *might* occur for other types of escorts (including independent escorts who maintain a social network with other escorts and agency-based escorts who have some interactions within the agency), some of the experiences described may not represent the "typical" route in which escorts attain greater proficiency and comfort with their job. Instead, they likely rely on learning various aspects of the job (e.g., providing clients with emotional and physical satisfaction, managing stigma, organizing work versus personal time commitments) that occurs directly from accumulated experiences through structuring their work and with their clients.

Going It Alone and Finding What Works

Many of the men we interviewed described both the informal and formal types of mentorship which we have been discussing. However, when engaging a client either at the agency's in-call facility or at the client's home/hotel, nine times out of ten, escorts could expect to be alone with the client. In these intimate one-on-one situations, escorts were left to draw from their discussions with mentors and, perhaps more importantly, from their prior interactions with other clients. These experiences often included sexual (either with non-paying sex partners and previous clients) and social skills (i.e., adept social and conversational skills inherent to engaging in casual conversation with a stranger or new acquaintance) obtained through personal experiences. Many of the escorts recognized that they had "natural" skills when it came to carrying on a conversation with a stranger, and would draw upon these skills when with clients. Although client's appointments often spanned an hour, escorts rarely had sex for this entire period of time, thus impromptu social and emotional entertaining was often required in addition to physical sexual behavior. As escorts became more experienced, they began to intentionally plan for their social time with clients and would inquire as to clients' preferences, bringing music, food, drinks, candles, massage oil, and so forth in order to enhance this aspect of an appointment.

Unlike the men we interviewed at *College Boys*, many independent escorts—those who advertise on the Internet and street-based escorts who are less likely to have a formal escort-mentorship structure—likely rely exclusively on previous sexual and social experiences as a primary mechanism for engaging clients. However, doing so establishes a training model based on trial-and-error which may lead to difficulties earlier in an escort's career through negative client feedback, dissatisfaction within the encounter, and/or lower wages and tips. Over time, most escorts who remain in the business learn a variety of means to maximize outcomes (e.g., receiving a tip from a client, quid pro quo emotional and physical involvement with a client). Among the men we interviewed, some described how they learned to limit their emotional and physical investments with a client. Typically, this learned physical and emotional restraint resulted from a previous experience when an escort had overextended himself during an encounter (both sexually and emotionally). For example, some of the escorts described how they assumed an intense emotional or physical investment was necessary with all clients, as this was typical of their behavior with non-clients (boyfriends, etc.), but they soon learned how to modify this investment to suit clients needs while maintaining their own personal limits.

Emilio described how he thought that, as a sex worker, he needed to do all the physical/sexual work in order to satisfy his clients, "When I started, I did all the work and was like, 'There is something not right about this, it's not fun.'" Emilio went on to describe how he soon learned that many clients did not expect an escort to do all the work. Much like non-paying sexual partners, Emilio found that clients often enjoy *mutual* sexual intimacy and can derive much sexual pleasure from (for example) giving oral sex, as well as receiving. As a caveat, many escorts described that the physical behavior during their "typical" encounter with a client often centered on them receiving attention from their customer (i.e., receiving oral sex, having a client watch the escort masturbate) and not the reverse. In a similar vein, some escorts described how they were uncertain of the exact sexual behaviors they were expected to perform with clients. Nick described how he assumed clients expected anal sex, but soon learned that was not always the case: "There are some things that have changed. I had [anal] sex with one of the first people [clients] I went out with, because I thought that was something that I *had* to do. In order to be a good escort that's something that I *needed* to do" (emphasis added). In many circumstances, the escorts we interviewed described how they learned to place limits on sexual behaviors with clients.

In addition to physical boundaries, *College Boys* escorts often described the need to place emotional barriers between themselves and clients highlighting how some clients can be particularly demanding on a relational level. Marc described this often unforeseen aspect of sex work in how he learned not only to place physical boundaries, but also emotional ones, "Some people really take everything out of you. It's like, 'Oh my God. I haven't felt that way in a long time.' I learned where my barriers are. I know what to give and what not to give, and I think that I can see what people need." In a latter portion of his interview, Marc described the need to emotionally disconnect with clients in order to limit his emotional commitment to a relative stranger and to maintain a personal comfort level with sexual activities occurring with clients. In this excerpt, we see how what he learned from previous experiences with clients led him to establish these boundaries:

Marc: It was it was because I didn't realize where my level needed to be. I didn't realize where I needed to stop.

Interviewer: What happened to the "degrading" feeling? You explained what happened to the energy.

Marc: I think that me putting up boundaries is what happened most.

Interviewer: So staying inside your comfort zone in terms of sexual activities with clients?

Marc: Well sexual activities and even sometimes, depending on whom it is and like what the situation is; sometimes even emotional stuff.

Jerry also described the need to set physical boundaries in order to manage emotional and relational boundaries with clients:

I have rules. I don't kiss, period. I don't. There are a few people that I have but it's very, very, very few and far between. It's an emotional thing for me; also kissing and fucking. I won't penetrate. I will not have any sort of anal sex at all. And the older men that are begging you to do it are like constantly coming up and throwing their lips on you. If you're not strong willed you'll just break down and go, "fine do whatever you want." And I won't do that because I want to respect myself at least a little bit when I walk out. So you have to be able to say no to people that are extremely pushy.

As Jerry suggested, learning how to set limits with clients allowed escorts to maintain their sense of personal integrity and emotional security before and after calls. Men who could learn how to do had longer escorting careers than men who did not.

Many of the men we interviewed described learning to set physical and emotional boundaries with clients did not diminish the client's satisfaction. In fact, many escorts reported how they often had a more enjoyable experience with their clients, and thus believed their clients would experience greater enjoyment as well. Compared to being cautious and uncertain during an encounter, which could then impact the quality of the experience with a client, escorts found they were more confident in pleasing their clients while also maintaining a sense of personal integrity. Without such confidence, escorts would focus more on managing their own discomfort or anxiety instead of attending to the client's needs; they may have appeared distracted or "uptight" to a client. As we have indicated, much of this process was learned through escorts own trial-and-error with clients. In the next section, we describe how escorts learned to modify their own attitudes and beliefs about sex work in order to become a successful sex worker—managing the emotional impact of their labor, generating positive feelings about their work, and learning to balance their personal and professional lives.

Attitude Adjustment

In the previous sections, we highlighted the various ways in which Martin established a formal and informal mentorship structure with his escorts. We also described how many escorts drew from personal experiences (social and sexual) when working with clients and how to more effectively navigate physical and emotional boundaries with clients developed either through a process of trial-and-error or from some type of mentoring process. In this next section, we spend more time talking about escort's transition into the field and how this process was often "bumpy" in the beginning.

Not all escorts reported positive feelings about their transition into escorting regardless of the mentorship they had received or how good they thought their social or sexual skills were. Andrew described how, when he began escorting, he was often not attracted to his clients and how his initial clients rarely tipped:

When I first started, there's a wreck in here. When you first start you get the shit calls. And when I first started I got the shitty calls: old people, dirty people, nasty people, people who paid you exactly what the fee was, didn't give you any tips whatever—and those were the worst because they made you the worst. And now I'll get repeat calls [repeat customers], people that I know that I can deal, and he'll tell me who I'm going to go and see, and what it's going to be like and all this other stuff so it's different now. And now I'm ok with it. I could probably do two [calls] in a night.

Andrew went on to describe how he later developed a friendship with one of his clients. This client happened to have been a "retired" escort himself who gave advice to Andrew about creating an emotional wall through manufacturing an alternate identity. Andrew learned to use this alternate persona as a way of distancing his personal feelings when working with his clients:

Because I was talking to this one client. He's like, "I escorted all through college and I put myself through Harvard law as an escort. You really just have to develop a different person [mind set] and this [other] person has to go and do this [call]. While you're in there [with a client] you 'blah, blah, blah,' like my name is Johnny Cash." As soon as I go into a call, I'm Johnny Cash. As soon as I leave I'm not Johnny Cash. I go back to being John Doe.

Many of the men we interviewed described an adjustment period after they first began escorting. Many times, the negative feelings escorts reported centered on the stigma associated with sex work itself. Escorts reported how they felt "dirty" for having sex with men with whom they normally would not have done so if it had not been for the money. Escorts often described how negative social views about escorting were ingrained in them, "After doing a couple calls you just feel a little bit bad about yourself doing it and like it doesn't feel right doing it. There's other ways to make money" (Brian). Many also expressed stereotypes about sex workers (e.g., they are drug addicted, homeless, mentally unstable, or abused) and how this description did not match how they viewed themselves. Some worried that others would apply these stereotypes to them if their escorting became known. In learning to cope with being involved in the business of sex work, men working at *College Boys* described how they learned to modify their own negative attitudes about prostitution. Frank talked about how his feelings changed over time:

At the beginning I was really leery about it. I was always like a nervous wreck and like watching what's going on in the room. I'd talk to the people and get to know them before anything else happened. Now I go in there, get, go and do what needs to be done and I leave pretty much it. I'm not so . . . I'm not so much ashamed of myself and what I'm doing. It's just something I don't want to be doing.

Managing this type of stigma included changing one's mindset about the nature of their work and dismissing stereotypes about sex work and sex workers.

Some escorts related how they changed their mindset by focusing less on escorting as a *sexual* act and more on escorting as a *service*—viewing the encounter as a business transaction. Nathan framed his work in such a way and it allowed him to maintain an emotional distance from his feelings about prostitution: "You just kind of like push it in the back of your mind like you try to separate it from your personal life; you're just doing it for money. You just like go in and you think about something else. You just do the work and then you leave." Similarly, Jeff told us about how he did not see sex work as "degrading" because he viewed it as a job, "It's not degrading myself at all like everybody else says it would. Everybody's telling me, 'Don't do it, don't degrade yourself. You're going to have nightmares for the rest of your life.' People get too worked up, I don't know why. I just see it as a regular job and like I said just talk to the person and you don't always have to always have sex. And you'll be just fine." Consistent with the idea that escorts also provide social and emotional services to clients, Jeff also described how his time with clients was not entirely spent engaging in sex. Instead, he often spent a significant portion of his appointments entertaining clients through conversation, having a drink, or watching a movie together.

Other escorts described the importance of being a "good listener" or communicator with clients, and how this often constituted a majority of the time during client calls. Non-sexual aspects of their job were often viewed positively, detached from the sexual (prostitution) part of their job. This mixed role (sexual and non-sexual) often helped escorts feel more positive about their work because (1) it incorporated enjoyable activities in with the sex which they often did not enjoy, (2) more time spent socializing meant less time having sex while still providing a service the client valued, and (3) social aspects of the appointment provided a more natural and normative transition to having sex with clients—escorts felt like they could develop a more personal basis in which sexual behavior would be contextualized.

Other escorts described how the amount of money they were paid and the speed in which they could earn it helped quell negative feelings about sex work: "Escorting kind of weirded me out, but I thought to myself, 'Yeah I think I'm going to be able to handle it. It's easy money.' I made, yesterday and today, more than [2 days pay] working for a construction company in just a couple of hours. So I'm like, 'Holy crap its easy money.' I pretty much push myself to do that [think about the money], you know" (Daniel).

In addition, some of the *College Boys* escorts described how they varied their behavior (i.e., often limiting physical contact in some way) with clients in an effort to feel better about being involved with sex work. For example, Pete, who identified as heterosexual, would masturbate in front of his clients or let them massage him, but did not engage in physical sexual contact with them (e.g., oral or anal sex). While his behavior was sexual (both he and his clients would be naked, masturbate together, and orgasm) he felt comfortable escorting because he did not view his behavior as "prostitution":

When I first started I was like, "Oh God I can't do this . . . [it's] too much like prostitution." And then I got into it and its like, "Well it ain't prostitution. No one's doing anything [sexual] for me. I'm not doing anything [sexual] for them." They're just buying an hour of my time because of my looks and their just looking at me just like at a strip club . . . Except you sit there and you play with yourself.

Erick described a similar phenomenon:

Erick: Wow, didn't know it was this lucrative. Just how much money you can make off of it and I was just blown away.

Interviewer: You mean by the clients?

Erick: Correct. And we [myself and another friend who started escorting the same time as me] both were kind of like, "We can't do this, it's against our ethics, our morals, our values, religion." But it didn't stop us.

Interviewer: What made you change your mind about starting to work here?

Erick: My beliefs? I kind of started to think, "The money, started to pay the price." And that made it almost better, more doable to work here.

Interviewer: Because the money was so good?

Erick: Very indiscrete, made it seem okay in our heads, even though it's typical knowledge that this is not normal, this is not something that should be offered as a service.

Interviewer: Why?

Erick: Sex for money is just, I think, ridiculous. I honestly consider myself old fashioned. Meeting the right person and having sex with only them and being monogamous.

Another way that escorts learned to cope with any negative feelings about sex work included viewing prostitution as a temporary means to achieve a longer-term goal. Although the reality was often not the case, men indicated they were just escorting temporarily, for a little extra cash, or to help them get back on their feet—to have enough money for a down-payment on a car, security deposit on an apartment, etc. Hector described his viewpoint on how long he was going to work:

My thought was if maybe I just do a couple of times it will give me some kind of help. At that point I probably didn't even have $10 in my bank account. So making $160 an hour was a big attraction. You know, like, "Hey maybe I can just work three times a week and that should be fine for me." When I was serving I made about $300 a week. And this I will just have to do three calls a day, or week, and I will be fine. And once I get some payments down on my credit card and on my car I can just quit and get a normal job. And thinking like escorting will be able to help me out.

Escorts like Erick and Hector often described how being successful and feeling good about what they were doing required them to view their work in a way that was consistent with their own identity and needs. Such a mindset might also require an escort to adjust his identity in an effort to match his attitude regarding his work behavior. As we have mentioned, this could entail creating an alter ego or imagining that the client was someone else (i.e., putting the escort's mind in a different place during the encounter). Although we have highlighted how some escorts reframed their work in an effort to cope or "deal" with any negative feelings they had about sex work, we wish to also note that many escorts (often those remaining in escorting longer—several months to several years) generally felt very positive about their work. Escorts gained personal emotional satisfaction in knowing that they were able to please their clients and some found that being paid for sex was a boost to their self-esteem and self-image. Some men felt more empowered or more attractive given that clients found them appealing enough to pay for their time and body. In the excerpt below, we see how Erick's self-image changed as a result of being a sex worker. In his personal life as well as his professional one, Erick felt like he took better care of his hygiene, was more outgoing, and reported an overall boost to his self-esteem:

Interviewer: You were saying it [escorting] builds you up?

Erick: I'm realizing that, "Maybe I *am* cute." And a lot of it has to do with the dates I'm going on probably. The guys have been getting cuter. I've been taking better care of myself, health-wise, too; so maybe that's helping. Since I've started escorting, I've started dressing better, spending that extra half hour in the bathroom. I think hygiene is a big issue when you do this [escorting]. When you do this you have to have amazingly good hygiene. You don't want to go in smelly. You don't want to go in with gross fingernails, greasy skin, that kind of stuff. I've been crazier since I started escorting.

Interviewer: Meaning?

Erick: Before escorting, I was kind of a shy guy; I'd go to the [gay club] maybe once a month. But now that I know more people, you get to know a lot of people through this . . . The nice thing about me is that I think I make people think differently about escorts. Because they do know me as a good person, and they find out that I do this later, and they're just kind of like, "Shit, but he's a nice guy.

Erick's reframing and reevaluation of his personal self-worth over the course of his career in escorting was common among many of the escorts we interviewed.

Incorporating the Trade into One's Social Networks

Thus far, we have discussed the ways in which escorts learned the trade. These methods have included formalized and informal mentorship, trial-and-error, and modifying one's own attitude about sex work (through the dissociation from negative social and personal views about prostitution). Sustaining a career as an escort required men to maintain a positive view about their profession. Although escorts often turned to each other (and to Martin) for support and as a resource to cope with the emotional and physical demands of their labor, other sources such as family, friends, and partners also played key roles in these men's working lives. Many men described how they initially did not disclose being an escort to people in their personal lives outside of the agency and how this non-disclosure created a double burden. First, escorts felt like they were living parts of their lives in secret—lying to people they cared about or evading questions about their source of income and their whereabouts at odd hours of the day and night. Second, many escorts felt that their non-disclosure was also a denial of access to key sources of social and emotional support from those who were otherwise central figures in their lives.

Some escorts reported positive experiences in disclosing their profession to family, friends, and partners; however, this was contingent upon receiving positive social and emotional reinforcement from said individual(s). In essence, simply having gotten the topic "off one's chest" was not enough to generate positive feelings for oneself, and a negative reaction generally resulted in negative feelings about having disclosed. Those to whom escorts disclosed were often incorporated into some of the professional aspects of the escort's lives. For example, several boyfriends and girlfriends of escorts visited the agency frequently, sometimes for hours at a time and socialized there. These individuals became familiar with the business of the agency in addition to the other escorts and manager at the agency.

Some men felt disclosure was not an option for them. These men often reported that their families would not understand their involvement in escorting, citing religious and moral objections to the profession. Escorts who felt they could not disclose to their partners also highlighted religious and moral objections in addition to citing a belief that their partner would feel that escorting equated to relationship infidelity even if the relationship was otherwise non-monogamous. Richard described why he concealed escorting from his partner: "Because of the whole stigma attached to it, and at the time I had just broken up with a very judgmental individual. He pretty much put me down all the time and I was afraid he would find out about this and it would be awful, so I kept it a secret, which was fine, but it helped." In some cases, fear of rejection was the reality—negative or judgmental reactions from those who found out a participant was escorting.

Despite potential stigma from family members, partners, and friends many escorts found social and emotional support from other escorts or by establishing friendships with those who felt more neutral or positive to escorting. This may have included limiting social interactions and contact with those who regarded escorting negatively, while increasing social interactions with those who regarded escorting more positively. Gay-identified escorts often described this process in similar terms to their coming out as "gay," whereby they surrounded themselves with those who were supportive of homosexuality (or gay also themselves) and limiting social interactions with those who expressed homophobic sentiments.

Some escorts felt disclosure was inevitable. In essence, people were going to find out. Rather than attempt to conceal and be the subject of gossip, some escorts were forthcoming about their work. Chase described how, when he transitioned into escorting, he decided not to conceal his identity. For him, this meant his picture on the agency's website would include his face (as opposed to cropping the picture from the neck down or having his face blurred/obscured):

> Because you know it didn't take long for people to find out because Michael [another escort] and I decided we wanted our faces on the website because we figured we'd get more calls that way and it didn't take long—probably a week for everybody that I know to find out. People judged us, and when I went into this thing, I went in with the attitude that, "If you're going to judge me for what I do for money, and judge me on solely that, and you know I don't care, then you're not going to be my friend if that's what you're going to base our friendship on and that's what you're going to judge me."
>
> It would be like judging you because you're gay, "I'm not going to be your friend because you're gay. I'm not going to be friend because you work at Friendly's [a restaurant chain]."
>
> You know, it's the same exact thing. Maybe this is not a respectable job, and certainly most people view it as not a respectable job, which is fine, But you know, if you're going to find out what I do for a living and disapprove of it, that's fine if you tell me, but you know, leave it at that and don't judge me as a person because I'm so, there's so much more to me than *College Boys*, you know. And it helped me see who my true friends were. I helped me see the people who judge me who I do for a living and that decide not to talk to me because I'm a *College Boy* and the people who were just like, you know, "Chase, I really don't like you doing this, but I understand that it's your life, it's your choice, you're the one that has to live with it and I love you for who you are." And it helped me see who my true friends are. I think it's about those things. I don't want to deal with people that are going to be fake and closed minded and judge me for that.

Escorts often had a difficult time gauging the type of reaction they would receive from someone close to them. For example, Tom reported how he was not expecting a negative reaction from his partner, and instead expected stigma from his mother. In reality, the opposite happened:

Well, I was kind of seeing this person and he found out I was a *College Boy* and he started saying how gross I was and how disgusting and everything else, and started calling me all these names. We since then patched things up but he won't date me because I do this for work. And I told him it was just the same as him saying something about a stripper or somebody coming out being gay or an ex-convict. You don't have to degrade the person. I have a couple of other friends but some of them are just asking questions. They're just very curious about why I do this and what the job entails, and stuff like that. It's just like my mom. She's ok with some things and others not. She's a mother. Of all the people, I thought my mom would be the one asking so many questions and just degrading me. But it just happened to be the person I was seeing. And my mom's the one that loves me.

In all, many escorts recognized the importance of social support to their longevity as an escort, and how this support could come from family and partners. In the event such support was unavailable, escorts recognized that they could turn to each other, Martin, or surround themselves with friends who were more understanding of their profession.

CONCLUSION

Despite the lack of formalized training options, the escorts we interviewed reported a variety of ways in which they learned how to perform their job. These experiences encompassed the physical, social, and emotional aspects of being an escort. From a sexual standpoint, escorts learned the behavior that would be expected of them with a client and how this behavior was often not identical to that which would be anticipated with a traditional sex partner (e.g., anal sex). From a social standpoint, escorts learned how to draw from their repertoire of social skills to entertain clients during the times together that did not involve physical intimacy. From a social standpoint, escorts also learned the benefits and consequences of incorporating and disclosing their profession to their social/personal networks. Escorts recognized the powerful mechanism of support that those close to them could provide, but balanced this against the potential for a backlash of stigma and judgment. Finally, escorts learned to manage the emotional aspects of their profession. They recognized the need to distance themselves from the stigma associated with sex work and the need to limit their emotional investment with clients such to avoid burnout.

Many of the mechanisms we have described in this chapter may be pertinent to all those involved in the sex work industry (men, women, transgendered individuals) regardless of their type of sex work (e.g., escort, erotic dancer, adult film star). Certainly, not all of the experiences we have described may be the case for any one individual. In addition, given the lack of formalized mechanisms by which sex workers learn about their occupational roles, we do not wish to discount the potential for other innovative ways that they may have adopted for themselves, but that we have not discussed in this chapter.

Chapter Five

FRIENDS AND BROTHERS

OVERVIEW

College Boys evolved into a tightly knit community between the time Martin established the agency and when we conducted our first interviews on a cloudy spring weekend two years later. What began as a means of support after being laid off had become Martin's family business. He was at the center of the whole enterprise, pleased with how the agency had grown and how it allowed him to have so many friends, supporters, and hangers-on all around. For the most part it was an all-boys club, and few doubted Martin's ability or right to lead it. He was no longer alone and out of luck. Martin now provided services that the type of men who once downsized him out of a job paid handsomely to receive. He was an entrepreneur, a businessman, and the leader of a small clan of handsome young escorts. The agency took on the appearance of a family, fraternity, or thriving enterprise depending on how deeply involved one became in its social network. People learned about the agency, often by accident from surfing online, going to the house with a friend, or seeing *College Boys* out at a club. Learning more, some people wanted to be part of the action. They hired an escort; they talked about becoming one. Once inside, escorts looked without, some never wanting to leave while others counted their days. This chapter tells that story—of an escort call service that became something more and about how Martin's personal and financial situation created a dynamic social organization that sold companionship to men of means. We speculate to what degree this represented a unique outcome given the personalities involved, versus to what degree such a development might reflect the social and emotional needs inherent for many sex workers in similar circumstances.

A Network of Fellows

Anecdotal and research reports suggest that many individuals working in prostitution and escorting form some type of social network with other sex workers, especially if employed by an agency. People seem to form groups either in person or online, despite prostitution's illegality and a desire in some to remain hidden for more personal reasons. Many sex workers connect to share ideas, provide emotional and material support, establish business contacts, and make friends. Prevailing negative social attitudes associated with sex work may, in some respects, enhance such affiliations by creating clear psychological boundaries between those who sell companionship and sex and others who do not. Such "in group" versus "out group" ("us" versus "them") perceptions are a well-documented phenomenon in social psychology. They reinforce normative behaviors and shared identity among group members (e.g., Kruglanski, Shah, Pierro, & Mannetti, 2002). Membership exaggerates perceived degree of similarity between people in the "in group" while maximizing such differences between this group and the rest of the world (e.g., Rhiannon & Crisp, 2010). Group membership helps to create a common identity and a buffer against negative messages from the "other."

As we have argued in other publications (e.g., Smith, Grov, & Seal, 2008) and elsewhere in this book, an enhanced group identity allowed escorts to manage challenges posed by their work and provided other more typical benefits of belonging to a social group. Not all sex workers wanted or needed to take advantage of such an opportunity—certainly not all of the *College Boys* did so. However, if the agency's experience provides any guide, then a significant portion of male escorts would appreciate associations with other sex workers in the same way that Martin valued relationships with his staff. In the face of denigrating social opinion regarding sex work, the group provided a safe haven of approval and a sub-culture where escorting became acceptable, even desirable and where one's efforts could be valued for their quality, frequency, or panache. A young man could feel better about himself when the larger world was putting people like him down. An escort could be honest about his work within *College Boys* and talk about its problems and benefits, receive support, and not worry about disapproval or rejection. He would not have to "hide," not at least from people within the agency's network. Instead, the escort could gain relief from a double life that often proved emotionally difficult to maintain. Although such tensions were not always prominent, all of the escorts used the agency as an emotional safety valve at one time or another. Whether in talking to Martin or by making friends with other *College Boys*, each of the young men working at the agency needed some type of relief from the pressures of sex work once in a while—whether this occurred through receiving social support, benefiting from mentorship with more experienced escorts, or just decompressing after a call by hanging out with the other guys.

Escorts also appeared to be mindful of the business potential in developing connections within the world of the agency. Men working for *College Boys* sometimes received referrals from each other, for instance when an escort was too busy or did not enjoy seeing a particular type of client for whom another escort might be better suited (e.g., with a client requesting a certain sex act). Escorts also passed along information about client preferences, quirks, and dislikes to associates who might be working with that client in a future appointment. This occurred directly when a client hired another escort who then spoke with someone who had a previous call with that client. Information exchange also occurred indirectly; while talking among themselves escorts described experiences with their work and clients. Reese said, "I do remember asking a lot of questions when I began. I would always ask, 'What does this client want? What is this client looking for? What do they expect? Do they know I don't do this, that, and the other thing?'" An escort who maintained connections within the agency could benefit from these exchanges more frequently than one who did not. He could more easily learn strategies for managing certain customers or have the chance to talk about what he would and would not be willing to do on an appointment. Such conversations permitted him to think through the job and its impact on his life with people he knew the work from the inside and from whom he would not need to fear rejection.

Martin and the escorts also strove to build good working relationships with each other. Often these connections grew much deeper and more personal. The business advantage of good mutual communication between the agency owner and his employees was obvious to everyone. As the owner, Martin needed to know a great deal of personal information about the escorts—information about sexual and social preferences that they might not disclose to just anybody. Thus, Martin could better match escorts with clients if he could gain their trust and confidence. He could also become aware of any strengths and weaknesses in his employees so as to develop management or mentorship strategies accordingly. Martin kept careful mental notes on the relationships *among* his escorts by noting who got along with whom, which possessed better social skills, and who among his escorts took more active roles in the agency or even leadership positions among the other escorts.

Likewise, all of the escorts realized the advantages of being on their boss's good side. The escorts often jockeyed for Martin's favor much as any employee might. They too kept notes on who was in, who might be out, and which escort had annoyed or pleased Martin in some way. Martin tended to give important calls to men he knew as reliable, friendly, and available; escorts with whom he tended to be more familiar. Even among newer escorts or when a client made a specific request, Martin preferred sending *College Boys* upon whom he could depend to provide good customer service. This was well known among men working for the agency, and most strove to meet Martin's expectations. They found it easy to like Martin who was naturally gregarious and caring. He tried to help the escorts whenever he could by providing support, money, and a place to live if they needed one. Just as many of the men became friendly with each other, so too did the majority develop genuine bonds of affection with Martin, augmenting whatever relationship they had with him as an employer.

Combined with the different categories of people inhabiting the agency's social fringe, the interacting relationships at *College Boys* created a multi-layered relational space represented in Figure 5.1. Everyone affiliated with *College Boys* agreed that Martin represented the agency's social nexus, the hub around which activity unfolded. Thus, where an individual could be placed on this map often depended primarily on their degree of personal and

Figure 5.1.
Relational Map of the Agency

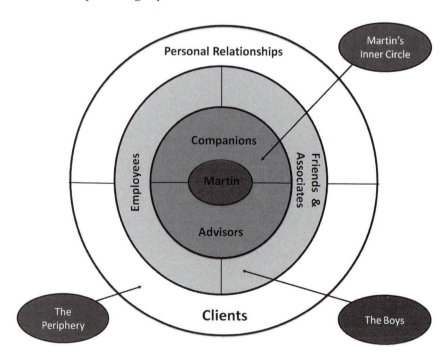

business involvement with Martin. As will be seen, Martin often appeared to encourage this blending of roles and felt comfortable with it. Escorts, clients, friends, family members, and partners also interacted with one another; these dynamics may have not directly involved Martin as owner, but they almost always related to events occurring within the agency and so could be thought of as indirectly affected by the tone Martin set and the various players' relative standing with him.

Martin's Inner Circle

Although Martin had many acquaintances and contacts outside of *College Boys*, nearly all of his closest friends were current or former escorts with the agency. Most of Martin's relationships prior to forming the agency had drifted away between his coming out of the closet and being laid off. He no longer kept in contact with his former girlfriend. As he was still closeted with his family, those relationships tended to be even more tenuous than they already had been. Furthermore, as an entrepreneur in a service business, Martin had to be constantly available to answer phone calls, respond to emails, drive escorts to appointments, and otherwise conduct any of the endless tasks needed to keep *College Boys* in operation. Maintaining ads on websites was time consuming as many required constant reposting or made subscribers log-in to the site on a regular basis. It really was a 24/7 job, 365 days per year. Unless you were part of that scene, it would have been difficult for Martin to find the time to connect. It would have been hard for you to understand him, or his goals.

By the time we met him, the agency he started encompassed nearly all of Martin's social life. Martin appeared to like it that way and to be fulfilled with the life he had created for himself. He was his own boss in the center of a buzzing hive. It required creativity and an almost manic constant energy to manage, qualities Martin possessed in abundance. Martin could always be on stage, he could always have people around him who needed him. He never had to follow someone else's schedule or follow another person's rules. The wealthy, professional, and influential sought him out, treated him well, and provided him with a living. Instead of working for them, he worked with them—temporarily their equal. They made each other happy. He gave them the escorts they wanted; they gave him an income and with it his independence. It was a good deal. However, the cost was to be consumed by the business and have little beyond it. Martin never lacked for company even though he was sometimes a little lonely for true love: True love, the one thing that you could not rent from a *College Boy*.

Martin instead surrounded himself with good friends; some of the most interesting and capable guys among an intriguing assembly of young men. The closest to him were his *Advisors* who were Martin's best friends and his lieutenants, and with him they formed the core of the agency's social world. Emilio, Andrew, Tommy, and Nathan did not fit any one type or mold, but they were all loyal—Martin trusted them implicitly. He sometimes gave over the operation of the business to one or more of this group when he allowed himself a day off or needed to travel. All were excellent escorts. They each had clients who hired them regularly; new clients frequently requested them off the website. Martin did not need to work in order to keep the four busy as he would often have to do with less personable or savvy escorts. Even when each stopped actively seeing clients at some point over our time interviewing the *College Boys*, all four continued their close friendships with Martin and helped him run the business. He depended on them.

- Emilio—A handsome young Latino man who looked equally good dressed as a woman. He was a drag performer, hair dresser, and costume designer: moody, loyal, sensual, and fun. Emilio was the first escort we interviewed. Stunning, new clients often wanted to hire him when they saw his pictures on the website. Protective, Emilio set the tone for a client coming to the agency for an incall. He mentored other escorts, watched over Martin, and knew how to have a great time. However, Emilio's strong personality and sharp wit could sometimes alienate people on the receiving end of an outburst or barb. He seemed to feel comfortable just living in the endless moment.
- Andrew—A brilliant and attractive guy with a quirky smile and innocent face whose New Year's resolution "was to not be so mean." Andrew could compete with Martin as the center of attention in any room through a combination of charm, looks, and smart banter. He was one of the few people who could get the better of his boss and best friend—he even made Martin speechless on a few occasions; stories that were told over and more to eager audiences who had never heard Martin bested in a verbal duel. Andrew possessed a dominant personality and a darker side to his nature that many clients relished. Dating Nick, an escort in the other half of Martin's *Inner Circle*, Andrew spent a great deal of time at the agency with his boyfriend. Martin loved their company and asked them to come by the house as often as they could. He enjoyed the constant sharp back-and-forth Andrew kept up with him, and valued the younger man's insights into staff and clients. Andrew seemed to enjoy the access he had to his boss and the status it gave him among many of the other escorts.
- Tommy—The fashionable golden-haired boy with long curls and a wicked tongue who rarely sat still long enough to cool down. Of all the escorts, Tommy may have been the one whose company Martin most enjoyed. If Andrew kept pace with Martin's stream of consciousness, Tommy could outpace Martin in pure verbal production. Tommy lived with his boyfriend, Michael in the sunny front room on the agency's second floor. Lively and immaculate, Tommy always had something glib and fun to say—even if it was sometimes at the expense of another. In the midst of transferring to another college when we interviewed him, Tommy possessed a sharp analytic mind that he did not often let others see—just as only those closest to him knew about his struggles with depression and a rejecting family.
- Nathan—Martin trusted Nathan the most. Nathan exhibited a strong, quiet, masculine personality and was a little older and more mature than many of the

other guys. Raised in the country and an attractive high school football player with short blond hair, Nathan spoke relatively little but smiled often. People were attracted to his understated polite charm as much as they were to his muscular build. We met Nathan one summer day when he was elbows deep in a car engine behind the house. He wiped the grease onto his jeans and pumped our hands grinning. After introducing us, Martin related that Nathan tended to attract and keep longer-term clients—highly placed men in government and business circles who enjoyed spending the weekend with him and wanted to do so regularly. Nathan was often in Washington, D.C. for long weekends during the time we worked with the agency.

Emilio helped Martin the most with new escorts and with publicizing the agency at clubs and events. He had lived in the house the longest, tending to keep an eye on what was going on upstairs among the various and shifting combinations of men. Andrew and Tommy took on the roles of Martin's playful buddies and confidants. Not as involved with the business side of things, they were perhaps the most similar to Martin personally. Martin and Tommy were inseparable during the year or so that Tommy lived at the agency. Nathan represented calm, steadfast, and loyal dependability. Martin relied on Nathan for solid advice and a confidential ear. He may have shared the most secrets with Nathan, who was the first person Martin tapped to take over the business on those rare times when Martin would not be available. Nathan also acted as the agency's informal treasurer, helping to keep track of Martin's finances and making sure all of the bills got paid. Money management consistently eluded Martin, who spent as freely as he received.

It was interesting that none of the men in Martin's advisor circle were particularly close with one another. Although on friendly terms, only Tommy and Andrew spent a significant amount of time together outside the agency, and that was typically while going somewhere with Martin such as a dance club on Saturday night. Tommy and Emilio, living together in the house, tended to say relatively little to each other; they instead provided mutual space to maintain their cordial relationship. Nathan remained more on his own, not living at the agency and increasingly occupied with his work, classes at the local community college, and a new relationship with one of the younger escorts. Perhaps, Martin sought to fulfill different needs with each other these very different men: Emilio as a major domo for the house, Andrew and Tommy as personal companions, and Nathan as the trusted lieutenant. As such, they had personalities that may have been too distinct to blend well with one another, despite their connection through Martin.

Nick, Michael, Dennis, and Becky comprised the other half of Martin's *Inner Circle*—his *Companions*. The three guys involved themselves less in the operation of the business; Martin did not typically rely on them for advice or emotional support to the degree he did with his *Advisors*. Martin frequently hired Becky, the only woman in the regular *College Boys* network, to drive escorts to and from appointments. However, her main role within the agency was as a close friend to Martin and many of the guys. The relationships in this half of the *Inner Circle* centered less on the agency and more on the social side of life, having fun together and providing support for one another.

- Nick—In love with Andrew, he feared that his affection was not always fully returned. Nick bubbled with enthusiasm and loved the party scene, but he would confide in those close to him that he worried about becoming an alcoholic. Nick's natural warmth and open nature won him many friends at the agency, and his high energy level gave him a good deal in common with Martin. Martin also enjoyed how he could just relax and be himself around Nick, who always had a kind word and a funny joke to relate. Coming from a deeply religious family, Nick had a quiet and serious side to him that few people got to see.
- Michael—Quiet, but with a fast temper, Michael could be possessively jealous of Tommy. A skilled dancer, tan, and very good looking—Michael had finished some education beyond high school and had a decent job. His looks and masculinity attracted many clients, who developed into a loyal group of regular customers. He could be eclipsed by Tommy's sunny and outgoing personality, but Martin very much enjoyed Michael's company and the three of them were often together. Martin often played the role of peacemaker between his two emotional younger friends.
- Dennis—One of the original escorts from when Martin first founded the agency, Dennis had run afoul of the law and had been in prison. When released, Martin picked him up and gave him a place to stay. Dennis had started to work again for the agency while seeking out more regular employment in his skilled trade. Although he and Martin had a close relationship based on years of association, Martin tended to keep Dennis a bit at arm's length compared to his open lively relationships with other members of the *Inner Circle*. Perhaps, Martin felt more loyalty to Dennis given their years working together. However, when alone, Martin and Dennis got along well and had many deep conversations together.
- Becky—Vibrant, moody, and a little insecure. Becky felt completely at home within the agency. Saying that she always got along better with men than women, and especially with gay men, Becky and Martin maintained a constant banter of teasing insults flying between them. She was especially close with Tommy, with whom she often spent much of the day; they made quite the rambunctious pair. Becky made people laugh. She was sensitive, but rarely showed it except in a fit of temper when a joke had gone too far or when she felt left out. A close companion for many of the *College Boys*, Becky became the ever-present kid sister, caretaker, party girl, and confidant all wrapped into one swirling package.

Others in the agency may have occasionally risen to the level of a *Companion*, but these four individuals consistently maintained close bonds with Martin throughout their involvement with the agency, and afterward. Although they were not as involved in helping to run the business as were Martin's *Advisors*, they still developed the same relationship with him as did the other half of his *Inner Circle*.

What we really see in the *Inner Circle* is a surrogate family running a successful business. These were people with loose ties to their own families who came together through their involvement in *College Boys*. Dennis described how it felt when he said:

> I'm part of the agency; I've been here since the beginning. I feel a sense of belonging, something to believe in, and somewhere to go, a place to be. It's like I actually belong somewhere; it's a family I guess. When you think about it, it is kind of twisted because it is kind of like a sense of family. Them two, Martin and Becky, I really look up to them a lot. It's just one of those things.

Their work in escorting allowed them to form close bonds to Martin; most also created lasting relationships among others at the agency. All of the men in Martin's circle of *Advisors* were dating *College Boys* at the time they were interviewed. Two, Nathan and Tommy, were still involved in these same relationships at the time we last spoke with them several years after our last agency interviews. Tommy and Michael, living an hour away in a home they had just purchased together, kept in regular contact with Martin and visited him from time to time. Emilio continued to work for *College Boys* off and on until the agency closed. Becky was there until the end—Martin's vivacious and flirtatious "work spouse." As Nathan gradually moved more into his own career outside of escorting, Becky assumed many of the responsibilities of the trusted second-in-command. Thus, she became more of an *Advisor* during the last year or two of the agency. Martin remained at the center, wrapping the shifting fabric of these relationships around himself like a warm wool comforter. His *Inner Circle* supported him in almost every way, materially as well as emotionally; and he gave back to them whenever he could, whatever they needed.

The Boys—Friends, Associates, and Employees

Navigating outward from the agency's *Inner Circle* to its orbiting fringe of clients, friends, partners, and family members, we first encounter a large and complex intermediate zone. As you can see in Table 5.1, this layer represented most of the escorts working for *College Boys*, men between the core relationships holding the agency together and the outer edges of its social map where it interfaced with the larger community. Even though some of the men at this level enjoyed relatively close friendships with Martin and the *Inner Circle*, none of the relationships marked them as a *Companion* or *Advisor*. These center-most roles within the agency reflected a reciprocated personal connection with Martin which was not usually evidenced between him and men at the intermediate level. Thus, while many of the escorts held Martin in very high regard and considered him to be a friend, these were less emotionally

Table 5.1.
Number and Percentage of Escorts at Each Social Level of the Agency

Level of Agency Involvement	Number (%)
Advisor	4 (10.0)
Companion	4 (10.0)
Friend	6 (15.0)
Associate	9 (22.5)
Employee	17 (42.5)

intense relationships than those in the *Inner Circle*. As such, even though his feelings would often be quite warm toward the escorts, Martin maintained an emotional boundary that limited the intimacy he shared with them—a distance he did not establish with people in his *Inner Circle*.

One might think of men in this intermediary range as the journeymen staff of any company or social organization. Given their numbers they provided most of the services to clients and brought in the majority of monthly revenue. Although often on friendly terms with their employer and other staff, relationships between the escorts and management were typically more social than intimate, more activity-based than personal. Such would be the case for many smaller businesses, and especially family-operated ones, a type of company that perhaps most closely resembles the social organization of *College Boys*. There was the most mobility between the three categories of men at this level than in the inner or outer spheres of the agency. Likewise, the escorts moved closer to and farther away from the agency's social center more frequently. Connections to the agency at this level often existed in a greater state of transition.

Figure 5.2 presents the three levels of social engagement among the three different types of escorts at the agency. We have presented the various roles at this level as progressing from *Employee* to *Friend*, signifying that escorts often developed closer ties with Martin and other *College Boys* over the course of working for the agency. Some may have even worked their way into the *Inner Circle*, whose members (except for Martin, of course) had all at one time or another been much more peripherally involved with the agency and its staff. This is not to say that all men working for *College Boys* developed deeper integration within the social fabric of the agency during the course of their employment. Many entered the agency as *Employees* and did not increase their connections to other escorts beyond the role of co-worker. Others made friends and became closer with Martin, but then developed some stable equilibrium point from which they did not advance. Some regressed over time in that ties to people at the agency loosened as friends left the job, personality

Figure 5.2.
"The Boys"—friends, associates, and employees

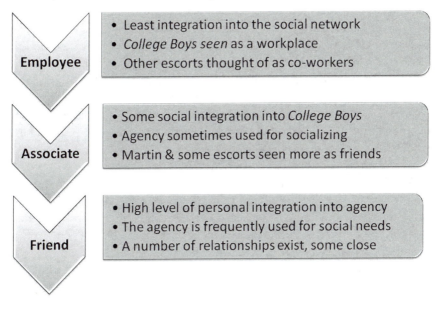

Employee
- Least integration into the social network
- *College Boys seen* as a workplace
- Other escorts thought of as co-workers

Associate
- Some social integration into *College Boys*
- Agency sometimes used for socializing
- Martin & some escorts seen more as friends

Friend
- High level of personal integration into agency
- The agency is frequently used for social needs
- A number of relationships exist, some close

conflicts emerged, or events and relationships outside the agency assumed greater priority.

A number of men starting with the agency as new escorts did not work out. Their span of employment would be quite short and their opportunity to build relationships within the agency subsequently limited. These individuals may not have been able to manage the emotional strains and stigma inherent to working as an escort. They may have found escorting not congruent with their values, and the reasons for escorting not strong enough to overcome them. Having sex with undesirable partners may have been too difficult to manage. A significant proportion of escorts worked only three or four months at *College Boys*—not long enough to penetrate more deeply into the agency's social network. Most of them would have remained at the *Employee* level unless they had pre-existing friendships with agency staff. In this case, such men would have come into the agency as *Friends*, but not have remained in the role for very long given their relatively short-term employment at *College Boys*.

Other escorts may have adjusted well to the work and remained, but may have not needed to work as often or for as much time. Some men might have had short-term financial goals that were accomplished before they built close ties with others at the agency—entering the agency as an *Employee* and leaving at the same level. These escorts would often get used to the money, and stay for much longer than they initially might have predicted. A more common occurrence involved men escorting to supplement their income. As we have seen in previous chapters, these *College Boys* may have worked full or part-time jobs with sex work providing a boost to these earnings. Some students used escorting to raise their standard of living; they wanted to work less to focus more on their studies, but also had financial goals they wanted to fulfill. Men in these situations would not have seen as many clients, and consequently did not spend as much time at the agency. Their time may also have been more consumed by work or study, leaving less time to socialize with other escorts. Such escorts would not have become as integrated into the fabric of social interactions at *College Boys* when compared to escorts who worked more frequently and/or over a longer duration.

Another variable influencing integration into life of the agency was the degree to which escorts inhabited rich pre-existing social networks. Some young men possessed deep connections to friends, families, and partners outside the agency which limited development of more significant connections within *College Boys*. Many enjoyed socializing at the agency and thought highly of Martin, but were too occupied with extant friendships and family relations to develop greater intimacy with people in the agency. Furthermore, as we will discuss more in Chapter six, negative social attitudes regarding prostitution prevented many men in this group from disclosing their sex work to friends and family, and most escorts were highly motivated to hide sex work from them. Needing to maintain a barrier between sex work and cherished relationships significantly limited the time and types of activity men in this sub-group had with others in the agency. It typically meant that these individuals tended to work less frequently for Martin, even though they might do so over a long period of time.

Men working over a longer duration, but seeing fewer clients for whatever reason, often settled into a long-term position within the intermediate zone either as an *Associate* or *Employee*. They rarely entered the role of *Friend* given limited involvement in the life of the agency. Their interactions with Martin and other agency people mostly centered on seeing clients and they spent less time and developed less intimacy within the agency's social world. Men assuming an *Associate* role tended to be at the house before or after calls; they might also stop by when in the area or when Martin had invited them out to eat or to a dance club. *Friends* held the most positive views of Martin and the other escorts among men in this intermediate range.

Employee escorts saw their affiliation with *College Boys* in purely business terms. Though they typically had cordial relations with the staff, their views were less positive or personally warm and they often had more complaints about the agency's social culture or about individual personalities among the *College Boys*. They did not express a desire to socialize with agency members or with Martin beyond what their work required. Escorting for them represented going to a job, and then leaving when the work was done. For example, Paul told us, "I just do it as a job you know. I try to do my best. That's what I would do in a regular job except it's sexual." It is difficult to say whether these somewhat more negative attitudes limited an *Employee's* social integration into the agency, or if that lack of involvement encouraged development of less positive opinions. *Employee* escorts' level of personal gratification from their work and personal connections through the agency were not as developed compared to men in the other groups—they enjoyed their jobs less and did not find the social aspects of the agency to be particularly rewarding, at least not more so than their pre-existing relationships. This same conclusion could not be reached for the *Associate* or *Friend* escorts and it definitely was not so for members of the agency's *Inner Circle* where the boundaries between personal and work lives significantly overlapped.

The Periphery

Although individuals in this outermost sphere of the *College Boys* universe may have been close to people within the agency, no one in the *Periphery* worked for Martin and none had substantial impact on the business other than as clients. Contact with the agency itself was more intermittent and superficial. Interactions with *College Boys* by those in the *Periphery* took the form of personal relationships with someone in the agency (friends, family members, and partners) or as clients hiring an escort. All in the *Periphery* knew of the agency and that its escorts provided relational and sexual services for hire. This differentiated them from other friends, partners, and family members who lacked such knowledge about someone they knew. Without this kind of awareness, people in various relationships with the agency's staff could not directly impact *College Boys'* social functioning. They would have been *Outsiders*, those for whom the agency did not exist. They would not know that their son, friend, or fiancé worked for a male escort call service.

Clients

Clients represented the majority of individuals within the social *Periphery*. Men hiring escorts interacted with the agency more as one would with a hair salon than a retail store. One develops a relationship with people providing a service as part of the purchase, rather than simply buying an object to take home and use. Martin cultivated this sense of relationship with clients as a way to ease their decision to hire an escort, make them feel comfortable with hiring one of the men from *his* escort agency, and to encourage repeat business. Martin became friends with some of the clients through long association and mutual trust-building, even if only over the phone. When clients came to the agency for an incall, relationships developed more quickly and often on a more personal level. Sometimes clients would bring food for the staff, socialize at the house before or after appointments, and even go out on the town with staff on a weekend night. All of this benefited the business; Martin worked hard to insure good customer relations.

As we will see, clients typically learned of the agency through its online presence and had an idea of who they wanted to hire when they first contacted Martin. Mostly married White professionals, new clients often took some time to get to know the agency before setting up an appointment with one of the escorts. Many clients held negative stigma about hiring escorts. They also feared that knowledge of their involvement in the agency would leak out into their personal or professional lives. Martin sought to normalize their decision to hire an escort and conveyed a sense of collaboration as well as discretion with the client. He said:

Martin: I would say most of the people that hire are pretty closeted about doing it. I'd say, pretty top secret for most of them.

Interviewer: Because they're not going to tell other gay people they hire?

Martin: Yeah, just the stigma around hiring escorts. If it were me I wouldn't tell people.

Interviewer: Why?

Martin: Because it's looked at, it's a stereotype that's looked at as very negative.

Clients reciprocated by developing trust in the agency to meet their needs in a safe, confidential, and satisfying way. Problems that inevitably arose with appointments or scheduling became easier to resolve when a positive working relationship had been established between Martin and his customers.

Escorts for their part also developed relationships with their clients—whether this was only during the frame of a single call or something more akin to friendship due to repeated return business with the same client. *College Boys* differed in the types of relationships that they preferred with clients and strove to develop with them.

- Emotionally Distant—Escorts in this group attempted to minimize the social and emotional interaction with clients. They tended to focus more exclusively on finishing the sexual act with clients, and then leaving the call as soon as possible. Tommy felt this way and phrased it in his typically direct manner, "Go in there fuck their dick, they cum. That's what I like to see, nice short calls. I don't want to be there. I'm like, 'Ok cut the jibber-jabber let's go.' " Although other escorts understood this motivation, most of them believed it to be somewhat rude or that it reflected poor customer service.
- Cordial—Most of the *College Boys* represented this category of client engagement. Here, escorts reported that they developed a polite and conversational working

atmosphere, allowing both parties to relax. When an escort talked about being "professional," they most often referred to keeping some emotional boundaries with clients while engaging with customers on social level. Steven expressed this point of view:

When I come to the room I'm like, "Hi, I'm Steven blah, blah, blah." I just sit with them and like, "So where do you work?" And they tell me about their job, like that's pretty nice. It all depends on what they say, you know? I like compliment them on their place and all that stuff.

Dennis spoke about putting on a cordial face so clients thought he was having a good time even though, like Tommy and many others, he really did not like much of the work:

I'll do it, if that's what you want. I'll do it and I'll put a smile on my face and I pretend I enjoy the entire thing. And you'll think that I'm loving it, but I don't. It sounds harsh but that's what you're paying for, for me to look like I love it. So that's what you're getting.

This type of involvement style could be used with most any type of client, even those who expressed their chief interest in the sexual aspect of an appointment. Escorts saw cordiality as synonymous with providing good value to the customer and reducing negative emotions resulting from sex work—it kept the escort engaged, but distinct.

• Friendship—Although most escorts had at least one client with whom they had grown more emotionally connected, few believed that one should seek to make friends with clients as a matter of course. Most of the *College Boys* believed that growing too friendly with most clients made it difficult to set sexual and personal boundaries—they also worried that clients would start to believe a romantic relationship existed with the escort. Most thought that becoming "too" emotionally involved with clients would make it difficult to maintain a professional interaction. However, those couple of escorts who believed in a friendship orientation argued that it provided the best way to help them feel most at ease during appointments. They found themselves looking forward to appointments because they had taken the effort to develop a "real" relationship with their clients.

One's level of social engagement with other agency staff did not seem to influence the type of relationship escorts preferred to develop with their clients. Developing personal connections within *College Boys* appeared to be largely unrelated to how emotionally involved escorts became with customers.

Personal Relationships

Although fewer individuals could be placed in this half of the *Periphery*, the relationships characterized in this area held much more importance for the escorts than did interactions with clients. However, the potential costs of disclosing one's escorting to people in key relationships were so high that most *College Boys* did not do so. Escorts attempted to carefully manage which friends, romantic partners, and family members learned about their sex work. Less than 40 percent of *College Boys* intentionally disclosed their escorting to someone close to them, which means that 60 percent or more did not feel comfortable doing so. They feared rejection, negative judgment, and disapproval. Most did not surmount these concerns and lived a double life that they managed with varying degrees of success. However, for some, acceptable opportunities to disclose their sex work to significant others presented themselves on at least one occasion. We will consider the people to whom escorts disclosed their involvement in *College Boys* and some of the factors related to taking this risk in the next chapter.

CONCLUSION

Starting with a few employees who barely knew each another, *College Boys* quickly became a complex social network centered on a tight inner circle of deeply interwoven relationships. Lacking such close bonds in much of their personal lives, central players in the agency created a surrogate family for themselves to provide these relationships. The family fought, it grew, it shrank, and it made money. It had its hidden dysfunctions and its favorite sons, and it had a benevolent somewhat hyperactive "mother" at the center for whose approval and affection almost everyone competed. *College Boys* was an intentional creation with far-reaching unintentional consequences for those who became embedded in its social milieu. It was an opportunity that changed many people's lives, often for the better from their own point of view despite what those on the outside might have believed at the time.

Even those less connected with the agency reacted to it in ways they might not have anticipated at first. Clients may not have thought they would ever spend a half hour on the phone with Martin talking about their marriages or business plans. The fathers and friends of escorts could not have anticipated learning that someone they knew worked for a male call-boy service or the complex and contradictory emotions such a revelation typically provoked. Escorts who themselves did not navigate more deeply into the agency's social world still connected with Martin and their clients. They often discovered elements of themselves that they at once enjoyed and which sometimes repelled them; that they could have sex for money and not care that much about it afterward, shocked many of the men we interviewed. It often gave them more self-confidence in the end, and a different perspective on their morality that could sometimes work for the better, or sometimes not.

What the social web described in this chapter did accomplish was to nurture people's needs. It gave clients an outlet for what they believed was unattainable in their personal lives. It provided escorts with income along with the mentorship and emotional support needed to earn a living through sex work. For Martin and many of the *College Boys*, the agency gave them a second home, a network of like-minded brothers whose companionship they could enjoy and come to rely upon. Although their lives did not always turn out for the better, and for some escorting created self-doubts and recriminations they could not accept, most escorts believed their involvement with the people at *College Boys* impacted their lives in positive and often unexpected ways. And they all felt connected to Martin in one way or another—he was the linchpin upon which that interlocking whorl of relationships hinged. He held it all together. It is to this personal impact of escorting for *College Boys* that we will now turn out attention in the next chapter. What happened in the outside lives of young men after they met Martin, and entered this unexpected world of Internet prostitution?

Chapter Six

MORE THAN A JOB

OVERVIEW

The amount of time that the men at *College Boys* had been involved in escorting varied from as little as one month to as many as five years. On average, men had been with the agency for a little more than nine months. As in other forms of work, successfully maintaining longer-term involvement in escorting often required men to integrate it into their personal, professional, and romantic lives. We believe that such accommodations would need to occur for most anyone working in this business. Escorts are faced with complex and deeply emotional decisions about how to navigate the process of developing and sharing their occupational identity. Escorts must select with whom to disclose and also determine the extent to which they will incorporate sex work within the broader context of their lives. Some *College Boys* blended boundaries between escorting and the rest of their lives; meanwhile, others developed comprehensive, complex, and often strict rules designed to maintain divisions between personal and professional activities. As such, this chapter will focus on how men managed this sensitive boundary—how they decided whether to disclose or conceal their working identity within three types of key relationships: family, friends, and partners. We also explore the unique ways clients participated in the escorts' lives and how escorts themselves sometimes softened boundaries with their customers, particularly clients with whom they developed longer-term associations.

Disclosing Sex Work

Many *College Boys* disclosed they were escorting to at least one person they knew outside the agency. Escorts often described conducting a complex risk-benefit analysis whereby they evaluated to whom they would disclose and to what degree. We have categorized our discussion based on the *types* of people escorts told about their sex work: family members, friends, and romantic partners. For some *College Boys*, the decision-making and disclosure processes were similar regardless of who was being told; other escorts described how they incorporated different strategies (and varied the amount and type of information) they revealed depending on their relationship with the other person.

Disclosure to Family

It is unsurprising that family relationships occupied a central role in their lives for many of the men we interviewed including both immediate (such as parents and siblings) and extended members (such as grandparents, aunts and uncles, and cousins). Only six of the escorts had done so. Two-thirds of these disclosures were to one or both parents. Two men had told siblings and one revealed his sex work to a favorite aunt of his. For those escorts who disclosed to at least one person in their families, most reported positive experiences when it involved members of their extended family and siblings. In contrast, experiences were typically not as positive when disclosing to parents. Cousins and siblings were generally more neutral, whereas parents expressed disappointment or worry. Although reactions from family members included expressions of concern for the escort's safety, they also tended toward the negative in ways that differed from friends or partners along moral lines. Parents especially responded with disapproval of sex work itself, critical of their child's involvement in prostitution. James related his experience when he disclosed escorting to his parents:

> My parents really look down on it. I think they're more or less like disappointed because they know my abilities; they know what I know what I can do with my life and, you know, how much better I can do. My dad's just like, "I can't believe it." My mom, she thinks it's the most disgusting thing in the world. It's probably because she never was introduced to it. She doesn't know you know what exactly goes on.

Only one of the disclosures to family members was said to have resulted in an exclusively positive response. This was from a sister with whom the escort reported a very close relationship and was someone he viewed as his best friend.

A Complicated "Coming Out" Process

The men in our project were all fairly young, a time in life when many gays and bisexuals, who were the majority of escorts in the agency, navigate the process of integrating their sexual identity into relationships with others through "coming out" (Grov et al., 2006; Rosario, Schrimshaw, & Hunter 2004; Savin-Williams, 2006). Escorts at *College Boys* often crossed the "coming out" milestone of disclosing their sexual identity (as gay or bisexual) in tandem with disclosing their work as an escort. Thus, when men described disclosing their escorting to family members, these conversations may have included concurrent narratives about "coming out" with respect to their sexual orientation. Many of the escorts' families learned that their son, brother, cousin, or nephew was escorting around the same time they discovered he also was not straight. This dual disclosure likely impacted family member's reactions; hence for male sex workers, it would be difficult to tease apart the unique impact of learning one's family member is escorting versus learning they are gay when the two events happened in such close proximity. Even when disclosure did not happen at the same time, the revelation of one's sex work might reignite emotions or concerns regarding issues related to sexual orientation. Some family members, especially parents, might have an "Oh no, not something else!" reaction to a disclosure of sex work. The two issues complicated each other, both for the escort and his family.

Threats to Family Identity

Families may have more invested in the *identity* of each member. They have known each other all of their lives. For one person in the family to announce that some aspect of their life radically differs from that which the family has come to know over their long association could cause more emotional turmoil than it would with a friend where relationships are built first upon shared interests instead of kinship. One's identity and behavior also impacts others in the family differently than for a friend. Given assumed similarities between people who are related to each other, revelation of one's sex work could lead family members to react defensively in order to protect their own sense of self or their perception of what people in the family are like. Families have strong, long-standing ideas about how their members should act. They have clear expectations about the characteristics and values members would typically assume—shared identities and beliefs that are not easily changed or countermanded. When a young person deviates from such powerful group norms, they rightly fear disapproval, misunderstanding, and even outright rejection. They might also worry about causing family members pain or grief in a way that would not occur with friends or relationship partners.

The desire to hide one's sex work from family members seems to be more intense than it would be for other types of relationships—the consequences of doing so may be viewed as more extreme and the benefits too tenuous. In a worst-case scenario, rejection by some or all of their family would be emotionally catastrophic. Such relationships are irreplaceable in a way that friendships are not.

The potential for such dislocation would be unacceptable to most people, leading to non-disclosure of sex work to family members. As most escorts anticipated working at *College Boys* for a few months or years, the potential for long-term heartache within the family did not seem to outweigh the benefit of increased understanding or support regarding the escort's sex work. Why should a young man risk permanent disruption of key relationships in which he probably had a great deal of himself invested and upon which much of his identity was based, over what would likely be a relatively brief period of employment? In such an analysis relatively few people would disclose sex work to people in their family; this is exactly what occurred.

Disclosure to Parents

Parents typically expressed the highest levels of concern when their son's disclosed his sex work. These concerns generally revolved around at least one of four factors. First, parents worried that their sons would catch a sexually transmitted infection, especially HIV. Interestingly, it is uncertain how much of this concern was related to their son's having sex for money, versus learning that their sons are having sex specifically with other men (irrespective of the exchange of cash—STIs and HIV are not spread on money). Second, parents expressed concerns for their son's physical safety. Escorts recalled discussions where parents' worried their son would be killed and "left in a ditch," or robbed/mugged. These concerns centered on their sons having sex with "strangers." Third, given the illegal nature of sex work, some parents expressed concerns about their child being arrested and developing a criminal record. Finally, some parents were afraid that public knowledge about their son's escorting would somehow bring shame to the escort as well as the family. For example, Mike noted that his parents were uncomfortable with his escorting, but did not outright forbid it. In Mike's case, his father worried about the reactions of others outside the family:

> Yeah, my dad saw the website and he just asked me, "Can you please just take your face off the internet?" He's like, "Because it's, because I don't want anybody that I know to think that." My dad knows that I'm not gay. He knows what I do. He's like, "People see that shit and they start to think all kinds of stuff."

It is interesting to note that Mike's father may have expressed more concern about sexual orientation issues than escorting per se. Because of the problems that disclosure presented, most escorts avoided the topic of their profession with their parents altogether. Some escorts did not seem "bothered" about not being able to talk about escorting with their parents. In interviews, men often portrayed this by shrugging it off by saying, "It doesn't matter" or "It's not important."

Meanwhile, other *College Boys* believed disclosure damaged and strained relationships with their parents. This was sometimes framed in terms of feeling greater social and personal distance, less of a connection. Given the complicated nature of some men's disclosure—parents learning their son is gay right around the same time they learn about his escorting—it was difficult to differentiate the isolation an escort experienced from his parents because of his sexual identity versus that resulting from his sex work.

Not all disclosures to parents resulted in emotional distancing or disdain. Some escorts who disclosed reported very positive relationships with their parents overall and generally felt they could talk about "anything" with at least one parent. These men often described their relationship with their parents in terms of a "friendship" (e.g., "My mom is my best friend, we can talk about anything"), and that their parents' "style" was generally more laissez-faire and less authoritative or restrictive. In these instances, escort's disclosure to parents did not "damage" their relationship, but it did not necessarily improve it either. In essence, no escorts said, "My relationship with my mom *improved* as a result of telling her about my job."

Disclosure to family was more common among escorts who self-identified as "gay." Bisexual and heterosexual escorts were far less likely to tell their parents. This concealment among bisexuals and heterosexuals was probably a result of the escort's fear of being stigmatized for having sex with men. For example, many bisexual escorts were not "out" to their parents as bisexual—their parents thought they were straight—and disclosing escorting would require they also tell their parents they were, in fact, not heterosexual. In contrast, heterosexual escorts were concerned about their parents (among others) calling their sexual identity into question were they to learn their son engaged in escorting with male clients.

Disclosure to Other Family Members

Approximately equal proportions of gay, bisexual, and heterosexual escorts had disclosed to at least one family member who was not a parent (e.g., a cousin, sibling). In general, escorts described how non-parental family members (uncles, aunts, cousins, siblings) were more receptive and generally more accepting of same-sex sexual behavior. Those family members who were more accepting tended to be closer in age to the escort (perhaps indicative of generational divides in attitudes toward sex work and/or homosexuality); the ties escorts held with these family members tended to be more social rather than hierarchal-authoritative (as was often the case with parents). In some instances, these family members even visited the agency and "hung out" with other escorts and Martin. Given the communal and social atmosphere of *College Boys* (largely a result of Martin's efforts to keep the facility as a welcoming "open" space), this was not at all out of the ordinary.

Disclosure to Friends

About one in three escorts at *College Boys* told friends they worked for the agency. The chance of disclosing one's sex work to an "outsider" increased with the amount of time a young man had worked for the agency. Several escorts had friends who were former or current sex workers themselves, and in all of these cases disclosures were made due to the comfort level with the job these individuals must have had. Overall, men tended to disclose most to roommates and close friends whom they had known for many years and shared a strong connections. In such cases, fear of rejection appeared to be minimized. The need for honesty in the friendship and for emotional support with respect to the job sometimes overrode concerns about potential strains on their relationships. When close friends expressed a negative reaction, it usually took the form of concern for the escort's safety (e.g., with respect to diseases or legal problems) rather than disapproval of sex work itself.

Escorts described their friends as essential resources for social and emotional support. In contrast to the mixed types of responses that family members gave, escorts often regarded disclosure to their friends as a positive experience. As with family members, friends were welcome to visit and socialize at *College Boys*. They incorporated friends into aspects of their escort work in a variety of ways. Most often friends acted as someone for an escort to talk to about his experiences with clients and his feelings about the work in general. In this capacity, friends played key supportive roles in helping escorts to navigate the emotional impact of sex work. The escort could talk with friends about his feelings about being involved in sex work which were sometimes in conflict with the escort's personal values. In a few cases, friends became more involved with the day-to-day operations of the agency. Sometimes friends would chauffeur escorts to and from calls or help Martin to track down an escort when he had trouble getting hold of him. Because friends were welcome to visit the agency, they often socialized with other men working at the agency or with Martin, thus blending the social networks between escorts and their outside friends.

Escorts believed that they could gauge what their friend's reaction would be before they disclosed to them. This could create stressful situations for escorts who had disclosed to some friends but not others. This was particularly evident when escorts transitioned from spending time with one friend (who "knew") to spending time with another (who was naïve) back-to-back in a given day. Or in situations where escorts were collectively "hanging out" with a group of friends, some who "knew," and others who did not. In each circumstance, escorts needed to consciously monitor their discourse with friends; they could not accidently let something slip in the context of a jovial conversation. Escorts at *College Boys* had to have a menu of excuses prepared were a friend, who did not know about the escorting, to ask about an escort's income or question where the escort was going—especially when an escort went out on a call at an odd time of the day or for an extended time period. Escorts also had to actively take steps to prevent friends who knew from inadvertently disclosing to friends who did not. The most common strategy was to prevent naïve friends from socializing with those who knew—they kept the two groups of friends apart. This created multiple sets of friends who did not overlap with one another. Doing so required a certain amount of finesse and attention—constant awareness of who knew and remembering exactly what they had been told.

Of course, not all escorts reported positive experiences after disclosing to friends. Many men reported "losing" at least one friend because they did not approve of sex work. Most escorts described this in terms of a *distancing process*, whereby over time there was a mutual disengagement from that friend. They would speak less and less often on the phone, neglect to return messages, and socialize less often. Eventually, this led to the full dissolution of the friendship. Escorts who lost friends often reflected on this experience as a means to identify who were their "real" friends.

Negative reactions were most likely when disclosure occurred with less intimate friends or acquaintances. Such disclosures were typically not made by the escort himself. Often, less intimate friends shared information with each other or someone recognized an escort's *College Boys* profile on the Internet. Unlike acquaintances, close friends almost never told anyone else about the escort's sex work. Brian related his experience with being involuntarily "outed" as a sex worker:

> It didn't take long for people to find out because Paul and I decided we wanted our faces on the website. We figured we'd get more calls that way and it didn't take long, probably a week, for everybody that I know to find out. People judged us. When I went into this thing, I went in with the attitude that if you're going to judge me for what I do for money, and judge me on solely that, you know I don't care. You're not going to be my friend if that's what you're going to base our friendship on and that's how you're going to judge me.

Anger and defensiveness were typical reactions among the *College Boys* when a friend made disparaging comments about their sex work. Often, such remarks were enough to end less connected friendships—thought it is difficult to know which party ended things first.

As was the case in talking about their sex work with parents, heterosexual escorts had a more difficult time disclosing to friends. For these men, most of their friends were heterosexual themselves. Straight escorts believed that their friends would not understand how a heterosexual man could engage in sex work with male clients—simultaneously questioning his work and sexual identity. Interestingly, some heterosexual escorts did not regard themselves as "prostitutes" or even as a person conducting "sex work," because they did not engage in physical sex with clients; intercourse was never involved. Some heterosexual escorts engaged in mutual masturbation with clients, but not oral or anal sex. Heterosexual escorts' concealment apparently grew from fears over being seen as a "prostitute" as well as over being seen as "gay."

Finally, the length of time one escorted was related directly to the number and proportion of friends a escorts had disclosed sex work. Those in the business longer generally reported a sense of "pride" in their work. They had learned to cope with stigma around sex work and often managed to establish close friendship with other escorts. Growing experience and comfort often resulted in a perceived obligation to be open with people close to them. Escorts also discovered that many people held neutral views about sex work or were open to learning more about it. Patrick, who had been escorting for two years, found that talking with others about sex work was a normalizing experience. He described how in being open about his escorting he often learned that those close to him also were involved in some form of sex work, "I feel like it's a little bit more socially acceptable than I thought it was when I first began, because I've been meeting people who have done it for other agencies and I've been meeting people who are checking out escorting [for themselves]."

Disclosure to Partners

Twenty-one *College Boys* were in some form of relationship at the time we spoke with them, ranging from casually dating to more serious longer-term commitments. None were legally married, which overall is fairly typical for people in this age range. Twelve (or 57 percent of escorts in a relationship) had told partners about escorting, though to varying degrees of completeness and accuracy. However, two-thirds of these men were in relationships with other sex workers. As with friends, it might be safely assumed that the risk of disclosing one's sex work to another escort was quite low—in fact, all men dating other escorts had partners who knew. What might be more surprising is that four men not dating another escort had nevertheless told their partners about working for *College Boys*. This represents about one in three men not dating someone with experience in the business.

Unlike what might be the stereotype about sex workers (that they do not value emotional or sexual commitment), the men we met said that they valued love and commitment as much as anyone else. In fact, many often indicated how they planned to "retire" from escorting and settle down with a single monogamous partner. Most men apparently disclosed to partners out of a sense of loyalty or obligation. They felt that their partners had a *right* to know about the escorting. Commitment to their relationships also meant that escorts believed partners had a right to know given some of the inherent downsides of sex work, such as the possibility of sexually transmitted infections or even just an unpredictable work schedule. Additionally, these men wanted to be honest in their relationships—they did not want to lie about where they were going or what they were doing when Martin sent them on an appointment. These *College Boys* felt uncomfortable claiming monogamy for the relationship when their job required them to have sex with clients. They wanted their partners to have "full disclosure" so that they were fully aware of the escort's life, and made a decision to be in a relationship with the escort with their eyes fully open. This degree of acceptance was very important to the young men who disclosed their sex work to relationship partners; it was worth the risk of alienating someone in order to find a person who valued the escort for the entirety of his experience.

Relationship length and depth of emotional commitment between the escort and his partner were significant factors in disclosure. For example, Erick said he would not disclose to a partner who he had just met or was only "casually dating." He would instead wait until the second or third date before bringing up the escorting. Meanwhile, Joshua said he would wait upwards of six months before telling a partner. Rick said, "I don't keep the fact that I escort from people I'm dating. I'm very truthful about it, but I don't like to bring it up right away. I'll wait until the second or third date to tell them so they can get to know me first." Escorts described how such "delayed disclosure" represented an effort to prevent outright rejection from someone who they were just getting to know, a way to let someone else get close to the "real" person without knowledge about escorting biasing a dating partner's perceptions.

Escorts at *College Boys* sometimes dated other men working at the agency; there were four such couples during our interviews, two of whom remained together at the time we ended the project. As with any form of dating within the context of a work environment, this created its own "drama," typically after the relationship dissolved. Nevertheless, escorts favorably described having a relationship with someone who also was involved in sex work. They believed these partners better understood the nature of sex work and the reasons for why one would enter the profession. This would ameliorate many issues that arose in relationships when only one partner was involved in sex work. Partner jealousy surrounding sex "outside" of the relationship (with clients in this case) was less of an issue if both partners were escorts and neither escort had to worry about their partner judging them for being involved in the sex work industry. Meanwhile, having a partner who also escorted provided a more understanding and informed listener with whom to share the many emotional and physical issues arising with clients. A partner who escorted could help deal with some of the broader stigma associated with sex work. Andrew illustrated this point when he said:

> It's like having a best friend and that's what makes it so easy, because you have someone to talk to about escorting. Sometimes it's cool to have someone to talk to about it because we'll go on a really shitty call, or a client really sucks, and like you

cannot even understand [what its like]. Sometimes it's really hot [with] some of the clients . . . and you want to talk about it. Like, "I just got laid!"

This does not suggest dating another escort was all roses, and we will revisit this point soon. It could present unique challenges as well as the benefits. No relationship is without its problems. Furthermore, it is worth us mentioning that the "permission" escorts granted each other to have sex with "outside" partners was often limited to paying clients. In essence, escorts who were dating other escorts often only allowed sex outside of the relationship if with a *paying* client. More conventional rules around the expectation of monogamy were often expected.

On the other hand, men who were in relationships with *non*-escorts noted how escorting often infringed on their time with their partners. Mike described how receiving a call while on a date put him in a difficult position: Should he spend time with his partner and lose the opportunity for income, or take the opportunity to work but then risk an argument? Would Martin still send him business if he refused to go on too many calls in order to spend time with a partner? In addition to time away from a partner, escorting infringed on sexual desire. Some escorts described how they had little sexual interest after seeing a client, especially after a multiple appointments. Conversely, they also worried about an inability to perform with a client if they had just had sex with their partner. Escorts in relationships had to strategically plan their sexual behavior with their partner as not to interfere with clients. This could reduce the escort's spontaneous enjoyment of sexual intimacy in his relationship. Emilio, whose partner was not an escort, described some of these concerns within the context of his relationship:

Emilio: It really affects our relationship and that's the reason why I don't want to do this anymore.

Interviewer: How does it affect your relationship with him?

Emilio: A lot of the times when he actually wants to have sex, my sexual drive isn't going for it, because I basically had sex all day. So, by the time we go to bed, or we're laying down watching TV or something, and [he] starts rubbing me or whatever and says, "Do you want to have sex?" I'm like, "I can't. I don't want to."

Such concerns were amplified among escorts who were dating other escorts, as *both* could be potentially called away to see a client at any given hour. In addition, both men had to worry about managing their sexual libido with clients as well as with each other.

Although escorts dating other escorts found they could disclose more about their work than men not doing so, issues of jealousy still sometimes arose. In one case, Chase described how his partner received more calls than him. This created an imbalance in their financial and sexual relationship. In essence, one partner was perceived to be more "valuable" or attractive. This partner would make more money from escorting, have more sex "outside" of the relationship, and overall be perceived as the more "attractive" partner. In addition, Chase described himself as more of a "bottom," while his boyfriend was more of a "top" during anal intercourse. In the context of the rules they created within their relationship, Chase's boyfriend was allowed to top clients, whereas they had agreed that Chase should not bottom for his clients. Receiving anal sex for this couple was perceived as a more intimate act, representing a moment to be reserved for one's boyfriend in a way that giving anal sex was not. Chase did not like the imbalance of power and sexual prowess this created within the context of the personal relationship, and it caused some conflict with his boyfriend. For some escorts, this boundary extended to kissing, such that kissing was an intimate act to be preserved within a relationship and creating a boundary between personal and professional sex lives.

Single escorts "on the dating scene" worried about the impact that their sex work could have on finding a committed relationship. Many escorts had already experienced problems in dating because of their work. James told us:

> Well, I was kind of seeing this person and he found out I was a *College Boy* and he started saying how gross I was and how disgusting and everything else and started calling me all these names. We since then patched things up but he won't date me because I do this for work and he was just too crazy. And I told him it was just the same as him saying something about a stripper or somebody coming out being gay or an ex-convict. You don't have to degrade the person.

Such reactions appeared to be the norm among the single men we interviewed, but only among the gay and bisexual men dating other guys—straight escorts either did not reveal their prostitution to partners or had girlfriends who themselves worked in the business. As the agency's reputation became more widespread, escorts dating other men encountered increased barriers to dating outside the profession as a result of the stigma their work carried.

Escorts who self-identified as heterosexual or bisexual faced added challenges disclosing to female partners in ways similar to when they told family members and friends. As with gay escorts, men in this situation also feared their partners would not understand the nature of escort work; that partners would have difficulty accepting sex work as a legitimate profession. Heterosexual and bisexual escorts also saw a second problem—their partners' shock and often disapproval of being hired for homosexual activities. These female partners frequently did not understand how their boyfriend could maintain his heterosexuality when being hired for sex with other men. Although heterosexual escorts typically engaged in a reduced set of behaviors with their clients when compared to gay escorts, this sexual repertoire still encompassed mutual masturbation, body worship, or receiving oral sex from a client. As we will describe in the next section, most escorts (and particularly heterosexual escorts) engaged in a variety of strategies to avoid disclosure with partners—maintaining a strict boundary between their romantic and sex work lives.

Hiding Sex Work: Living Two Lives

Escorts who disclosed to friends, family, or partners often regarded this as an important facet of personal their integrity and overall honesty. Many had attempted to hide their sex work, often with success, but experienced prolonged internal conflict about doing so—often feeling like they were "living a double life" by lying to the people they loved. Escorts who experienced repeated negative reactions from their disclosure were often reticent about telling others, especially people they just met and friends or family whose morals the escorts thought would result in another negative reaction. As such, many escorts described reasons why they chose not to disclose their sex work to those who were close to them.

Concealment from Parents and Family

Given the age range of the men we interviewed, nearly all had already moved out from their family homes. The ages in which men left their homes were on par with other young adults; these were not men who moved out at age 14 and then "took up" escorting. Establishing this independence also was sequenced similarly to other young adults—most finished high school and then moved out or went away to college. Similar to many young adults leaving home, living separately from parents provided greater freedom to foment their own personal and social identities. Certainly these escorts' families had provided a foundation of morals and cultural expectations, but living away from home allowed personal identities as young adults to mature independent of daily parental involvement. As a result, men did not have to explain their work schedule or social activities on a regular basis, making it easier for an escort to avoid disclosing sex work to his family.

A primary challenge for men hiding their escort history from parents involved finding ways to explain their income and work schedule. Many men felt quite guilty about deceiving their family, but would rather navigate the daily complexity of maintaining elaborate, yet fabricated excuses than face the expected backlash and rejection were others to know the truth. Patrick described the mental exhaustion caused by keeping his escort work a secret and how this strain intruded into his time with clients:

Interviewer: What might go through your head that could affect your call with a client?

Patrick: Family, friends. If any of them found out I'd be one lonely person.

Interviewer: What do you think would happen?

Patrick: Well my parents probably wouldn't talk to me because of the fact that I'm a male prostitute.

Interviewer: Does anybody know about your escorting besides people associated with the agency?

Patrick: No.

Interviewer: What's made you decide not to tell them?

Patrick: The fact that having to go through and deal with it, the embarrassment, yelling. It would embarrass me without a doubt. My mom and dad would probably disown me. There are like two or three people that I've ever told, [and] they were bisexual, so they kind of understood—they're fine with it.

Concealment from family was the primary strategy of most heterosexual escorts and almost all bisexual escorts. As with gay escorts, straight escorts skirted the topic of work and money when possible, and maintained a comprehensive set of stories to explain one's whereabouts and income in the event conversation could not be avoided.

Concealment from Friends

Although many escorts talked about their sex work with at least one friend, most remained "in the closet" to a majority of their closest friends. As we previously indicated, disclosure was related to amount of time that escorts were involved in the business; those with longer employment histories tended to have disclosed to a greater number of people. In addition to fears of rejection, many escorts expressed that they did not want their friends to "worry" about them. Such worry often centered on physical danger in the context of a call and about HIV or STI transmission. *College Boys* often indicated that friends "would not understand" and they would not comprehend how the work could be safe, enjoyable, or lucrative. Escorts often specified their friend's sexual orientation as a way to explain or contextualize why one friend might worry more than another, noting that their "straight" friends would experience more anxiety than gay friends. This perhaps speaks to a perception that escorting was viewed more favorably within the gay community (Bimbi, 2007; Parsons, Koken, & Bimbi, 2004).

Escorts who actively hid their sex work from friends did so to maintain a boundary between their personal and professional lives. Many men who concealed their escorting also took active steps to maintain this boundary over time. Even if sex work was framed to others as "temporary," escorts feared that disclosure in the present would come back to haunt them in the future. Zack articulated this anxiety well when he said:

Because the detachment would help me compartmentalize it; I could eventually return to the ["real"] world where escorting wasn't actually a part of my life. I wouldn't have to deal with it. The real dealing with escorting or the most forefronting of it is the social aspect you know—having to confront people about it and have people be concerned about you and people think that maybe since you do this one thing you do all these other things. The judgment that comes with it, that's at the forefront of my mind, and what's going to affect me, and what's going to be the biggest hassle to deal with. And, so, if I can keep the secret, then I've got the biggest problem out of the way. And of course that in itself comes with a lot of emotional turmoil—the having to deal with it with other people. Recently I was confronted about it and I lied, and it felt so weird because I hate to lie, because I feel like I'm not being myself, and I pride myself on being able to be honest, you know. I shouldn't be anything that I can't be open about. I love that about myself and I know that other people love that about me too; and it hurts my sense of self when I do stuff like that [conceal my escorting]. Anyway I found myself in this situation just two weeks ago. I'm lying to this person who confronted me and I have this sense of injustice. I'm just like, "How dare he accuse me of this thing" that I'm actually doing? And I was like [to myself], "This is ridiculous! How does this thought process go through my head? I am guilty. I am doing this."

What is interesting about Zack is that he is very open to his friends about having a criminal record. It is well known that there is substantial stigma attached to having been in jail, often independent of the severity of the crime. In essence, the fact that someone served time is seen as a "black mark" on their standing in society, irrespective of the fact that the crime might have been petty marijuana possession, versus vehicular manslaughter. Is it possible that the stigma associated with escorting is perceived as worse than that of having a criminal record? As an aside, Nick described how his family was aware of his drug and alcohol use and a prior DUI arrest, but feared his parents learning about the sex work because they would "mentally disown" him—a complete emotional disengagement. The imagery escorts sometimes used when describing such disconnection from loved ones is similar to that depicted in films such as *Torch Song Trilogy* (1988) when a disheartened mother tells her child, "You are dead to me. I no longer have a son."

Concealment from Partners

Because of the stigma associated with sex work and concerns about maintaining the appearance of monogamy, many escorts struggled with maintaining honesty in their romantic relationships. Some escorts reported taking a break from sex work whenever they entered a serious relationship. In some cases this might have included full reprieve from escorting; they stopped altogether. Other men described "scaling-back" whenever they were in a relationship. This may have included seeing fewer clients (i.e., accepting fewer calls) or engaging in a reduced set of sexual acts with clients (e.g., only having oral sex, but not anal).

Like escorts at *College Boys* who did not tell their friends and family, escorts who concealed sex work from relationship partners had to fabricate elaborate excuses to belay their partner's interest in sources of income and daily whereabouts. As partners had more regular contact with escorts, these excuses had to be even more believable. Two escorts described how their partners thought they were drug dealers at various points in the relationships because there were too many "holes" in the escort's stories. These partners believed that the "secretive" calls that escorts received at odd hours of the day and the escort's subsequent departure for several hours seemed too similar to what drug dealers would need to do for the escort's story to be believed. Both escorts never reported being accused of sex work by suspicious partners; male prostitution did not enter their boyfriend or girlfriend's mind.

Escorts sometimes blended the truth into efforts to conceal their sex work from romantic partners. One escort told his partner that he worked for the agency, but only as a chauffeur. Patrick told his girlfriend that he "keeps men company" for money, but with no mention of sexual behavior. His girlfriend did not ask many questions, perhaps out of fear of what the truth may have brought. Several escorts told their partners they were strippers or exotic dancers. Stripping and erotic dancing are certainly forms of sex work, but often not perceived as "selling" sex, exchanging sexual behavior for money as would a "prostitute." Some partners found the idea of their boyfriend working as an erotic dancer exciting and expressed their approval. These partial revelations of escorting allowed an escort to disclose some aspects of his involvement with the agency to a partner, but keep the most salacious hidden. It could serve as a test for gauging a partner's reaction to even more information, or it could serve as a long-term solution. Partial revelations seemed less like overt lying to escorts and were perhaps less emotionally difficult to manage as a result.

Oil and Water? When Personal and Professional Lives Intermix

Patterns of disclosure and concealment tempted the boundaries between escorts' personal and professional lives. When talking to others about his sex work, an escort melds key facets of the two, and barriers between them are difficult to maintain in either direction. When concealing sex work from people in his personal life, a man must actively manage the flow of information from activities as an escort and prevent them from spilling into his relationships. Opportunities for sex work to interface, and thus interfere, in escorts' personal lives abounded.

Although many men reported satisfaction with the work flexibility and income that escorting offered, *College Boys* described facing tough decisions in choosing how much to prioritize escort work over spending time with family, friends, or partners. Sergio described how he had become accustomed to detaching the mental and emotional aspects of sex from the physical during his two years working as an escort. He discovered that this type of mindset could result in unforeseen complications; it was hard for him to "reattach" the two when he was not working. Sergio began to experience difficulty obtaining and maintaining an erection in his personal life:

> I've been having erectile dysfunction and I don't know if it's physical or mental. I'm trying to figure it out if it's mental. The best guess that I have is that it's from me detaching myself from sex so often that it's become a habit. Like, I found myself, the last time I was with my boyfriend I kept interrupting sex. I was like, "Let's talk about something random." I don't even know how many times, and I don't know if I was annoying him, or not. I couldn't read him. I think it's because I wasn't in the moment completely. I tried to ask my doctor for meds.

A second type of problem that men highlighted often centered on the escorting-schedule operating in conflict with other aspects of their lives. Although flexible, an escorting schedule was sporadic. Men loathed being called away from partners and friends, particularly for calls in the early morning hours between four and nine o'clock. Escorts would sometimes refuse to take calls at these times; determining that their social lives and personal needs outweighed the importance of the extra money. However, such a "choice" might not be possible for escorts possessing fewer financial opportunities, such as men working in the developing world or those experiencing homelessness. Even many of the escorts at *College Boys* accepted these less desirable appointment times because they needed the money to pay for important expenses, or out of anxiety that the manager would assign them less business in the future if they did not jump at opportunities when they were offered.

A second example of how the professional aspects of escorting conflicted with personal time can be seen with Daniel. During our interview, Daniel described time-management difficulties he faced while attending community college that led him to withdraw from two courses in one recent semester. Both courses were difficult and escorting did not leave enough time to make sure he could succeed in them. Daniel found that the variable schedule was a particular impediment to attending classes and studying. Emilio indicated that going on a call always involved a greater time commitment than the one or two hours he was actually at the appointment. He had to get ready to go and then clean up afterward—and then there was the commute. Because *College Boys* was situated near several urban areas, escorts were often sent to calls an hour, or more away. Some escorts were sent as far as a three-hour drive, each way. Thus, a one-hour call could easily turn into a time commitment of three to six hours depending on where the client was to be seen.

When Clients Become More than Clients

Thus far we have focused our discussion on ways in which men incorporated escorting into their personal lives, or the degrees to which they did not. This analysis has centered upon three major aspects of men's *personal* lives: family, friends, and partners. However, there remains a fourth integral group of individuals involved in the lives of the *College Boys*, a group of individuals who men encountered as a *result* of their professional endeavors: their clients. In this final section, we take up the varying roles that clients assumed for escorts.

In the context of our interviews, we asked men to tell us about their perception of an "ideal" client. Often, men described this person using a series of "not" statements—not too old, not too overweight, and not unattractive. Delving deeper beyond a client's physical attributes, most escorts also described how much they enjoyed developing a personal relationship with their customers, something beyond the physical they could experience with clients. Escorts appreciated socializing with clients in the context of their calls; they liked getting to know them. Although certainly not the case with all clients, the escorts' general sentiment was a preference to engage in the social aspects of their work over-and-above the sexual ones:

Interviewer: What's your favorite kind of call?

Jeff: Conversation.

Interviewer: What do you like about that the most?

Jeff: Like I said, I like the getting to know people, a complete stranger. I'm just going to get to know something about them and share some experiences that they had and maybe look at my life and think or realize that maybe that could have happened to me. Things could be worse right now, something could relate to me that happened to a client. I can see how they bettered themselves and I can learn from that.

Because escorts often sought opportunities to know clients more personally, they liked having clients hire them for multiple hours, on overnight appointments, or for weekends. Not only would these calls earn more money, extended appointments allowed time to know each other better. Joshua described his overnight clients as being more "romantic" and highlighted how the evening's events often mirrored a traditional date that progress from going out to dinner and then to a show, having sex, falling sleep, eating breakfast, and then departing. It made the whole experience seem more "legitimate" and less like prostitution. Joshua also he felt he could be "himself" more with multi-hour clients. Such calls mimicked non-commercial interactions with personal partners, providing a ready script that seemed to help both men feel more comfortable.

Even more desirable from the escorts' perspectives was a "repeat" client or someone who hired an escort on more than one occasion. *College Boys* were aware of the characteristics, needs, and preferences of repeat clients; it was easier to work with them because such repeat business lacked the "unknown" that occurs when seeing a client for the first time. Berto expressed increased comfort when seeing clients more than once:

> Like I said, I'm very shy, my social anxiety. Stuff like that, especially if it's the first time I meet someone I'm really shy. But after that, after I meet someone the first time, it's a lot easier for me. So, like I have a regular in [Location]. I go up there and we'll sit there and have a couple of beers or something like that. And we'll sit there and talk for an hour and just chat, or whatever. It's cool because I can relax and he's actually one of my better friends that I can stay and talk to about anything. Even though he is a client, I don't consider him a client. I consider him a friend. Now it's like, especially with my regulars, I can go in there and relax.

Escorts knew what to expect and were already acquainted with the client. It made the situation more predictable and manageable. *College Boys* feared that new clients could be part of a police "sting," or cause an unstable situation in which the escort's safety would be at risk. Most, if not all, of these concerns were belayed *after* seeing a client just once.

Such feelings occur on both sides of the business transaction. Many clients likely experience similar levels of anxiety about escorts upon first meeting them—uncertainty if the escort will look like his pictures, perform well, have an engaging personality, or represent a reliable safe partner. Client concerns are evident from the customer review websites where clients post and read reviews of escorts, using this information as the basis for selecting which men to hire. In contrast, there is little such infrastructure available for escorts to "review" clients, which is one of the benefits of working for an agency—the agency maintains records on all clients, and escorts often casually discuss their experiences with clients among themselves and with the manager in the context of socializing before and after calls. The *College Boys* certainly did. Unacceptable clients could be easily "blacklisted" from an agency and Martin maintained such a mental list of clients with whom he would never do business again.

Escorts also noted that repeat clients provided a greater sense of financial stability. Sometimes, clients would hire an escort on a regular basis over a period of several years, hiring one or more times each month. In addition to repeat business, escorts highlighted that regular clients generally tipped better. Tips could double or even triple the normal hourly rate and were therefore greatly valued by the escorts. Over time, regular clients would often give other incentives in the forms of gifts. For example, Zack described how he opened up to one of his clients about his desire to go to college. The client took Zack on a three-hour shopping trip to a local electronics store, purchasing for him a $2,000 laptop computer and several hundred dollars in software.

Martin, the agency manger, recalled instances when clients would cover an array of an escort's costs. In one case, a client paid off an escort's credit card debt. In another, a client gave an escort a credit card so that the escort could make purchases with the client covering the balance. Taking this to a more permanent level, both Ethan and Jeff described how clients extended offers for them to move in; the client proposing to cover their expenses so that they no longer needed to escort. Neither Ethan nor Jeff felt enough emotional connection with these clients to accept the offer. In contrast, the manager also described how he lost a few employees who "quit" working for the agency and instead just saw a couple of clients (or even just one) through this type of longer-term and more exclusive arrangement. Martin talked about how clients paid a former escort's rent, took them to exotic destinations as a "travel-partner" while covering all of the previous escort's costs, or provided an escort with a luxury car while staying with the client on an extended visit. These clients were often regarded as "sugar daddies."

Receiving gifts from clients was considered acceptable among the escorts at *College Boys*, but only to a certain degree. It was fine when such gifts and monetary incentives represented tokens of generosity and nothing else. Nevertheless, some escorts highlighted concerns that these "extras" might also be advanced payments for future encounters in which the escorts were expected to be *more* emotionally and sexually invested than might otherwise be the case. Concurring with this idea, Martin highlighted how it was necessary for escorts to maintain a stronger emotional investment in a client who was providing "extras"; it was necessary to show more feeling than what was typically invested in a one-hour encounter. Escorts often did not mind the "understood" nature of this agreement (e.g., "This client treats me well, so I will return the favor in kind."). However, "returning this favor" was contingent on the escort having somewhat mutual feelings for the client. He would ideally not accept additional gifts from a client whom the escort found personally or physically "repulsive," knowing that he would not be able to reciprocate with a deeper emotional or sexual commitment. Escorts described men who "faked" such connections with a client as "stringing" someone along. It was considered unethical and unprofessional behavior among the escorts at *College Boys*. Martin talked about such an instance, "One of my escorts didn't want to hurt people's feelings. Clients offered to buy him trucks or give him incredible amounts of money, stability, or whatever. But if he [the escort] wasn't on that same emotional level with that person [client], he felt that was using someone; even though, to a degree, that is what our whole business is almost about."

Although many escorts like the idea of having a "sugar daddy," this was rarely a long-term commitment for the men at *College Boys*. Escorts often acknowledged the unequal emotional investment between them and a sugar daddy— escorts being the less invested party. Furthermore, finding a sugar daddy or becoming a "kept boy" was not necessarily regarded as a goal for escorts who recognized that their relationship with clients was commercial and not emotional. These bonds lacked the staying power to support a longer-term commitment. Were an escort to have multiple sugar daddies, or "retire" from escorting after finding the "right" sugar daddy, he would likely be looked down upon by other escorts. In essence, the fairy tale ending to Edward Lewis' (a big-money entrepreneur played by Richard Gere) relationship with Vivian Ward (a street-based prostitute played by Julia Roberts) in the 1990 movie *Pretty Woman* was not a goal the escorts at *College Boys* had for themselves.

There were other ways clients became involved with escort's lives in addition to the financial incentives and gifts. As we have highlighted, escorts usually enjoyed opportunities to get to know their clients. In some cases escorts and clients became friends. Escorts "hung out" with clients (perhaps over a lavish dinner at a restaurant the escort could not afford himself), but without the evening leading to sexual behavior. Over time, escorts found themselves opening up to some clients about topics and concerns that would normally be reserved for people in their personal support networks. Some escorts told this type of client their real name, or talked candidly about family, friends, school and other aspects of his personal life. Joshua discussed how some people he met through escorting were often more central in his life today than many people he had known before working at the agency:

> A lot of the people that are now important in my life I met through escorting. A lot of my friends are people that I worked with [clients]. The boyfriend previous to this was actually a serious relationship that lasted six months. He had actually hired me. And we ended up sitting there, sat at his house over night, and we just talked and talked and talked. The next morning, he came over and I was working on a home improvement project at my house. And he came over and helped me with that.

In addition to escorts spending time with clients outside the agency, some non-sexual socialization between escorts and their clientele occurred at the agency. Martin described how some more regular clients often dropped by the house for extended periods of time, bringing take-out food, playing video games with escorts, and generally socializing without the exchange of payment or sex. Certainly, such extended visits were reserved for clients who were wellknown to the agency and had managed to integrate themselves into the lives of the escorts and the culture of the agency.

CONCLUSION

Escorting was more than just a job for many of the men at *College Boys*. Because of its stigmatized nature, men carefully managed who knew about their sex work and to what degree details were revealed when the escort self-disclosed his involvement with the agency. Each man developed his own process for telling others about sex work although commonalities occurred among the escorts we interviewed. Whether choosing to be completely open or to conceal escorting from those around them, all escorts faced some level of conflict and rejection. As a result, thoughts and emotions about escorting often occupied a central role in these men's lives. Even when they kept their sex work segregated to the periphery, attempting to do so subsequently placed escorting (and the desire to keep it hidden) in the midst of one's mindset. Thus, in this chapter we have explored similarities and differences in how men navigated the disclosure/concealment process with friends, partners, and their families. In addition, we have noted the unique challenges that heterosexual men encountered, often resulting in their full concealment of escorting. Finally, we explored how interactions with clients were woven into escorts' personal lives. Commonly, this was through repeat or multi-hour encounters, gift giving (incentivizing), and through the use of personality, charm, and wit. In kind, escorts enjoyed getting to know their clients and viewed socializing with them as one of the most rewarding aspects of the job. Escorts were challenged to identify appropriate professional, romantic, and personal boundaries with clients that maintained the commercial relationship as well as their own personal integrity. Escorting was more than just a job for the men at *College Boys*; it became part of their lives.

Chapter Seven

THE BUSINESS

OVERVIEW

So far most of our book has been spent describing the people and relationships that constituted *College Boys*. Doing so allowed you to become familiar with the agency from the ground up. As you noted, people often worked with each other to meet their social, psychological, and material needs. You have come to know Martin and some of the *College Boys* as individuals, so that now as we shift our focus to the agency as a whole and particularly to its functioning as a business, hold onto that individual perspective and remember the people involved in this thriving "family" concern.

Being a small highly centralized operation, the interaction of separate personalities greatly impacted the agency as a business organization. As we will see, an escort's location in its social network vis-à-vis Martin and other members of his *Inner Circle* significantly impacted the nature and even the success of their employment. Moreover, Martin delegated so few of the agency's management functions that *College Boys* could not long maintain its organization or operation when he was absent. No one was fully able to assume Martin's duties because no one really knew how to run the entire business, had the contacts, or enjoyed the confidence of the staff and clients in the way that Martin did. This arrangement, so common in many small companies, eventually led to the downfall of *College Boys*, something we take up in Chapter Ten. But for now, at this point in our story, the agency is humming along—pulsing with activity and making a lot of money for everyone. *College Boys* is more successful than Martin ever expected.

Basics of the Business

As we discussed in Chapter One, Martin began *College Boys* in response to his own financial situation. He had been laid off and saw few prospects for regaining the income he enjoyed at his previous job; other ventures had not produced what he hoped. Martin needed to make a living; he perceived escorting as a means to generate income. As Martin realized he was getting older and that his physique could not compete with younger or more athletic men, he reasoned his talents as an organizer and salesman could still be put to use. Martin leveraged these skills to compensate for his declining sexual capital—he got other men to do the actual escorting while he handled all of the logistics. By doing so and keeping a cut of the hourly fee, Martin could make more money than by working alone with an ever-shrinking clientele. This situation represented a pathway into business not all that different from that of many entrepreneurs. Working for others has not paid off for Martin, so why not start his own business and work for himself? He brought on his first escort and *College Boys* was up and running.

The agency expanded over the next several years averaging 20 to 25 escorts working at any one time, although this number could vary significantly given the nature of the business. More important, progressively less of Martin's personal time was spent seeing his own clients. At the point we began our interviews more than two years into the operation, Martin saw only one or two clients per month—and these were almost always his old customers who specifically requested Martin's companionship, sometimes with a second escort coming along for the "ride." Martin joked about "taking one for the team" when going out on a call, which only endeared him more to the staff. Continuing to work occasionally also maintained Martin's credibility with the escorts, a fact he relied upon when giving them advice on how to act with clients, in helping them deal with the downsides of escorting, or when reinforcing his expectations about their job performance.

Martin's typical day was busy, and he rarely took one off. Like many entrepreneurs he got up early and stayed up late to run the shop. He almost never put down his cell phone because he needed to be available for clients and escorts. Martin used the same phone for personal as well as business purposes; there really was little difference. We usually saw him seated at his desk in the front room. Martin bantered with the men wandering around the first floor, scanned the Internet for new escorting websites or independent escort listings, responded to email inquiries from current and potential clients, or talked on his cell phone—mostly he did the latter handling dozens of conversations per day. The men expected it; they knew he had to answer most of his calls so they just turned to another person in the room or did something else when Martin's phone chimed. When he was done, Martin came back to the previous conversation full of apologies, news, and opportunities.

Phone calls came in at any hour of the day or night, but most frequently in the afternoon and early evening—say from three to nine P.M. Before calling *College Boys*, clients often emailed Martin to inquire about a specific escort or ask questions about how to set up an appointment. Many clients "felt out" the agency to determine its legitimacy and level of discretion, concerned about the potential personal, professional, and legal problems that could arise from a breach of confidentiality or a police sting. After one or two email exchanges, Martin wanted to talk to clients over the phone. He never set up an appointment from emails or texts alone given that he too had much to lose should a security breach occur or too many clients fail to pay for services they had contracted. Moreover, Martin could only do so much through email when trying to match clients with a *College Boy* who would best meet the client's interests.

Martin chatted with new clients to determine their interests and seriousness in following through with appointments they might schedule. He wanted to know if police or other law enforcement groups were infiltrating his agency. Martin had friends, sometimes clients, who taught him how to spot suspicious cell phone numbers. He devised methods of identifying individuals who might not appear to be what they seemed. There were certain catch phrases that law enforcement could not use else their operation be ruled entrapment in future court proceedings, so Martin made sure that he worked these into conversations. He assessed the willingness of clients to hire and to pay, and was suspicious if a client demanded too much information about the personal lives of people working for the agency or details about its business operations. Only once did Martin believe the police had contacted him. He evaded the call. None of his escorts were ever arrested for their sex work, and the agency was never raided.

Legal entanglements were only one reason to be careful. Many of the *College Boys* wanted to work for an agency because Martin carefully vetted their clients. Independent escorts can run into real problems with their clients ranging from the more mundane (refusal to pay) to the more dangerous (physical violence). Furthermore, some clients hoped to have unprotected sex (to "bareback") with an escort and often offered more money to do so (Morse, Simon, Balson, & Osofsky, 1992; Bimbi & Parsons, 2005). Others may have agreed up front that certain sexual activities would or would not occur, but later tried to push an escort's boundaries even further once they were together. Such concerns appear to be even more prominent for men working the streets and who work individually (Scott, Minichiello, Marino, Harvey, Jamieson, & Browne, 2005).

Thus, having an agency to negotiate boundaries with clients, check out their intentions, and establish payment and other expectations made Martin's role as middle-man especially desirable despite his cut of their fee. Several *College Boys* talked about the security they felt working through the agency:

Wes: I trust Martin to set me up legitimately. He knows who these people [clients] are. I know something about them and I feel safer. He or someone at the agency knows where I am, because that was a big thing for me. I couldn't go if someone didn't know where I was. I know I'm less at risk for someone hurting me or killing me because he knows where I am; he knows who I'm with.

Interviewer: And they know he knows?

Wes: Right so if something happened to me, they know that if something happened to me it would fall back to them. There's a little security there. But I would never pick up someone off the street or "work the street corner."

At its height, *College Boys* provided services to about 250 different clients per month who hired escorts for around 300 separate appointments. The agency charged $160 for an hour with one of its escorts. As you will read in Chapter Eight, one-hour appointments were the norm. However, escorts could also be hired for extended appointments lasting longer than an hour, with reduced rates for each half or full hour beyond the first. Typically, Martin charged $50 for an additional half hour with one of the guys, and $100 for a second or third full hour. Beyond three or four hours with an escort, clients would pay what was called the "overnight" rate (as most of these longer appointments ran until the following morning). Overnights were billed at $600 for up to an eight- or ten-hour appointment. Some clients wanted the escort for a weekend or longer, especially if they desired a travel companion. At this point, there was no real set rate. Martin would negotiate multiple-day appointments on a case-by-case basis; however, such extended stays typically ran into the thousands of dollars.

An escort kept $110 of his hourly rate and Martin received the remainder as the agency's fee. Martin retained a proportionally smaller amount of fees beyond the first hour as a way to encourage escorts to develop clientele who hired for longer periods of time. Escorts might also need to pay for a driver if they did not have their own transportation. Drivers were often other escorts or their friends. Given the cost of gas and a nominal fee for a driver's time, most escorts paid around $25 to be taken to and from an appointment. Martin helped to arrange drivers and often rode along with escorts being taken to and from a call—if it were a short distance, Martin would sometimes compensate the driver himself. In an effort to promote better customer service from the escorts, the boys kept all tips or gifts from clients without having to provide Martin a cut of any such extras. Tips were a normal part of escort work, much as in any service industry operating in the United States; escorts could make good money beyond the regular fee if they provided service that satisfied their customers. Sometimes, they could double or even triple the hourly rate when clients tipped well—savvy escorts did what they could to insure clients were pleased enough to tip generously.

When considering the amount of business Martin conducted at the zenith of the agency's operation, one can reasonably estimate *College Boys* was netting an average minimum monthly intake of about $40,000 with the agency's cut of that figure at around $12,000. Martin indicated that approximately 60 percent of his escorts worked only a few hours per month, making several hundred dollars to supplement other income or give them money at school. However, other escorts worked on a more "full time" basis seeing a number of clients each week. They tended to cultivate multi-hour and overnight appointments and to develop a set of regular clients who would provide better tips and gifts as well as more frequent business. Regulars also carried the advantage of being known quantities, men with whom the escorts had more of a relationship where expectations were clear and comfort levels better established. Escorts working on a full-time basis could earn a thousand dollars per *week* or more, and could make several tens of thousands of dollars per year. For example, Tommy and Michael both worked a good number of hours per week and eventually bought a house together with a substantial down payment saved from their escort money.

All of this business was conducted on a cash basis, although during the last year or two of the agency Martin did accept payments from trusted clients through a commercial online billing service. No records were kept of the financial transactions and no paperwork existed for scheduling appointments; even though customer inquiries might be kept in Martin's email for a week or two and phone numbers could be stored temporarily in his cell phone. It was chiefly a business conducted verbally, using Martin's memory—*College Boys* operated on the discretion and the trust that this built; discretion for clients and escorts alike. On the other hand, it made running the business difficult for anyone other than Martin, even for one of the *Inner Circle* who knew him well. They simply did not have the depth of memory Martin possessed, or the trust of his clientele developed through a shared history of mutual interactions.

Agency Operations

As with any small service-oriented business, managing *College Boys* involved the several interlocking functions shown in Figure 7.1. Although some of these required daily attention and were central to the regular operation of the business (e.g., scheduling), all of them demanded consideration if the agency were to maintain itself over time. We now discuss these four functions in turn, showing how *College Boys* responded to the demands inherent in each and how they impacted the agency's business outcomes.

Figure 7.1.
Operating functions

Staffing

Managing *College Boys'* workforce always challenged Martin and was perhaps the most difficult of the functions to coordinate. Recruitment and retention required constant effort. Chapter Three discussed several reasons young men considered a job with *College Boys* and Chapter Four explained how new escorts learned their trade. Although we will not reprise the discussion of training and mentorship here, we do need to address Martin's efforts to locate new escorts and the criteria he employed when deciding whether or not to hire someone. Martin became more selective over time in the ways he looked for new *College Boys* and took less of his own time doing so. He no longer needed to spend hours talking to men in gay-oriented chatrooms, asking escorts to bring friends over to the house, or going to clubs in order to meet promising new hires. By the time we interviewed him, he did very little active searching at all. Potential escorts came to *him*—primarily through someone already affiliated with the agency and typically from being friends with one of the escorts. A small percentage, Martin estimated it to be less than one-fourth of new hires, found information about the agency via the website. He received several email inquiries per week. Few of these men actually came to meet with him, let alone got to work as a *College Boy*.

Martin preferred having people come to his attention through a friend or similar pre-existing connection. Often, they would tag along with their escort friend to hang out at the agency and spend time watching movies, playing games, or talking with the other guys. They would go out to clubs together. Martin would buy food or take groups out to eat. As they socialized with his staff, Martin got to know them informally which provided him with more detailed information about whether they might be worth recruiting. Should he decide to make the attempt, he did so through humor. Other *College Boys* typically beat Martin to the punch, joking with their friends about going out on a call for some extra money or about having sex with this one guy or that. It often made friends on the *Periphery* think about working for Martin. He encouraged them to "just try it once or twice" as a way to see whether or not they wanted to do it more often.

Martin attempted to replicate this informal atmosphere when someone had contacted him online. An interested party called him and they would talk several times before Martin invited them over to the house. Once a man came to the agency, Martin interacted with the potential hire in the front room. Inevitably, several escorts would be present and could join in the conversation. Current staff also provided more details about the job, and Martin could watch them interact with the new person. Afterward, Martin polled his escorts about their thoughts on whether to give the potential hire a trial appointment or two. He not only received a number of different opinions with which to inform his own, but inviting his employees to participate in a management decision made them feel appreciated and involved; it strengthened their relationship with Martin and gave them a sense of ownership over the agency.

Martin envisioned a definite set of characteristics that *College Boys* should possess. These were based on his knowledge of the client market and on what worked best for retaining and operating a high quality staff:

- Youth—Most clients preferred younger escorts and consistent with his business identity, nearly all of the escorts were between the ages of 18 and 25. The oldest man working for Martin was in his mid-30s, but was advertised as being in his late 20s. Together with several other older escorts, this permitted some variety in client preferences. Escorts needed to document their age as Martin would not hire anyone younger than 18.
- Attractive—Martin only hired lean or athletic young men given the strong client bias in this direction. Further, escorts needed to possess good hygiene and

attractive facial features. Martin did not hire men with too many piercings or tattoos, finding that most clients found such features unattractive.

- Open-Minded—Over the years, Martin found that escorts who had reservations about prostitution, possessed a more conventional sexuality, or who disliked having sex with men in relationships often did poorly in the business. Thus, he talked with potential hires about their values and attitudes regarding sexuality and relationships. He tried to gain an understanding of their initial comfort level with the work to prevent adjustment problems down the road.
- Reliable—Escorts needed to be available for appointments, deliver services as agreed upon, and be on time for their appointments. Most of Martin's problems in running the agency came from failures in this area; nearly all escorts dismissed from the agency had been unreliable in one or more ways on a number of different occasions.
- Sociable—Even on calls that were primarily sexual in nature, escorts still needed to engage in some level of small talk with clients. They had to care about providing good customer service. Escorts seen as friendly and masculine were in great demand, and Martin believed that clients resented men perceived as "rude" or "distant."

Escorts already working for *College Boys* agreed with Martin about these characteristics. Nearly all escorts viewed having a positive attitude and good social skills as much more important than physical attractiveness on its own. Everyone agreed that an average-looking escort could still be very successful if he possessed a winning personality and/or the skills to build strong working relationships with his clients. This list was influenced by Martin's personal bias toward masculine, "straight-acting" White men, preferences that influenced staffing at the agency which employed relatively few men of color given the city in which *College Boys* was based—something criticized by a number of the escorts when the topic came up with their boss.

Any employer would want to keep his best staff, so Martin actively sought to retain escorts that clients wanted to hire either because of the young man's looks, personality, customer service, or hopefully some combination of the three. Keeping good escorts reduced the number of new men Martin needed to recruit, allowing him to be more selective when he did need to hire, and spend less time hiring and more time managing other aspects of the business. Given the amount of support and training new escorts required, reduced staff turnover and increased selectivity decreased the need for development activities while simultaneously increasing the pool of successful escorts who could provide excellent role modeling and advice for newer *College Boys*.

Despite his efforts, men were always coming and going from the agency. Martin estimated that the average escort worked at *College Boys* anywhere from six to twelve months:

Martin: When someone's new, they wind up with lots of business because they're new and everyone wants to see someone who's new usually. But after they've been around for a while then that really levels off. You definitely get some regulars, but the majority of people [clients] that I deal with like variety. Very rarely do they stick with the exact same person all the time.

Interviewer: How does that affect your business?

Martin: It always makes me believe that I need to be hiring new people. It's difficult for some of the long term people; the longer they're around, the more they definitely develop regulars. But that newness levels out, so the nights of doing more than one call every single day and having a call every single day levels out too. It makes the business where your life expectancy as an escort generally dies off after about a year unless you're able to keep a regular group of clients or have something really special about you.

Martin tried to mitigate these factors with staff he wished to keep. He sent them more business with clients known to be reliable, friendly, and respectful of an escort's boundaries. Martin cultivated better personal relationships with higher quality escorts, giving them a more personal reason to stay with the agency when they inevitably wondered about moving on. It also reduced the likelihood that escorts would leave *College Boys* to work for themselves as independent providers. This appeared to be a successful strategy as escorts were reluctant to work on their own not only due to the perceived hassles and risks of doing so, but also from a sense of not wanting to "betray" Martin. Zack talked about having seen a longer-term client without Martin's knowledge and how it made him feel afterward:

> I did once [see a client without telling Martin] and I regret it. I told Martin about it afterward. I felt guilty and it's not just that I cheated Martin out of money. That money could have went towards things Martin needed, but it's not even about the money. It's like I think of him kind of as a dad. He's a really cool guy and also he's a safety net too, which if you do stuff outside of the company you don't know what you get yourself into. So I won't do that again.

Most of the guys expressed a similar high degree of personal regard for Martin. It helped good escorts stay at the agency longer and motivated them to do a better job, especially when they did have to see clients who were less desirable or more difficult to please.

Not all escorts succeeded at *College Boys*. Of these, the majority wound up to be poor fits for the job despite initial signs of promise. These men sorted themselves out of the agency, typically without urging or prompting.

- Moving Away—Men in their late teens and early twenties often live in a state of transition: Going away to school, relocating for a new job, wanting to live somewhere new or more exciting, moving to a new city with a friend or partner. Many new *College Boys* fell into this group, simply leaving town before they had worked very long for the agency.

- Undesirable Sexual Partners—Some of the escorts could not stand having sex with people they found unappealing. Interestingly, this did not often occur among straight escorts. It was much more common among gay escorts. It seemed that once a straight man had made the decision to cross the line to have sex with another man, the client's other characteristics mattered little. Gay escorts faced a more complicated situation. They already had sex with men, so multiple interacting factors (age, build, hygiene) influenced sexual desirability—simply more could go wrong. Whatever the reason, some new escorts could not find a way to make themselves have sex with people they found unattractive.
- Values and Attitudes—Most new escorts initially believed they could engage in prostitution. However, some became too uncomfortable once actually having sex for pay. Many indicated a conflict with their identity; they could not reconcile prostitution with their established sense of self. Others related that escorting made them feel "dirty" and dehumanized. They could not accept escorting in moral terms, feeling contaminated afterward or believing themselves to have become "just a piece of meat" to be bought and sold.
- Logistical Demands—The lack of stable work hours or transportation made the job too demanding for some young men. They found that being on-call disrupted their lives—it was too difficult to take appointments at any time of day given other responsibilities and priorities. Lack of transportation made it hard for some escorts to see clients, paying a driver for gas and time cut too far into their income to make escorting worthwhile.

Although Martin encouraged people to give the job a trial period and provided mentorship to help them adjust, men who left the agency of their own accord usually did so after only seeing three or four clients.

Martin needed to actually "fire" only a few escorts during our time at the agency; he worried that disgruntled escorts could maliciously reveal what they knew about clients and agency operations. Martin only ended an escort's association with *College Boys* when the staff member had proven to be consistently unreliable or when there had been complaints from too many trustworthy clients. Martin's most pressing needs were for an escort to be available when they had agreed to work, arrive at appointments on time, and provide a satisfying experience to clients within the limits negotiated between Martin, the client, and escort. Martin worked hard to insure that clients and escorts were matched on the basis of their interests and boundaries, but expected some degree of accommodation from an escort (or at least courtesy) when this was not possible or when clients arrived at an appointments with additional desires. Martin seemed to have a longer "fuse" with escorts who were more integrated into the agency's social network, providing them with more chances and a longer time frame with which to turn around their customer service. However, even then, there was a point at which he could no longer accept the quality of an escort's work performance.

Escorts who proved themselves unable or unwilling to meet these basic expectations could expect a conversation with Martin about what it meant to work for

College Boys. At first, this discussion would be friendly. It focused on helping the escort develop success-oriented skills and attitudes—professionalism if you will. Discussions became more direct and took on a sharper edge when they needed to occur several times. If remedial efforts did not succeed, Martin would gradually stop sending new business to the offending escort. He might give the young man one or two more "test" clients to provide "one last chance" at helping the escort change his ways. Or, Martin might only send clients to certain escorts if no one else was available to take an appointment. The usual means of termination was to simply let an escort's association with *College Boys* fade away. Should the former employee contact Martin, the young man would be told the reasons why appointments were no longer being scheduled for him. Sometimes Martin could be convinced to give the escort another try, but often he could not. Martin needed to protect the agency's reputation and minimize the likelihood of negative client reviews appearing on the Internet.

Advertising

No business survives without reaching a base of customers willing to pay for its services. And like any other businessman with a small company, Martin developed several cost-effective strategies for reaching potential clients and letting them know what *College Boys* offered. Two main types of strategies allowed Martin go get his message out: direct and indirect advertising.

Direct advertising placed the agency before potential customers. Martin always purchased space in the city's phone book under "escort services." Even though he estimated that it represented less than one percent of his business, Martin still felt obligated to place the phone book ad to reach men without access to the Internet. Martin also advertised the agency by taking escorts out to clubs. Most every Friday and/or Saturday, Martin and a group of the men would head to the city's gay bars. They would dance and have a good time; Martin bought all of the drinks. To "repay" him, the escorts passed around discrete business cards or left them on tables and counters. Martin got more than a few calls this way, especially once the agency had established a reputation and people knew him and some of the *College Boys*. Later in the agency's history, Martin established a relationship with several gay clubs in a large city two hours away. Martin sent two or three guys to these bars on most weekends where they would strip. Often they would already have one or more clients to see when they were in the city—if not, there were always men at the show who wanted to hire them afterward.

The lion's share of *College Boys'* advertising occurred online. Martin estimated that more than 90 percent of his monthly business came through the Internet, especially from the agency's detailed website. To get potential clients to his website, Martin peppered *College Boys* banners on several online "hook-up" bulletin boards and classified web pages directed to men seeking other men. These allowed a more general web user to become aware that a male escort agency existed in the area as well as a way to visit its website. Martin also placed advertisements on websites specifically directed toward individuals looking to hire male escorts. Martin bought space on several of them both for the agency itself and for individual escorts. Agency profiles featured several guys in a single advertisement whereas pages for individual escorts (typically men in higher demand or newer to the agency) focused on separate *College Boys*, their characteristics, and sexual preferences.

Interested potential clients could learn about *College Boys'* escorts and procedures when they visited its website. The website too represented direct advertising. A potential customer had demonstrated enough interest to click on a link found somewhere else (perhaps even through a more general web search) to reach the agency's virtual location. Once here, Martin had the task of communicating the variety of men available while being careful to avoid any specific discussion of sexual behavior for sale. It was often a difficult balance to strike:

> Usually clients have seen the pictures ahead of time; and most people are usually driven visually, based on what they see on the picture. First, I'll get an email asking specific questions about that, but I think it's easier for me to talk someone through that on the telephone than it is even to an email on it because of legalities. It's a little risky sometimes to put too many things in writing when an email can be printed out later on and wind up causing you problems down the road.

The agency emphasized that customers paid for an escort's *time* without expectation for sexual behavior, "The client acknowledges that escorts are being paid for their time, and that no sexual activity is either implied or promised when an escort is hired." Similar disclaimers are very common among online escort websites, and need to be. Although hiring someone for platonic companionship (such as for non-erotic massage) is completely legal in the United States, the same cannot be said of Internet-based prostitution.

How did the agency imply that clients could expect sex when they hired an escort without directly saying so in its advertisements? It did so through digital photographs. Any website with *College Boys* escorts would have pictures of them; often there were small galleries of six or seven photographs users could browse. None showed a fully clothed individual—all were erotic in nature. Escort profiles typically included a number of nude shots either showing their whole naked body or specific body areas (e.g., chest, arms, backside, or groin). Few escorts showed their faces, fearing identification and discrimination. We joked with Martin about how the guys would show their privates but not their faces. Martin answered in a deadpan voice, "It's less personal." We had to agree this apparent contradiction made perfect sense in the context of virtual prostitution in a way that it did not for the mundane world.

At this point, Martin's direct advertising merged with more indirect methods. Photographs posted online suggested regular sexual activity whereas the text of the advertisement omitted explicit references—threading the needle between what the customer desired and what the law permitted. Martin relied upon the *suggestion* of sexual gratification for much of his advertising efforts. To a certain degree he could depend on cultural stereotypes about escorting and massage to do some of the work for him; all he needed was to present his business in a way that activated this latent awareness. However, were he too subtle then a client might not understand exactly what *College Boys* had to offer.

Martin emphasized *companionship* as the service clients paid to receive. In fact, as we related earlier in the book, many clients did seek more than sex from their escorts. They wanted someone with whom they could connect, even if for only an hour. Martin reassured erstwhile clients about the sexual aspects of an appointment by showing pictures of what they could expect to see in person, and by emphasizing that an escort would focus on satisfying the client's needs while providing excellent company. Thus, simply seeing escorts dancing at a club or enjoying themselves at a gay bar could effectively advertise the agency by showing customers what they might be able to hire for an hour, night, or weekend.

The agency could also rely to some degree on word of mouth, always said to be the best form of endorsement as it comes unsolicited from a client himself. Other clients are much more likely to believe someone else hiring an escort. Here the legal aspects of what can and cannot be said are much freer. Clients posted reviews on websites related to hiring escorts or to a website specifically dedicated to clients communicating their experiences after hiring. The official line would be that if sex occurred between a client and escort it was not because this had been expected as part of the fee—sex occurred because the parties enjoyed each other's company and wanted it to happen regardless of the monetary arrangement that had first brought them together. Martin found that client reviews were extremely effective in generating new business and were perhaps his single largest source of new customers. With clients largely unable to speak with one another in person, such virtual spaces permitted them to share information about escorts and to recommend who to hire or who to avoid. Clients could also relate their views on the ease of setting up appointments, working through *College Boys* to have an experience they desired, and the level of satisfaction provided by their overall interaction with the agency.

Scheduling

Although one might think that scheduling could be a fairly straightforward aspect of running the business, it actually occupied most of Martin's time and effort. Scheduling escorts to see clients required successful completion of several interlocking steps, any of which could derail an appointment.

Staff Availability

No appointment could be scheduled without escorts to send. Martin needed to insure that he always had several *College Boys* on call and ready to see clients. This required a huge amount of time and coordination, especially as Martin kept no paper records. He remembered everything without writing it down, and was remarkably accurate in doing so. Martin had a number of escorts he knew wanted work. They would usually drop what they were doing to take some business. Often, these were men newer to the agency. They were just getting started and wanted hours. Otherwise, they tended to be men with whom Martin had more of a personal relationship. Martin perhaps leveraged personal bonds when asking them to see a client at inconvenient times. Some of the escorts resented this a bit, as did escorts who had less of a personal connection with their boss.

In addition to his fall-back options, Martin also required escorts to give him regular updates on when they could and would work. He gently cajoled staff more toward the "would" side of that equation rather than the "could." Often he made jokes with the escorts like, "If I called you when you were having sex with your girlfriend, you'd already be in the mood to take a call, right?" Martin also gently reminded staff that if they restricted their hours too much, other escorts would pick up the business instead. We frequently heard him say, "Well, you know, I need to be able to get hold of guys and I'll use the guys who have been most flexible and willing to work first." This reminded escorts that although Martin made every effort to accommodate their personal schedules, working for *College Boys* was a job and one that often had irregular and inopportune hours.

The agency's house almost always lent Martin an ace-in-the-hole when he needed one. Escorts lived at the house. They constantly socialized at the house. Many spent a good number of their free hours there enjoying the company of friends. Martin could always tap this pool to take a call if he needed an escort to go out with a client. Although he never said so outright, it made good personal as well as business sense to open up the agency as a lodging house and community center—the rentboy's equivalent of the local YMCA. Escorts had the dual benefits of a largely enjoyable social and/or living situation and could develop a better relationship with the boss. Therefore, these men could probably get more hours from him should they wish to do so. Likewise, from Martin's point of view, not only could clients coming to the agency for incalls meet even more eligible young men they might want to hire; they also built a more congenial relationship with the agency. Martin could keep better tabs on his staff, encourage their professional development, and build better working and personal relationships with them. It worked to everyone's advantage. Like many aspects of small businesses, bolstering one area of the firm had positive impacts on other areas.

New versus Repeat Customers

Martin's efforts over the years had paid off for his business—he estimated that 60 percent of weekly client calls involved repeat customers. Martin took this as a sign that the agency provided good service and enjoyed a decent reputation. Although there were always complaints and miscommunications, Martin believed that he managed these quickly and sensitively. His own experience as a client taught him what he did not want when working through an agency, and he sought to provide better service at *College Boys*. New clients involved more pre-screening. It was difficult to discuss the sexual nature of what the client sought given Martin could not promise that sex would occur during any given appointment, even though he believed that more than 95 percent of client-escort contacts involved some type of sexual activity. He had more difficulty making recommendations for new clients regarding which escort might best suit their interests. *College Boys* often provided perks (e.g., discounts, free transportation, preferential scheduling) in order to retain good customers and encourage their more frequent business.

Selecting the Right Escort

One advantage of the Internet for small businesses is that customers often do a great deal of their shopping and information gathering online, requiring less staff time once the customer finally decides to make their purchase. Martin often found this to be true at *College Boys*. As the majority of his business came through the website, the average customer had already read through many escort profiles, obtained information about agency scheduling and payment policies, and made some preliminary choice about who they might like to hire, for how much time, and for what activities. When they called Martin, only the new clients needed him to explain how one went about arranging appointments and making payments. Moreover, most clients new to the agency had hired an escort elsewhere such that they understood the generalities in doing so. Only a small number of new clients had never hired at all.

Once past the nuts-and-bolts conversation about how to hire, Martin helped clients finalize their choice of escort(s). The majority of clients contacted the agency to set up an appointment at least a day or two in advance, less than half called for a same-day appointment. When calling in advance, Martin had more flexibility in scheduling clients with their first choice in escort—he could verify the escort's availability and get back to the client relatively quickly. Same-day calls were harder to manage given limitations on who might be available. Clients often were not able to see their first choice even though Martin tried to accommodate client preferences whenever possible.

When discussing the selection of an escort, Martin tactfully interviewed the client about what would ideally occur during their appointment. Sometimes, clients had selected an escort based on looks or other features without fully considering the sexual and non-sexual aspects of what that *College Boy* might provide. Some escorts were better at conversation, more presentable at a fine restaurant, possessed a more relaxed attitude, or would engage in certain sexual acts but not others. Martin needed to help clients match their preferences for physical attributes with an escort's personality and behavioral characteristics in order to maximize the likelihood of a successful call. It would not do to send a dominant young man to a client who preferred submissive, meek partners regardless of how physically desirable the client found that escort.

Martin needed to consider other factors as well. He tried to distribute business more or less evenly among the escorts currently seeking hours, at least among the ones Martin found dependable and customer-oriented. He knew that some escorts complained about one of their fellows getting more hours as a sign of favoritism. It could cause some ill will in the agency and led to more than one serious falling out. Martin tried to smooth over these concerns by being as fair as possible, and also by explaining to his staff that (a) newer escorts were always going to get more requests, (b) the longer someone worked for *College Boys* the more he had to rely on developing a set of regular clientele to counteract client preferences for the "new kid" at the agency, and (c) he gave more business to escorts who proved to have more flexible schedules, a greater degree of reliability, and did what it took to insure client satisfaction. Although he tried to be respectful in outlining these considerations, Martin could also be quite blunt talking to his staff about how he arranged their appointments, particularly when pushed. It helped that escorts often heard Martin's end of the conversation given that they could listen to him talking on the phone with clients. Most knew the deal, those that did not adapt tended to have relatively short working lives with the agency.

Following Through

The appointment was set; Martin and the client have agreed upon a time and place. They discussed who will go and what will generally occur when the escort arrives, and for how long. A fee has been arranged. The client knows to have the money in cash at the start of the appointment, even if the escort does not ask for it. Many escorts find it rude, not to mention legally precarious, to ask clients for money. Clients should offer to provide the "gift" on their own without prompting—it's just polite. Martin has reinforced expectations with the client in terms of using condoms for anal sex, respecting the escort's boundaries, and communicating one's desires to the escort so he could provide as much satisfaction as time permitted. All the client needed to do was wait for his escort to arrive.

Getting to an Appointment

Arrangements could be a little more complicated on the escort's side of the equation. The convenience or inconvenience of the appointment depended on his transportation, personal situation, and time management skills. Martin provided transportation to escorts without vehicles of their own. He would get another escort or a friend to drive staff to an appointment. Even some escorts with their own transportation preferred to go with a driver, especially with clients not known to the agency. They felt safer knowing that someone else was close at hand in case something should go wrong, if the client became pushy, refused to pay, or even grew dangerous. However, Martin preferred men to have their own rides given potential problems with coordinating schedules for three people (driver, escort, and client); working with two calendars was bad enough.

Escorts could also have difficulty with their personal situations. Unexpected commitments with partners, friends, or another job would arise during times when an escort had said he was available to work. Martin may have set up an appointment days in advance only to have that escort tell him that his other job needed him to work or that his parents were having a family barbeque. People in the escort's personal life, even when they knew about his involvement with *College Boys*, could be less than understanding about sudden changes in plans or for the escort's need to take appointments at all hours of the day and night. Seeing clients, especially if the escort wanted to work frequently, significantly disrupted his time for other people. Conflicting time demands between an escort's personal life and sex work represented a constant irritant for both him and Martin. The escort tried to juggle competing needs whereas Martin needed to get escorts to clients who wanted them.

Not all of the escorts managed these complex issues as effectively as Martin would have liked. Although Martin enjoyed spontaneity and spunk in his escorts, he also needed them to act responsibly and take their work for the agency seriously. Frequent problems arose when escorts made commitments, but then backed out of them at the last minute when something they thought more entertaining had arisen. Less organized escorts sometimes double-booked themselves, forgetting their work hours at other jobs or plans they had made with family or friends. Even though Martin continuously reinforced the importance of sticking to agreed schedules, a significant portion of his time was consumed by re-arranging appointments, finding replacements, and triple-checking availability with his escorts.

Delivering the Goods

Getting to appointments was only half the battle; escorts needed to deliver the type of experience that left clients satisfied about their hire. The situation is quite similar to ordering pizza over the phone. You have to talk with the shop about what you want, how much it will cost, and where to deliver the pizza. The pizza has to actually arrive around the time you want to eat or the moment is ruined. Even if it does get to you on time, the pizza itself has to be what you wanted. It might not be exactly what you ordered, but what you get has to be satisfying nonetheless—any unforeseen "surprises" should be pleasant ones. With respect to *College Boys*: The exact scene which unfolded during an appointment might not have been identical to what Martin discussed with the client, but it should have matched well enough and met enough of the client's expectations to satisfy and, therefore, feel successful.

Martin strongly believed satisfying clients depended on the escort's commitment to customer service. It was no different than the line he took during his career as a corporate trainer. He understood and worked to reinforce boundaries escorts needed to set with their sex work; expectations he communicated to clients up front. However, Martin also expected his escorts to act as professionals when seeing customers—a professional focuses on meeting the customer's needs as long as doing so remained within predetermined limits. Clients paid for a particular experience. Martin wanted to insure his staff focused on good customer service in four different domains:

- Timeliness—Get to appointments when scheduled, stay for the contracted period.
- Communication—Help clients understand limits, possibilities, and expectations. Listen to clients so that you understand theirs.
- Positive Relationship—Focus on the client's interests and comfort. Develop rapport with clients by remaining discrete, courteous, and pleasant.
- Satisfaction—Make sure the client relaxes, enjoys himself, gets the experience he wanted or more so that he feels like his money was well spent.

It was the escort's responsibility to make the client happy, and not the reverse. Some escorts had difficulty understanding this imperative in sexual situations, holding onto a view that enjoyment should be reciprocal. Martin attempted to disavow his staff of this notion, pointing out they were being *paid* to be with a client, not to enjoy themselves. They were *working*, not at home with their boyfriends or girlfriends. Pleasure could be a nice addition to the job but it was not required; whatever enjoyment there was with clients usually did not occur through the sexual part of an appointment, but through any social time beforehand or afterward. Most escorts enjoyed conversation with clients and getting to know one another. For example, Joshua said:

> We ended up sitting in the formal parlor of his Victorian bed and breakfast and we talked for four hours. And he seemed genuinely interested in everything that I said ...You give people a chance to find a similarity and they will. People aren't as different as they pretend to be.

Martin wanted the escorts to build relationships with their clients; he wanted his escorts to remember that the clients were *paying* to enjoy the escort's company and not necessarily the other way around.

Quality Control

Companies interested in long-term success actively seek feedback from customers; they do not wait for customers to provide it on their own. Unless such feedback is solicited, a company usually receives a smattering of complaints about either the quality of the product or the difficulty in navigating the firm's procedures for finding, purchasing, and delivering that product— these two elements represent the *content* and *process* of a commercial transaction. Savvy firms solicit honest customer opinions continuously, and then use this information to reduce problems and enhance positives. They also look to their employees for such information and for innovative ideas about new services, product quality, and customer service. If the "customer is king" then wise firms constantly insure that they know what their ruler thinks about practices and products. Martin understood this imperative, pursuing feedback about *College Boys* and looping it back into his business through his staff development practices and operating procedures.

Talking with Clients after Appointments

Martin usually asked clients to call him some time after their appointment so that he could check to see how things went. Most of the clients did so, and the great majority of their feedback was positive. By building the expectation the customers would speak with Martin after their sessions, he sought to develop the reputation that the agency cared about the quality and professionalism of its escorts and would work to fix any aspect of the appointment that did not go well. Martin believed that clients appreciated a proactive attitude from the agency and that it helped to build more congenial relationships with his customer base. Martin could not only gain a better sense of how sessions went by collecting information about most of the appointments, he also had another chance to advertise his business by reminding customers about other escorts they might like to hire, talk with clients about the future availability of the escort that they had already hired, and develop the type of relationship with his customers that could encourage repeat business. If clients did not call him within a day, Martin almost always called them.

Talking with Escorts after Appointments

The first piece of information Martin received was usually from the escort. Escorts typically returned to the agency right after a call, or Martin went out with drivers to pick them up from a client's home or hotel. Practically, this allowed Martin to collect the agency fee with as few hiccups as possible. In terms of the current discussion, speaking with escorts immediately following their appointments allowed Martin to debrief his staff about their experiences. He could better understand the customer service strengths and weaknesses of his staff and help them develop more appropriate expectations. Martin could also begin to identify aspects of the session that went well or poorly, providing correction or praise as needed.

Equally important, Martin gained insight into his clients through the eyes of the escorts. He better understood what they looked for when hiring an escortand how well they were able to communicate what they wanted while setting up their appointment based on what the escort said actually occurred. He gained a sense of the client's reliability in following safer sex expectations and in respecting the escort's limits with respect to sexual behaviors, drinking, or drug use. Martin also learned if clients paid the appropriate fee, tipped well, or provided gifts. He developed a better understanding of clients social behaviors, personalities, and needs so as to better match them with the right escort in any future appointment.

Checking Reviews on the Internet

Martin considered the possibility of online escort reviews when he spoke with clients after their appointments. Clients often already knew about how to do so and the websites where such reviews were posted. For his part, Martin checked the escort review sites daily to look for any new feedback on his employees. When a review was posted, Martin shared it with his staff whether the review was positive or negative. Many reviews contained elements of both. He used the reviews for several purposes:

- To reward good performance—Escorts were proud of their positive reviews and earned some respect from other escorts at *College Boys* when one was posted. Martin praised them lavishly.
- As teaching tools for other escorts—Martin used reviews as training tools for his staff. He talked with them about what clients said they liked or disliked. He highlighted how an escort may have prompted a positive experience through a certain aspect of the client's feedback. He noted where the escort could have done a better job.
- To build a sense of responsibility—When reviews were posted, Martin made sure that other escorts knew the impact it had on the agency's business. Good reviews generated many more client calls whereas bad reviews definitely produced a chill. Reviews about one escort affected income opportunities for everyone.
- For performance evaluation—Although Martin did not conduct formal personnel evaluations with his staff, he definitely kept mental track of who was up and who was down in terms of their job performance. Client reviews carried a great deal of weight, and the escorts knew it.

Given the importance of online client reviews to the business, they represented a key element of Martin's quality control efforts.

CONCLUSION

We went into *College Boys* expecting to find a fairly unique organization. We left surprised by how similar it was to other small "family-run" businesses. Martin and his staff faced the same pressures that many small companies confront: maintaining a quality product, reaching and developing a paying clientele, working to continually improve procedures and services. The solutions Martin developed for these challenges grew out of his own corporate experiences and also through his time running the agency. The largely illegal and sexual nature of his business did impact how it ran—employees were typically recruited privately, customers (especially new customers) had to be screened for security purposes, and public advertisements could not fully or directly disclose everything about what clients purchased from the agency. However, in large part, these considerations did not significantly alter more basic management or operational functions of the business. Escorts at *College Boys* still needed to provide good service at a price where customers found value. It had to recruit, train, and retain employees who could deliver that service. The business had to provide services efficiently such that customers could procure them without hassle or undue delay. The agency's business operations seemed shockingly normal until you forced yourself to remember that it was a male escort call service.

Martin and his staff created something together. The psychological and social space that they called *College Boys* served many divergent needs for staff and clients alike. Now that we have gained more of an understanding of these various aspects of the agency, our next two chapters go into more detail about what clients wanted or needed to obtain from the agency—needs that were strong enough for clients to risk relationship and reputation to acquire and pay for them. We have looked around the agency quite a bit up to this point in the book. We have met the staff and heard what Martin has had to say about his business. Let us now turn our attention more toward the client's point of view and see what they aspired to gain by renting time from handsome young escorts at *College Boys*.

Chapter Eight

WHAT YOU GET FOR A BUCK

OVERVIEW

Escorting involves more than just physical sexual behavior. As you have read in previous chapters, escorts also provide clients with companionship, emotional intimacy, and even romance. Time spent with clients varies from the politely platonic to the wildly erotic: From casual conversation and massage to typical "vanilla" sexual behaviors such as oral sex and on to more specialized erotic scenes colloquially known as "fetish" or "kink." In our time with the men at *College Boys*, we discussed the types of clients escorts regularly served and the variety of situations those clients requested. In this chapter, we discuss the different lenses through which escorts categorized their work and time with clients. We start to describe in more detail who hired men from *College Boys* and the types of services that they requested from these escorts.

Organizing Calls by Their Duration

Duration of the call was one of the major ways in which escorts organized their work conceptually as well as practically. When clients contacted Martin to schedule an appointment, among the chief questions they were expected to answer included, "How long would you like to spend with this escort?" Although escorts and their clients were not required to adhere strictly to whatever time initially agreed upon, this initial request set the parameters for the entire encounter.

The One-Hour Call

By far, the most common type of call men at *College Boys* entertained was the "one-hour" call. Escorts were contracted for a single hour at a standard pay rate plus tip. As you read in Chapter Seven, the agency took a cut of this rate with escorts keeping the remainder in addition to anything else that the client may have provided. One-hour contracting seems to represent the standard among escorting more generally, including for female escorts and with individually employed Internet-based escorts. In contrast, it may be less common for street-based sex workers, where clients and sex workers negotiate prices based more on sexual behavior (e.g., one price for oral sex and a higher price for anal or vaginal) and less on the amount of time that they will be together.

Although the men at *College Boys* were often paid by the hour, and most clients hired an escort for a single hour, the actual time spent with clients was more fluid than this label might suggest. To a great degree, an escort's work was complete when the client was satisfied—most commonly when the client achieved an orgasm; however satisfaction extended beyond the purely sexual. Escorts understood they may be expected to satisfy clients psychologically or emotionally as well as, and sometimes in place of, sexual satisfaction. Completion of the client's goals usually occurred within the 60-minute time frame, and often it took less. Occasionally, satisfying a client exceeded an hour. Regardless of how long emotional and/or physical satisfaction took, the fee was often structured around the pre-agreed one-hour rate—there would be no proration for a call that ended prematurely or an excess charge if a call exceeded the hour by less than 30 minutes. Additional billing was usually left to the escort's discretion. Instead, a combination of a client's needs and an escort's capability chiefly determined the duration of a call, with 60 minutes as the "suggested" window for the amount of time spent with an appointment.

Escorts understood that calls may end early or go over the one-hour allotment and were expected to adjust their behavior accordingly (i.e., express willingness to stay longer if a call seemed to be ending early or knowing when it is time to wrap it up were it to run long). Accordingly, escorts knew that strict adherence to time or "rushing" a call would be perceived as rude—clients and escorts who insisted on strict time adherence were often negatively referred to as "clock watchers." Communication ahead of the encounter helped ensure that escorts met client expectations within a given period of time. In *College Boys* and most other agencies, the manager asked specific questions about a potential client's interests, listening closely for their needs, identifying the best escort for the job, scheduling convenient time for the client and escort to meet, and communicating clearly the client's interests to the escort ahead of the actual encounter. Given the complex nature of such an arrangement, it is no surprise that clients often rehired those escorts in which they had a previous "positive" interaction and who were believed to take the time to satisfy their needs.

Most often, one-hour calls involved a sole escort. However, these calls sometimes involved more than one man from *College Boys*, with two escorts typically being the limit for any type of multi-escort encounter. Calls involving a second (or rarely a third) escort tended to be far more sexual in nature. In essence, these calls were less about the social aspects of an encounter and more about satisfying a client's sexual fantasies (e.g., a client watching, joining, or even directing a sexual encounter involving more than one individual). Escorts appreciated multi-escort encounters typically because they were being "paid" to have sex with someone who was also in the business, and who was also often close in age and more attractive. They also felt more comfortable with another escort given that they almost always knew him on a personal basis.

The Multi-hour Call

Although reflecting less than 20 percent of the agency's business, clients sometimes requested an escort for more than one hour. These were referred to as multi-hour calls. The most common duration for a multi-hour call was two hours. Clients who requested multi-hour calls were often well known to the agency, and often requested these calls with escorts they had seen previously. From Martin's perspective and that of escorts we interviewed, these clients seemed to be financially better off, capable of paying double or triple the hourly rate. Clients requesting a multi-hour call often did not want to be "constrained" to a single hour and typically used the additional time as an opportunity to socialize with the escort before and after sex, or to extend the amount of intimate time to be had with escorts. Extra time for intimacy could include such activities as cuddling before or after sex, additional foreplay such as kissing and massage, and sometimes extra time for sex. It was very uncommon, however, for clients to use this extra time *exclusively* for sexual reasons—most wanted the social and emotional aspects of their time with an escort to be extended, creating more of the "boyfriend experiences" you read about in earlier chapters.

Escorts appreciated multi-hour encounters primarily because of the financial incentive. Men understood that the extra time with clients was unlikely to be used exclusively for sex and thus were excited at the opportunity to be paid to satisfy a client's emotional, rather than sexual, wishes. The concept of "talking" with clients was pervasive in how escorts described the calls they enjoyed, in addition to being a central aspect of the encounter overall. Men described the importance of conversation during all encounters (one hour and multi-hour) often highlighting how the social aspects of appointments assumed equal importance to the physical, if not more. Emilio described how even an unattractive escort could be successful in the business by drawing upon his social skills and personality, "By walking into a room and talking to a client you can tell easily that you have to have a really flexible charming attitude that will win them over. You have to have really good sex appeal. You can be butt ugly and [still] have sex appeal."

Multi-hour calls sometimes involved a second escort, but it was much more common for the client to hire a single escort. There are two reasons for why multi-hour calls involving *multiple* escorts were rare. First, the price of hiring multiple escorts for more than one hour grew significantly, becoming cost-prohibitive even for wealthier clients. Second, calls involving a second escort were typically less "social" in nature, and more focused on physical sex. Most clients seemed able to achieve sexual satisfaction within a single hour. As additional time within a multi-hour call was typically used for socializing, hiring a second escort must not have led to additional satisfaction of these non-physical needs in the way that it did sexually. Emotional and social intimacy *declined* if more than one escort was in the room, contradicting the client's purpose in having an encounter last longer than the usual hour.

Given these considerations, it still was possible for a client to hire a single escort for a multi-hour call and then coordinate for a second escort to join for one hour during some portion of the appointment. Such arrangements were rare, probably in large part due to the logistics of attempting to coordinate multiple schedules (client and two escorts) with an added layer of complexity surrounding when the second "shorter-duration" escort would arrive in the context of the multi-hour call. As the cliché goes, "Timing is the key to everything." Perhaps more importantly, having another person join the escort and client might interrupt the relational aspects of the appointment; if multi-hour calls tended to be more like a date, then why would a client want a second person to intrude upon that experience?

Overnight Calls

The next type of call for which clients hired were overnight calls. Much less common, only about one-fourth of escorts at *College Boys* had ever been on one. Much like multi-hour calls, this extended time was used for socializing and for several sexual experiences rather than only one. Overnight calls often began in the late afternoon or early evening. They usually started with a meal either at a restaurant or via hotel room service and light drinking (e.g., wine with dinner). Appointments most often concluded just before or immediately after breakfast. All such meetings occurred at clients' homes or hotel rooms—none of these calls occurred at the agency's in-call room. Clients bore the costs for the hotel, meals, drinks, and other entertainment or shopping.

Sexual intimacy during overnight calls tended to follow a more traditional dating script than when escorts were hired for one or two hours. In a non-commercial "dating" situation, many people have sex before or after sleeping for the night; in an overnight call sex at both times was the norm. Relative to the amount of social and sleep time, escorts considered added intimacy as manageable, sometimes enjoyable, and well worth the additional pay. Even though escorts made less *per hour* on an overnight call, they much preferred to make this "lump" sum of money with a single client in a single night versus trying to achieve a similar amount with several clients over multiple calls spanning days, if not weeks. It was usually more relaxing, involved less sex, and maximized the social aspects of calls that the large majority of the men at *College Boys* appreciated most.

Martin carefully selected escorts to send on these long appointments, only choosing men upon whom he could rely to provide a superior experience; men who had demonstrated good social skills and the ability to engage clients in non-sexual interactions. Martin emphasized that escorts going on extended calls had to be able to carry on real conversations which included both listening to clients and contributing their own personal stories. Unlike single and multi-hour appointments, escorts often revealed extensive amounts of personal information in the context of these calls. Escorts talked about their families and where they grew up, their educational experience, and work history. In some cases, escorts even revealed their real name to clients in the context of these calls when they almost never would have done so during a shorter and more emotionally distant appointment. Many escorts that this level of exposure was a feature of the overnight call—part of the experience into which clients were buying. Escorts actively decided to reveal more personal information within the social aspects of these extended calls, just as they created a more intimate sexual experience with their overnight clients.

There were aspects of overnight calls that escorts did not enjoy. It was customary for escorts to sleep in the same bed as clients; however, escorts felt that their time asleep should be without expectation of intimate activity. Although this was not always the case, most clients recognized this arrangement. Tony described when a client did not, "I don't like to do overnights because the last person I was with . . . the guy is right beside you and you're sitting there trying to sleep and he's reaching over you and grabbing your penis. It gets really fucking annoying. You just want to reach around and slap him but you can't. That's like the only thing I hate [about] the overnights." Understandably, escorts reported not sleeping as well when on an overnight appointment, likely a result of multiple factors not limited to sleeping in a foreign bed with a stranger next to them, amplifying any social and emotional "baggage" that may be associated with their experience.

The Travel Call

The least common type of call involved extended travel, typically by air. Escorts referred to these as "travel calls" which might include traveling to a client who lived out of state and spending several days with him, often in the range of two to seven nights. Clients arranging travel calls could be on business trips themselves and want to hire an escort to join them. Often, escorts travelled on vacation with clients, either originating from the same location as a client or meeting a client at the vacation destination. The client held responsibility for all costs from airfare to meals, and even souvenirs. In contrast to other encounters, such calls were generally not initiated through a first contact with the agency. Instead, clients would take a liking to a particular escort they had already hired and then make the escort an offer to go on a trip. The escort would tell Martin about the offer and Martin completed needed arrangements with the client. In some cases, escorts were not paid a daily rate while traveling, but instead "treated" to an all-expenses-paid vacation complete with spending money, shopping trips, and casino expenses. In these cases, an agency fee was negotiated with the client separate from any arrangements with the escort.

Escorts often had a choice about whether to reveal their real name to a client in other types of appointments. In contrast, any travel involving airfare would require an escort to use his real name. *Clients* were responsible for the cost of airfare and thus, often obliged to book the escort's flights, meaning that an escort would have to disclose his real name and date of birth to a client. In order to avoid disclosing such personal information, an escort might arrange for travel himself with the client reimbursing him later; however, there was much incentive to having the client do this work. Foremost, by fronting the costs for airfare the client authenticated his financial investment in the encounter. In either event, escorts worried about arriving at their destination only to have a client fail to show up. At least if the *client* bought the tickets, escorts knew they had only lost their invested time, not the cost of a ticket.

Similar to overnight calls, travel calls required escorts to use their interpersonal skills, education, and other cultural capital. Escorts could expect multiple sexual encounters with the client over the duration of the trip. Like overnight calls, of which travel calls could be thought as an extension, sexual encounters usually included other intimate behavior such as massage and foreplay, depending on the client's requests and the escort's willingness. Combined with the deeper level of social interaction that escorts invested when they were hired over a number of days, it was common for escorts to frame travel calls in terms of a "romantic" getaway. They often referred to themselves as a "companion," something that was completely uncharacteristic of even an overnight appointment. In the history of the agency, a client had never booked *multiple* escorts for a single trip, although a few clients had paid for two escorts to drive a couple of hours and spend the weekend.

Out-of-state and international clients unknown to the agency very rarely wanted to schedule an escort to travel to them. Both Martin and the escorts were well aware that such a client would probably have better luck hiring an escort that lived closer to him (or resided in the city that he was visiting). An escort living closer would be more likely to "come through" with the call at a much less expense to the client. Thus, both Martin and the escorts often expressed skepticism if a potential client were to contact the agency with such a request. Similarly, Martin and the escorts felt uncomfortable with escorts being sent long distances when there was no previous business relationship with a client. They feared a scam or law enforcement sting, considering the wisest course of action being to avoid the situation altogether. In those few cases where such appointments did occur, it was almost always with a client who had hired an escort from *College Boys* while on a trip to the agency's home city.

Organizing Calls by Type of Act and Type of Client

Martin organized the *College Boys'* pricing structure around the time escorts spent with clients, not by the act or service provided. A client who wanted a massage would be expected to pay the same amount as one who desired oral sex. From Martin's perspective, this simplified the transaction for everyone: the agency, the clients, and the escorts.

- For the agency, calls resulted in a standard rate of return such that Martin did not have to worry about his escorts underreporting the services they performed with a client with a concurrent loss of income to the agency for what would have been more expensive activities.
- For escorts, it meant they did not have to keep a tally for a menu of services that may have provided to a client. They would not have to worry about clients pressuring them to engage in a particular act just because it was on the "menu." Clients could not ask them to delete certain behaviors from the bill in order to keep within a certain budget.
- For clients, time-based fee structures reduced the risk of being hassled (i.e., hustled) by an escort to do something they client had not planned—classic up-selling that so frequently occurs in other lines of business.

Escorts and clients could think about the time they had together as the object of the transaction, not the events and actions that filled that period. It discouraged them from conceptualizing sexual acts as financial commodities, but encouraged both parties to see them as relational; given the stigma around both ends of the prostitution business encounter, focusing on time and not sex was a way to avoid reducing sexual acts to specific dollar amounts. One could focus on providing customer service rather than a body to be used, a key distinction between escorting and prostitution among the men we interviewed.

It was no surprise that escorts often described their work in terms of being paid for *time*, and not sex given these considerations. Escorts believed this obfuscation blurred the lines around the legality of sex work and helped them to legitimize their work role. Marc said:

Basically I tell the person [client] right off the bat, "You know you're paying for my time and that's basically it. I'm not here to here to be a prostitute. I'm not having sex with you for money and, you know, things, and stuff." But you're going to get some cases where people are going to be dumb. For instance, say you get a gay escort goes in to the hotel to see a client and they say, "Well, the rate is $160 for the first hour blah, blah, blah." You can't do that. If you're not smart enough you're going to get caught [by the police]; or if you're not aware of your surroundings, if you're not aware of the people around you. You have to be smart and you have to be witty about a lot of things.

Frank expressed a similar sentiment and expressed a perhaps erroneous view that billing for time gave him legal protection:

They're paying for your time. And you know if he's paying me for an hour, he's paying me for an hour of my time and what we do in that time is between two consenting adults. It has nothing to do with money. That way it's legal; nothing illegal about it. It's not every client I go see that I have sex with.

Nevertheless, escorts often categorized their calls in terms of behaviors they performed with clients. They employed several dimensions when describing their interactions on an appointment: sexual behaviors, social activities during a call, and unconventional or "kinky" requests. The most common sexual acts between escorts and clients were oral sex and mutual masturbation. Less than half of appointments involved anal intercourse. In the case of heterosexual escorts, sexual acts often were limited to the escort masturbating while the client watched or the client performing oral sex upon the escort without reciprocation.

Although most escorts were open to engaging in oral sex with their clients, many indicated that anal sex was a personal boundary that they would not cross, "Yeah I don't get into that really. I would much rather give somebody a full body massage and have them do the same for me or even like, like oral sex" (Marc). Many escorts regarded anal sex as an intimate act, too intimate for them to sell—some expressed that payment "cheapened" the emotional importance of anal sex with a partner. It is worth noting that most gay and bisexual escorts did not have anal sex with their casual non-paying sex partners either. Among those who did engage in anal sex, they often did so as the insertive partner, the "top"—infrequently with clients and usually in the context of a relationship. Brian was one of several escorts who would engage in anal sex with his clientele as long as he felt comfortable with the man hiring him. Interestingly, he described calls where he was the receptive partner as the least enjoyable, "[I hate] The guys that like to fuck me all the time; [for example,] Like in several different positions. If I'm not turned on I really don't like to bottom. If you're not turned on, it hurts, so I dislike them a lot. I put myself as versatile on the [College Boys] website because I feel I'll make more money that way. I'll deal with it, but I don't like it."

Escorts reported that they did not have unprotected sex with clients and indicated it was unusual for a client to request it. Martin was clear with escorts that he wanted them to protect themselves and their clients from sexually transmitted infections and HIV. He also communicated expectations for condom use to his clients in clear, but respectful terms. Condoms were always available for escorts at the agency and the manager insisted that escorts take condoms with them when going out on appointments. The agency paid for condoms and lubrication. This type of safer-sex environment contrasts with that of street-based sex workers. Men working on the street have been more likely to report "survival sex," including unprotected anal sex with their clients (Greene, Ennett, & Ringwalt, 1999; Haley, Roy, Leclerc, Boudreau, & Boivin, 2004). Clients particularly interested in unprotected sex may offer additional money to an escort. In contrast to agency-based sex workers and independent internet-based escorts, street-based escorts may have more incentive to accept such an offer given that they often live under economically precarious conditions. In this circumstance, the immediate benefit of extra money that may help pay for food or shelter could outweigh longer-term risks associated with managing HIV infection.

The "Talking" Call

Escorts most enjoyed appointments that focused on socializing with clients—they got paid to hang out and talk. Although some "lighter" sexual behavior might occur at some point during the call, conversation encompassed the large majority of the time. Escorts appreciated getting to know their clients. For example, Brian related how the social connection he established with a client improved the overall encounter:

> And there was a guy that loved music. [He] Played a piece on his piano for me and stuff like that and talked to me a lot about the pipe organ and all the stuff—things that I'm interested in and I love to learn about. And it helps also to be personable with these people and then to go do things with them instead of just ... It breaks the ice and makes me not as nervous to go in there with them. I like talking to people and things.

Even when some sex occurred, most escorts used conversation to ease themselves into their calls as well as build a sound working relationship with their clientele:

> Well actually I like talking to them and making them comfortable because when I first started out *I* used to be the one that was nervous. Now whenever I walk into the room they're the one that's always nervous and doesn't know what to do. So I just sit there and talk to them, calm them down, try to get to know them. You know, tell them a little bit about myself. But I think that's about the best thing I do right there: Try to connect somehow. (Jeff)

Another advantage to conversation was less obvious to escorts when they first started to work, but soon became apparent with experience. Seasoned escorts recognized that time spent socializing in the context of a call reduced the proportion of an appointment available for sex—the activity with clients escorts enjoyed the least. In some cases, escorts purposely attempted to prolong the amount of time talking with this exact goal in mind, extending the social portion of a call so as to minimize its sexual component. Skilled escorts were considered to be those guys who could do exactly this and still have clients remain satisfied with the hire. Erick said:

> If they want sex right off the bat, I try to hold that off, try to talk to them, give them a massage, and just relax. I just start to tell them to relax and I try to just be dominant and tell them, speak to them first because I'd rather get to know the person before I do anything with them . . . [Get to know] The person, the person's life, what the person likes, and dislikes. How the person feels.

Moreover, escorts recognized that clients often wanted to talk and that not all clients were only looking for sex during an appointment. For example, when Chase was asked what made him want to get to know something about his clients, he responded:

> Because I feel they're lonely. A couple of calls I've been on, they just want to sit down and talk, just have a decent conversation. Most people are just lonely. They want someone there that can talk to them that they can relate to in some way just like a companion, a friend . . . I'm always up for meeting new people; that's why I love my job so much. I'm sure I made that person feel better, that somebody wants to get to know them.

Getting to know one's client was an essential feature of calls, and for many escorts the "talking call" comprised its own genre of interactions with their clients; one that added value for both the escort and his customer alike.

The "Business Deal"

Not all client-escort interactions were social in nature. When asked to describe calls that they liked and disliked, escorts frequently discussed what could best be described as the "business deal," meaning clients who were very direct about their exclusive focus on sex—men who wanted in-and-out with minimal personal interaction. Emilio described this type of client as the "businessman":

Interviewer: How come you put the businessmen into a different category?

Emilio: Because the businessmen, the way they ask the whole thing goes down is they will tell you what they want, they come in, they're very business about it. They come in they do what they said they were going to do, they're done, they pay you, they leave. There's no, like they don't want to talk about anything.

Although Emilio described this client as business-like, it was not to imply that this type of client was a businessman (i.e., white-collar professional) in daily life. Instead, he framed the context of the sexual interaction in terms of a business deal, an exchange of sex for cash—the commoditization of the escort's body and behavior and an emphasis on the prostitution aspect of his work. Such encounters usually ended when a client achieved climax. Rather than spending the remainder time socializing and getting to know the escort, the client paid the fee and went on his way.

Escorts noted the benefits and limitations of "business deal" clients. On the positive side, this type of appointment tended to be shorter in duration and clients tended to be very specific about the type of behavior they sought. Escorts appreciated earning the same amount of money in less time without any sexual "surprises." Clients rarely tried to coax escorts into activities beyond what had already been agreed upon. Escorts very much disliked when clients attempted to do so. This was particularly the case for heterosexual guys who loathed clients attempting to convince them to perform oral sex; even though they made it clear that their sexual repertoire was limited to mutual masturbation or receiving fellatio. For straight escorts, "business deal" clients often represented an optimal customer as social and emotional connections to their male clients produced more internal discomfort given the discordance with these escorts' sexual orientation.

On the negative side, most escorts appreciated social interactions with their clients. Cut-and-dry sex and pre-determined transactions tended to make some escorts feel "used" or, as some described, "like a piece of meat." The commercialization of their bodies and intimate behaviors became the discordant factor for them. Interactions with business-deal clients made these escorts feel more like "prostitutes" who were being sold for sex and less like "human beings" in a mutual social interaction. In the end, escorts recognized that it was the client's choice about the type of call he would have. Were an escort to attempt to "force" a client into a business deal interaction, he would be considered unprofessional and disrespectful. Similarly, if an escort became too social in a call, trying to jimmy conversation into the situation where none was desired by the customer, he might make the client feel uncomfortable or frustrated which could prematurely end the appointment. The client would not be pleased in either case, and neither would Martin.

The "Kinky" Client

"Kinky" clients were those who had sexual interests that escorts perceived to be out of the norm. As can be seen in the table, kinky sexual activities encompass quite a range of behaviors ranging from what people might consider relatively

Table 8.1.
Descriptions of Typical "Kinky" Sexual Behaviors

Activity	Colloquial Name	Brief Description
Hand-anal	Fisting	One partner uses multiple fingers or even his entire hand to stimulate the anus and rectum of his partner.
Delaying orgasm	Edging, cum control	One partner masturbates the other but ceases moments before the partner will achieve orgasm. The process is repeated for an extended period of time (e.g., 10, 20, and 30 minutes or more).
Electricity	Electro, electrostim	Self or other application of electric current to erogenous areas of the body to produce pain and/or pleasure.
Fecal matter	Scat, potty play	Watching one having a bowel movement into (for example) a toilet or onto another partner.
Foot play/massage	Foot fetish	Licking and massaging one's feet, licking/smelling socks and/or shoes.
Genital pain	Cock and ball torture, CBT	One partner inflicts pain on the other's penis or scrotum. This may include direct striking or use of tools such as clothespins, hot wax, and/or rods.
Oral-anal, analingus	Rimming, tossing salad	Using mouth and tongue to stimulate the anus and anal region.
Oral semen exchange	snowballing, swallowing	One or more partners ejaculate into the mouth and then "deep" kiss to pass semen between partners.
Restraints	Bondage and discipline, B&D	One partner uses restraints on another, to deprive movement (e.g., handcuffs) or other senses (e.g., blindfold). The discipline aspect may take on characteristics of role playing/power-play.
Role playing, power-playing	Dominant/submissive, Dom–Sub	One partner assumes a more dominant role (detailing commands for sexual behaviors, positions, activities) while the other responds to commands. Might include verbal "humiliation" and begging for privileges.
Sadism and/or masochism	S&M	Sadists receive pleasure by inflicting pain; masochists receive pleasure through receiving pain.
Urine exchange	Piss play, watersports	Deriving pleasure from watching one urinate, from urinating on others, or being urinated upon.

mild (such as having oral-anal contact) to very extreme (using feces or electricity during sex).

Escorts usually referred negatively to clients making kinky requests. Most escorts refused to engage in kink. Tony summed up this point of view though with some level of acceptance, "I think they're fucking weird, like the peeing, shitting, the anal—I think that's all weird, but that's their ... that's how they get turned on, I guess." Rick said that appointments involving kink were his least enjoyable:

Interviewer: And then the guys you really don't look forward to?

Rick: The weirdoes.

Interviewer: What are they?

Rick: They have fetishes that I'm just not into. Like I'm not into role playing very much, like feet, or being rimmed. That kind of stuff is just freaky to me.

In general, *College Boys* did not like being surprised by such requests, although some did oblige. Clients interested in non-traditional or specialized sexual behavior would often relate their request to agency manager with the hopes of being matched with an escort who was willing. For example, Ned was open to doing water sports with his clients, though not on the receiving end. Such boundaries were common among the men we interviewed; they represented a key area in which escorts felt most free to express their personal preferences during appointments with clients.

Client Characteristics

In addition to categorizing calls according to the type of activity that took place during the appointment, escorts also grouped their job experiences based on the type of client with whom they worked.

Age

Age represented a central defining characteristic as escorts considered different categories of appointments based on their customers. Men at *College Boys* divided their clientele into three age groups: Those about the same age as the escort, those that were older but still within a somewhat similar age range (less than ten years older), and then clients who were much older than the escort (typically greater than ten years). Older and much older clients were regarded as less and least desirable respectively. Not all of this hesitation was related to differences in appearance; some aspect of desirability was also attached to *role* expectations for clients who were much older than escorts. Men at *College Boys* often related that they would not want to have sex with "someone my father's age" let alone a man who was grandfatherly. This was true even for heterosexual escorts who also seemed to feel that sex with much older clients crossed interpersonal taboos similar to those that exist in families or schools. Given these considerations, the escort's own age appeared to play a role in determining what the escort himself considered to be "old." For example, Joshua (who was 26 years old) referred to his young clients as those under the age of 28, defined those "middle-aged" as those aged 28 to 45, and "old" clients were those over the age of 45. Thresholds for demarking the age in which clients were labeled "much older" varied according to the age of the escort making this judgment. For example, a 19-year-old escort might indicate that someone 20 years his senior is "very old," whereas a 29-year-old escort might categorize someone 20 years his senior as "middle-aged." Age differences mattered most for the younger escorts, becoming less problematic among those few escorts from our sample in their later 20s or early 30s. Such a pattern seems no different than how U.S. culture (more broadly) views age differences in sexual relationships where a significant age gap is often viewed with less taboo among older adult partners.

Few clients were similar in age to the men they were hiring. Younger men in general perhaps lacked the necessary disposable income to hire an escort, and were probably within an age range where they do not "need" to pay for a man in his early 20s to have sex. Clients closest in age to escorts tended to be closeted homosexuals who were unwilling to risk public exposure to find same sex partners. Perhaps, there also was less social and personal stigma associated with hiring an escort among older men. Although escorts preferred their clients to be younger, it did not seem that clients were ever turned away because of their age. That being said, escorts varied their sexual repertoires based on a client's age. Escorts were more likely to perform oral sex on younger clients, men they usually found more attractive. In contrast, escorts preferred to engage in conversation and massage with older clients. Joshua highlighted this, "There seems to be a, there's a space kept, on a personal level, between the older clients and myself that I don't really feel with younger clients." It is curious if this "space" that Joshua highlights was something perpetuated by the client (as he implies) or something more interpersonally derived.

Similarly, escorts noted that older clients were more likely to be "talking calls," as we previously described:

Chase: The guys that just want sex are usually younger and the strictly conversation is older, oldest.

Interviewer: What's your favorite kind of call?

Chase: Conversation.

We wonder to what extent clients understood how an age discrepancy between them and the escorts they hired affected social and physical connection during appointments. In kind, escorts highlighted that older clients were sometimes more "pushy" or assertive with regard to initiating sexual behavior or ensuring physical activity happened. Could this have been caused the escorts' own reluctance? Were escorts at *College Boys* much more resistant to sex with older men, versus being more eager to have sex with younger clients that clients had to be more direct in expressing their interests? Or, did older men perceive a greater degree of entitlement with escorts they hired because of the commercial nature of their relationship and inherent power inequities between client and provider?

Erick: Because most of the people are older so I don't enjoy that very much. Like in their 50s. I had some of those.

Interviewer: So, they're too old for you to be attracted to?

Erick: Yeah and some of them are a little forceful.

Nick also highlighted how older clients tended push his sexual boundaries, "I will not have any sort of anal sex at all. And the older men that are begging you to do it are like constantly coming up and throwing their lips on you. If you're not strong-willed you'll just break down and go, 'Fine do whatever you want,' and I won't do that."

Physical Attributes

Although a client's age was repeatedly mentioned when escorts classified the "types" of men they saw, some escorts also discussed clients' other personal physical attributes. The most common attribute escorts described was the client's weight, with overweight men being far less desirable. For example, Hector described how he scaled back his sexual repertoire with overweight clients, "It depends on the person, because the 350-pound fat guy, you know ... thinks that you're going to sit there make out with him, and it's not happening. You know, it's for self-respect, for myself. I'm not going to do that."

Another physical attribute that escorts described was the amount of body hair, with hairier clients garnering more criticism from the men at *College Boys*. Finally, some escorts discussed their clients' overall hygiene, typically referring to body odor or bad breath. Wes highlighted how he would overcome hygiene issues with his clients:

> People that are just gross, like have a body odor or something. Just yucky. I just want to get rid of you [finish the call] as quickly as possible ... Some people just don't have great hygiene. I'm like, "Can you take a shower, or something?" I don't have a problem telling somebody, "Maybe you want to go take a shower first."

In an effort to avoid potentially awkward situations surrounding hygiene, some escorts would eroticize the moment by suggesting they join the client in the shower.

Level of Outness

Finally, escorts often described their clients in terms of their orientation and the degree to which clients were open about having sex or relationships with other men—a client's "level of outness." The topic of a client's own sexuality typically only arose when clients identified themselves as heterosexual—and often only if married to a woman and/or a father. Escorts we interviewed labeled these clients in three ways: As "closeted" gay men, "closeted" bisexual men, or "heterosexual" men who just sometimes had sex with men with a strong tendency toward the "closeted" end of this spectrum. The idea that these clients were "closeted" conformed to social norms stipulating that that men having sex with men were really gay or bisexual, but living as a heterosexual. Few escorts believed that "heterosexual men who had sex with men" were genuinely straight, though a few actually did despite cultural prescriptions to the contrary. Mason described how the first client he saw was married to a woman, and his dismay about this client maintaining a heterosexual identity. It was a common reaction among the escorts at *College Boys*:

> I was like, "Oh my god, you're married?" I just thought it was like some type of, I don't want to say fantasy but, I just thought it was something that most people just said that they did. I mean straight men don't like gay men. I mean, I've turned straight men into being gay but I've never had a straight man *seek* a gay man out. I'm like, "You're in the wrong boat, because you should be on my side, not her side, she's over there."

Clients married to women were often described as being their own genre of a call altogether.

Those clients who were married and/or closeted generally requested a reduced set of sexual behaviors, compared with "out" gay clients. In essence, oral sex and mutual masturbation were their most common activities with escorts. Escorts appreciated these more restricted sexual requirements. Conversely, given their situation, clients in relationships requested heightened levels of assurance for discretion and anonymity, as clients' female partners (and co-workers, friends, and families) were completely unaware of the fact that they were (1) going outside their marriages for sex and (2) doing so with *another man*. Two sets of social values, heteronormality and monogamy, had been breached. Escorts noted that married men were likely hiring sex workers because of a need for discretion and a lack of access to male sex partners in their regular lives. When hiring an escort such clients would not have to worry about attempting to establish any form of relationship outside of the sexual encounter, which may not have been the case with a non-commercial partner. As the saying goes, "Escorts aren't paid for sex. They are paid to leave quietly once the sex is over." Ned described what it was like to see closeted clients whether they were married or not:

I've come to notice that a lot of the people that hire are usually professionals that don't want to jeopardize their job or their status in society by coming out and saying, "I'm gay or I'm bisexual." So instead they do something like this behind closed doors. That way, during the day they're still the lawyer or the professional doctor that works at the medical center. Obviously sometimes people tend to discredit you depending on what it is that you do. So certain people they just want respect. They just want to keep their good reputation and everything. Any of these people that call up [the agency to hire an escort]; I mean rather than pay somebody to come over [hire an escort]. If they were that open [out] about it, they could go to one of the [gay] nightclubs where they could find somebody. . . . [These are] the ones that just kind of do it on the side but still have their normal lives with the wife and kids.

All escorts were expected to be discrete regarding client information regardless of a customer's sexual identity, but were often more empathic to the need for confidentiality with closeted clients. Perhaps, the understanding was enhanced by escorts own desire for secrecy about their sex work (and male-to-male sex among heterosexual escorts). Escorts may also have had their own experiences in the closet and could understand their clients struggling with how "out" to be.

In contrast, some escorts described a sense of overall discomfort seeing clients who were married to women. Specifically, these escorts felt like they were contributing to, or enabling, these clients' infidelity. Cultural norms regarding marital monogamy held such strength that many escorts at *College Boys* experienced strong negative emotions such as anger or guilt when asked to violate them with a married client. They often found such reactions puzzling or ironic, but expressed them nonetheless:

Erick: But then I found out after everything, he was married. I was not ready for that, he was like, "Yeah, I'm married." I'm like, "Okay."

Interviewer: It sounds like this surprised you.

Erick: Yeah because he hadn't told me he was married . . . My heart just started speeding up and I just didn't know what to say at that time. Things got uncomfortable again. That was the only downfall that I recall. It was uncomfortable. I felt kind of gross that I could do that to somebody because I know that if I was married I wouldn't want that to happen to me.

Interviewer: So it felt gross for you?

Erick: Unfortunately.

It is difficult to say exactly what proportion of the agency's clients were married or otherwise closeted. It was considered taboo and unprofessional for an escort to outright ask his clients about their sexual orientation, thus the topic was broached only when a client initiated the discussion. However, Martin estimated that about 60 percent of clients were married to women, and an additional 20 percent were gay men in long-term relationships with other men.

CONCLUSION

The types of clients and calls the men at *College Boys* entertained varied widely. In this chapter, we have used escorts' own descriptions of their customers and appointments to delineate categories by which they organized such work experiences. Because *College Boys'* most common type of call was the one-hour appointment, this time-structured framework likely shaped how escorts mentally structured time with clients. Had *College Boys* required all calls to have a two-hour or two-escort minimum, or simply just charged more for a single hour appointment, the type of client using the agency would likely have changed dramatically. Clients who could not have afforded to pay the increased rate or those clients who were not interested in extended encounters would take their business elsewhere. Although single-hour encounters appear to be the standard among Internet-based escorts and most agencies, it is common for escorts and escort services who describe themselves as "elite" to charge much higher hourly rates and institute multi-hour minimums with the primary intention of attracting a different type of client (often termed "higher-end" customers). Thus, the types of calls and clients described in this chapter do not constitute every possible type or combination. Nevertheless, our descriptions likely captured a large majority of the experiences typical for agency-based male escorting services and Internet-based independent male escorts currently operating in the United States and most other economically developed countries.

Chapter Nine
PLACE AND CONTEXT

OVERVIEW

Escort agencies have been rapidly adapting to the new realities of sex work in the modern marketplace. In this chapter, we discuss the changing role that physical spaces play in the erotic services industry given Internet-driven transformations that have confronted more traditional providers, the sex work equivalents of "brick-and-mortar" outlets. Few industries have seen as much radical evolution in their business models as those delivering erotica; new opportunities abound for entrepreneurs in these fields whereas significant challenges have emerged for existing businesses. We compare independent escorting with agency-based work, highlighting benefits of independent escort work versus its detriments, contrasting increased autonomy with the downsides and risks of going solo. This chapter concludes with a discussion of the broader escort enterprise, drawing from economic models of supply-and-demand.

A Fast Business in Rapid Transition

Although one can classify sex work by the types of erotica provided (e.g., erotic dancing, adult film acting, and/or escorting), the field can also be described in terms of the physical space where the erotica is housed. Many of the mechanisms through which escorts and prostitutes meet their clients have changed over the years. These spaces may include actual establishments such as a brothel or a strip club; yet in the modern world they may also be *tenuous* spaces such as a virtual environment on the Internet such as a chatroom or classified bulletin board. Such virtual spaces are not really new. However, in its history sex work has vacillated between the physical and tenuous and has usually occupied both to some degree. What is new is that for the first time and just within the last decade, sex work has experienced a dramatic shift toward the tenuous environment via Internet erotica.

Brick-and-Mortar Spaces for the Female Sex Worker

In order to understand fully the evolution of male sex work within digital and physical spaces, it is worth looking at the ways in which female sex work has persevered through access to physical environments. In this section, we discuss the three main types of brick-and-mortar establishments used by female sex workers today: brothels, massage parlors, and strip clubs. All three represent *physical* spaces in which the women and customers directly interact, however the commercial aspects of sex work vary within each venue.

Brothels

In contrast to escort agencies, that typically operate as dispatch-and-call centers with no physical space for clients and escorts to interact, brothels oper- ate as facilities capable of housing the sex work itself. In so doing, brothels in most of the United States must operate discretely, giving the appearance of a hotel perhaps with an associated bar. Potential clients visit the brothel and select from a range of sex workers "employed" by the agency. In such a space, clients hold an overt expectation that sexual behavior will occur and take place on the premises. The client would contract an escort, typically via a Madam running the brothel, and have sex at the agency in a room he rented from the Madam. Law enforcement and the larger community often know the chief purpose of the location even though the business is usually conducted as covertly as possible. Such brothels have often been tolerated, though not necessarily welcome, in the community. And as a result, the physical locations of brothels were often in the poorer social and economic areas of a given city, frequently at its outskirts.

Business operations *within* a brothel might also vary from overt to covert. In a more overt operation, the Madam might take responsibility for the advertis- ing and sale of sex *within* the brothel, as compared to workers handling trans- actions themselves. The Madam would keep a portion of the profits and pay the remainder to her employees. Otherwise, a brothel may try to maintain the active appearance of a hotel or inn such that any escorts or prostitutes were not its official "employees." Instead, self-employed and often street-based sex workers bring clients to the hotel for sexual services. Either the escort or the client would pay a fee to the agency/hotel for use of a room. Agencies operating under this type of covert internal business model may have been attempting to skirt anti-prostitution laws by feigning a lack of awareness about the activities being conducted on their premises—"We simply rent out rooms and don't know or have any control over what happens inside them."

Massage Parlors

Massage parlors represent the second type of major brick-and-mortar business model used by female sex workers. These facilities operate similarly to more overt brothels, maintaining a storefront often equipped with a lavish neon sign advertising "massage," but usually nothing more. Or, operations may be more covert, such that the parlor is tucked away onto the third floor or a multipurpose office building. Massage parlors may function partially or even fully under the auspices of local laws. For example, they may be licensed by the city and employ licensed/trained massage therapists. In such as setting, perhaps only one or two of the employees were *genuinely* licensed, whereas others worked under the guise of the parlor, adopting an obfuscating title like "bodyworker."

Similar to the brothel, a client books an appointment via a receptionist (this person may function in the same capacity of the brothel's Madam). Clients are then taken to a private room and their session begins with a more traditional massage. Unlike a more traditional massage, his session would end with the masseuse performing some combination of sexual acts, colloquially termed a "happy ending." Most often, sexual acts included the masseuse masturbating the client to the point of orgasm. Perhaps less common would be her performing oral sex on him, or rarely full vaginal sex. Massage parlors attract clients through word of mouth and often via suggestive ads placed in the "adult services" or "classified" sections of local newspapers and magazines. These ads may feature a scantily dressed woman poised suggestively with the text promising "massage with full release." Overt advertisements for sexual behavior are rare. (For more information on massage parlors, see Nemoto, Iwamoto, Oh, Wong, & Nguyen, 2005; Nemoto, Operario, Takenaka, Iwamoto, & Le, 2003.)

Strip Clubs

The third major brick-and-mortar business model for female sex work still active today are clubs where sex workers strip off their clothes, dance erotically, and often interact suggestively with their audience. Although not characteristic of all strip clubs, many have private back rooms which clients can rent for a "private show" or "extended lap dance." In so doing, the client selects one or more strippers or dancers to join him in this secluded space for a limited time. Sexual behavior may or may not be allowed by the club depending on local laws and police activity; when it occurs providers often use obfuscating language such as "champagne room" to describe what a client might expect without directly saying so. In instances where sex may have been strictly forbidden *on premises*, strippers or dancers might arrange for after-hours encounters with clients at a different location, perhaps the sex worker's home or a nearby hotel with hourly rates for rooms.

Female Sex Work Facilities and the Law

Brothels, massage parlors, and erotic strip clubs continue to operate fairly conspicuously in the United States today. Although arguable, perhaps the most "tolerated" are erotic strip clubs which are licensed and often heavily regulated by local jurisdictions. As a result, permissible behavior at an erotic strip club varies significantly throughout the country. In some areas fully nude dancing may be allowed; in others only topless dancing may be permitted. And in more strict areas, topless dancing may be permitted, but only if the women's nipples are fully covered (usually with nipple pasties or electrical tape). Some jurisdictions may not permit the sale of alcohol in the same place as nudity. Others may not permit physical contact between dancers and patrons irrespective of whether dancers are nude. Club owners found in violation of local ordinances can face heavy fines, forced closure, liquor license revocation, and, in some places, criminal prosecution.

When examining the role of local ordinances in the business of sex, an interesting case to study is that of Nevada. In some parts of Nevada, prostitution has been legalized. In contrast, advertising for prostitution remains *illegal*. Thus, an agency may receive licensure to operate as a brothel; however, it would be illegal for them to market directly the services they provided. As a result, these agencies must use convoluted and suggestive language in any advertisements. Similarly, Nevada brothels often rely on word-of-mouth advertising and referrals among clients. All told, brothels in Nevada must be extremely innovative to keep their businesses operating. On one hand, they have to honor the laws governing them in order to keep an operator's license. In so doing, they tiptoe around the boundaries between what is legal and what is not in order to keep their customer base. This tug-of-war between brothels and the law is perhaps an archetypal example as to why the business of sex continues to be a business in transition; changes in values and practice create constant flux for this industry.

The Male Sex Worker and His Clients

Certainly, much of what we have said thus far *could* be applicable to male sex workers providing services. Nevertheless, much less is known about male sex work, probably because the industry is smaller relative to female sex work. For example, in Nevada there were no registered male sex workers until 2010 (Powers, 2010, January 6). Interestingly, Nevada's first registered man was heterosexual and intent on only providing services for female clients

(Daly, 2010, January 13). Thus, it is hard to state with any accuracy whether norms for female brick-and-mortar establishments correspond to those employing men. This is not to suggest the male sex work marketplace is non-existent. Instead, it operates via different venues. In terms of brick-and-mortar facilities, male sex work is typically found in the form of erotic dancing and hustling in bars and clubs. Less prevalent today are men (independent sex workers) who hustle in bathhouses given the precipitous decline in these businesses following the emergence of HIV/AIDS in the 1980s.

Dancing and Hustling in Bars and Clubs

The vast majority of the male-for-male sex work market continues to operate covertly. Its brothels and escort agencies are few and far between with the trade proliferating throughout other aspects of gay culture—originally via its bars and clubs, city strolls, and bathhouses; today it does so increasingly over Internet websites and chatrooms. In gay bars and clubs, go-go boys and other erotic male dancers still remain staples of the "scene" throughout the United States. In most gay bars and clubs "hustling" is not a *central* aspect of this environment. Nevertheless one might still expect to find dancers, often called *go-go boys*, whose primary job is to gyrate to the beat of the music and foster a sense of sensual fun. These men may be expected to work wearing next to nothing, perhaps a g-string or thong, and earn money via tips from patrons. Nevertheless, these go-go boys would be far less likely to label themselves as a "stripper" or even a "sex worker" as their daily activities are unlikely to involve "traditional" sexual behaviors with any clients. This may blur the line in defining exactly what sex work represents within American gay culture. And given the permanence, visibility, and variability of erotic "go-go" dancing present throughout the gay club scene, some have suggested that sex work is more permissible and socially acceptable within gay communities (Bimbi, 2007).

Although less common, some gay bars are known for catering to a concurrent "hustler" scene. In these places, the business is devoted almost exclusively to creating the ambiance of the more familiar female "stripper club." In contrast to a traditional gay club or bar, a hustler bar may have no dance floor or similar "social" area for patrons to intermingle. Instead the patrons situate themselves around a bar while dancers, who are hired by the bar's management, walk or sometimes dance around spending a little bit of time with each man in hopes of earning tips or obtaining after-hours business. Sex between the dancer and client may or may not be permitted on site; when it is, behavior often takes the form of brief massages, masturbation, and perhaps oral sex. Typically, sex is discouraged or outright forbidden—gay bars and clubs have a well-documented history of clashes with the police and public health departments. Hustler bars may be under particular scrutiny and thus, owners may worry about attracting too much attention. In contrast to female strip clubs, male hustler/strip clubs rarely have back or private rooms. Thus, "hustlers" who dance, strip, or just mingle casually with patrons may arrange for more "complete" encounters at a later time.

Gay Print Publications

Outside of physical establishments like stripper/hustler clubs, male sex work resides within gay communities via abundant advertisements for "body work," escorting, companionship, and other erotic services throughout many print magazines, fliers, and gay newspapers. Admittedly, these advertisements are often tucked away in the back of such publications, replete with elusive language so as not to directly suggest sex-for-pay. In contrast to the men working/dancing at a hustler bar or those represented by an agency, the advertisements found in print media are often independent sex workers. Certainly many agencies also advertise side-by-side with independent sex workers, but independent entrepreneurs substantially outnumber agencies in this medium.

For a case in point, we look at *Next Magazine*, New York City's leading gay-guide magazine. More than 59,000 copies are printed each week with over 200,000 readers. Toward the back, one can find listings for "models/ escorts." Advertisements include pictures of men in revealing poses, though with genitals pixilated or otherwise censored or obscured. The text suggests the possibility of sexual behavior, listing "model's" sexual preferences (e.g., top, bottom, versatile), and often with a description of his physique and genitalia (e.g., circumcision status, penile dimensions, body hair, and so forth). *Next Magazine* can be found in gay-oriented establishments throughout the greater metropolitan area and in many "typical" businesses within traditionally gay neighborhoods in New York City such as Chelsea, Hell's Kitchen, and the West Village.

The magazine's corresponding website (www.nextmagazine.com) formerly provided companion listings; however, *Next Magazine* expanded these listings by opening a separate companion website (www.nextboys.com) exclusively devoted to "online classified advertising service for gay male escorts and bodyworkers to promote themselves." *NextBoys* notes that they are not a gay male escort agency and instructs potential clients to contact advertisers directly. Similar male sex worker directories can be located in the back of local gay publications (and on the publication's corresponding websites) in major cities across the United States. For example, *HotSpots!* magazine, Florida's largest gay publication, provides sex work listings in the back of its magazine and on its website (www.hotspotsmagazine.com) with classifieds placed under "Adult Models" and "Services." And as you read in Chapter Seven, there are also classified websites independent of print media—stand-alone electronic venues where escorts, bodyworkers, and agencies posts advertisements for their businesses.

Thus, although most male escorts might not have as many opportunities to work via agencies or brothels, other mechanisms such as stripper bars, print media and the Internet, allow them to reach a wide base of potential customers. Of course, this is not to discount the presence of street-based sex work, which has persisted throughout history. However, as you read in Chapter Two, the number of men working the street seems to have declined significantly since the beginning of the twenty-first century. There is much evidence that much of this sex work marketplace, for both men and women, has transitioned to the Internet. Sex work really is a business in rapid transition, potentially the greatest era of change in its history since the invention of the street itself.

Tough Decisions: Go It Alone or List with an Agency?

A widespread virtual market for men seeking sex with other men has emerged to connect potential partners. As a result, many men who were considering escorting now have a greater opportunity to experiment within the sex work industry. A would-be escort can "dip" his toes into a vast and unfettered sex work marketplace from the convenience and (most importantly) privacy of his home. As you read in Chapter Two, he can enter and exit the sex work industry with a few strokes on his keyboard and the click of a mouse button.

Those men deciding to enter escorting face a series of options on how they will navigate their "career" (however brief it may be) as a sex worker. Will he post an ad on Craigslist? Will he invest in a month-long subscription on an escorting website? If so, what website and what type of subscription? Should he take an ad out in a local paper or magazine? If so, what will the ad say? Will he use his picture? Will the picture include his face? How much will he charge? What services will he perform? What are his limits in terms of sexual behavior or types of clients? Should he list himself with an agency? Should he try to take up erotic dancing? What impact will of this have on his personal life? Who will he tell? Who *won't* he tell? What will he do to protect his physical and emotional safety? For how long will he be an escort? Will he even call himself an "escort"? All told, these men dive into a sea of uncertainty and it is likely through much trial and error that they will traverse some of the many costs and benefits inherent to the sex work marketplace. In this next section, we explore some of these outcomes associated with choosing to be an independent sex worker or in partnering with an agency. For independent sex workers, our focus will be on those who are not engaged in street-based work. As you read in Chapter Two, street-based sex workers often have less autonomy than other independent sex workers. They are more likely to be engaged in survival sex and live in underprivileged social and economic situations.

Costs and Benefits: Independent Escorts Have It Worse
Generating Your Own Business Is Tough Work

An independent escort must generate his own business, without assistance to locate, screen, and schedule clients. In so doing, he may advertise on escorting websites like rentboy.com, or in print media such as the back of *Next Magazine*. Men who may not want to front the financial investment of advertising may look for potential clients in the men-seeking-men section of websites, in live chatrooms, or via an ad on electronic bulletin boards like Craigslist. The advertising aspect of being an independent escort can eat up a lot of time and money. Independent escorts must pay to have their ads posted online or in print, buy a URL or space on a blog, and provide their own sexual accessories (condoms, lube, massage oil, toys, etc.). Advertising alone (especially print advertising) could run a full-time escort several hundred dollars per month depending on where he placed ads and the level of exposure he selected for them (we will discuss this more soon).

Assuming an independent escort has successfully advertised himself, he then needs to negotiate with his clients, including screening and coordinating a meeting location. The escort may have to discuss the behaviors in which he is willing to engage, facets of his personality, and personal or other sexual interests. The escort would need to ask questions of this potential client to identify if this person is someone with whom he wants to do business. This may include asking questions to identify client's sexual needs or desires, questions to determine client's availability, and questions to determine where the client wants to meet. Escorts may need to communicate their "policy" with regard to certain sexual acts or condom use. Simultaneously, the escort must assess if the client will honor these policies. All of this has to happen in the context of a five-minute phone call, over email exchange, or perhaps text messages. It can take several such exchanges to clarify all of the client's interests and make the necessary arrangements.

Independent Escorts Are Easy Targets

In addition, the independent escort must establish some sort of tracking system for his clients. This could be something as simple as a list of phone numbers, or a more elaborate system such as detailed notes about the encounter, including the price a client paid (noting any tip), personal reflections about the encounter, the client's address, and so forth. There are pros and cons associated with keeping a more elaborate tracking system. Advantages include knowing how to interact with a client were he ever to re-contact the escort. For example the escort will not have to "relearn" what a client from three months ago liked or disliked as detailed notes about previous encounters will remind him. Escorts could prioritize repeat clients about whom he had positive notes and developed personal regard; likewise, an escort could avoid or even blacklist clients with whom he recorded negative experiences. One of the downsides associated with maintaining this type of elaborate tracking system would be the cost of the escort's time. And perhaps the most serious disadvantage would be any legal ramifications were the escort ever to be arrested for prostitution. The information could be subpoenaed, confiscated, and deployed against the escort and his clients.

Compared to agency-based escorts, independent escorts are also more likely to be subjected to scams and ripoffs. There are many ways in which an escort on his own can be victimized:

- The client does not pay the full fee after the encounter.
- The client does not show for the encounter or gives a bogus address.
- The client asks the escort to front certain costs such as travel or a hotel room, but then does not reimburse the escort, or does not show.
- The client negotiates one set of behaviors ahead of an encounter and then pressures the escort into something else. As an example, a client may hire an escort for an erotic massage (similar to what we described in Massage Parlors), but then pressures the masseuse into additional sexual behaviors. Escorts often charge a lower price for erotic massage.

An independent escort can blacklist a client after a foul encounter, but by then he has already lost time and money. In contrast, an agency (and *all* the escorts represented by the agency) can only be burned once by an unscrupulous client. The manager would quickly identify an undesirable client and prevent escorts from seeing him in the future.

In addition to client-perpetuated scams, independent escorts are also easy targets for other types of financial scams or ripoffs. Although many people have received bogus emails from someone overseas telling us we have inherited (from a relative we have never met) or won (from some lottery we never played) a large sum of money, independent escorts (perhaps because of where they advertise) receive many more. The scam promises to transfer funds into our bank account, once we respond with personal and financial information. Another version of this fraud includes an email asking the recipient to act as an intermediary in the transfer of large sums of money. The message indicates that a check will be sent to the recipient. The recipient is to cash the check and pass along the money to another party in the form of a money order. We are allowed to keep a portion of the money as a transaction fee. The check, of course, is fraudulent. Many people can see through these scams, but escorts who are working independently without support and perhaps strapped for cash, may be more susceptible and thus easy targets. Their situation and mindset create a may create vulnerability similar to other groups who seem more susceptible to these unscrupulous practices.

Independent Escorts Might Be Subject to Greater Physical Risks

Perhaps, the most serious concern confronting independent escorts involves their personal safety. Independent escorts maintain one-on-one interactions with clients, often beginning with a simple phone call and ending without the benefit of a third party to monitor the transaction; no one else becomes involved. These escorts may travel alone to locations of a client's choosing; they would be in real danger should a client turn violent or abusive as when a client becomes argumentative if unsatisfied with the outcome of an appointment (such as if the escort insisted on using a condom). During a call, an escort may realize he does not want to continue but is then forced to by the client—he is raped by the client. Admittedly these risks exist for agency-based escorts as well; however, agency-based calls are coordinated by an interested third party. Typically, agency-based appointments are organized several hours or days prior to an encounter and the agency temporarily records the meeting location along with a client's contact information. Although the opportunity for an abusive client may be "equal" for independent and agency-based escorts, the chance of a violent client being caught after the encounter is greater when the encounter is coordinated via an agency. This is something of which potential clients are well aware.

Escorts also risk entering a situation where someone poses as a client, but actually intends to commit a hate crime or robbery. Because of the illicit nature of sex work, escorts may be reluctant to report crimes, something of which clients and many criminals know. This, too, makes the independent escort an easy target. An example of the most extreme danger independent escorts and other sex workers face can be illustrated with the 2009 case of Philip Karkoff, dubbed the "Craigslist Killer." Karkoff purportedly[1] used craigslist.org to hire masseuses and female exotic dancers. Women met Karkoff at a hotel where he detained and robbed them. Karkoff's case came to light when he was arrested for the murder of Julissa Brisman, a masseuse, who was shot multiple times during an alleged struggle with Karkoff.

To mitigate such risks, independent escorts sometimes communicate their whereabouts to friends or other escorts. Escorts may ask this friend to periodically check in before, after, or sometimes during the escort's sessions with clients. This requires escorts to disclose their sex work to at least one other person. Many independent escorts may forgo maintaining this type of security given the complexity of coordinating with a third party or friend due to the requirement that they disclose their sex work (something highly stigmatized). Instead, an independent escort may choose to take their chances.

---

[1]Mr. Karkoff committed suicide in jail while his case was awaiting trial. He pleaded not guilty.

We imagine escorts who are working *occasionally* or *temporarily* would be less likely to create a formal security system. For example, someone who needs extra money at the end of the month might post an ad on Craigslist. This person might not consider himself a sex worker and might not recognize the need to have any type of security system in place. His sentiment may be, "I am just doing this once. No need to tell anyone else. I am sure I will be fine." Similarly, such security measures may be difficult for street-based sex workers who interact with clients and organize encounters ex tempore, often entering a client's vehicle and driving to a location of the client's choosing. Street-based men depend much more on a client's goodwill and honesty.

Costs and Benefits: Independent Escorts Have It Better

Although there may be added work and risk in managing their business, independent escorts preserve a sense of greater autonomy. Independent escorts do not have to surrender a portion of their income to an agency; however, note our earlier discussion on advertising costs for which independent escorts are responsible. In contrast to agency-based escorts, independent escorts can set their own pricing structure. They also have full control over the types of clients they see. In contrast, some agencies may not allow escorts to refuse certain clients, particularly ones that bring a good deal of business to their agency.

Independent escorts may also have a greater array of options in the "types" of work they do and for which they advertise themselves. For example, an independent escort may be interested in only doing erotic massage (without oral or anal sex) or engaging in specialized forms of sex work such as bondage and discipline (for which escorts can charge premium rates and clients will gladly pay). These other "types" of work may not be germane to a more "mainstream" escort agency's business model or clientele, and thus are ideally suited for an independent provider. Independent escorts can also make their own schedule. Agencies may require escorts to be available for large amounts of time, whether or not actual calls take place. Agencies might also require escorts to keep a set schedule of hours, something that might not be ideal for someone who is working more than one job, attending school, or who just wants to maintain more of their personal privacy.

Finally, agencies may place constraints on the other types of sex work in which their escorts are involved. Some agencies may require that escorts list themselves exclusively with that one agency. This prevents price wars between escort agencies were an escort to list himself with multiple agencies. In addition, an exclusivity agreement prevents clients and escorts from skirting around the agency to negotiate sex work directly and independently. For example, an agency may charge $200 and keep $50—the cost for clients is $200 and the escort's profit is $150. Those skirting the agency may negotiate a direct price of $180. The agency would lose its profit, the client would have paid 10% less, and the escort would have banked an additional $30 (20% more!).

Have Your Cake and Eat It Too

Thus, far we have discussed some of the pros and cons of working independently versus listing with an agency. Nevertheless, we do not wish to suggest that sex workers are relegated to participating in only one or the other, such as choosing to work independently or listing oneself with an agency. In fact, some escorts may work independently, perhaps listing themselves on multiple websites as well as listing with an agency. More to the point, some escorts may list themselves with *multiple* agencies. Additionally, opportunities for *other* forms of sex work outside of escorting may also present themselves and can augment the individual's sex work business. Escorts commonly act in adult films where producers often pay a single fee with the talent receiving no residuals on sales. As you have read, escorts also frequently work as dancers or strippers, with the additional bonus of meeting potential clients. Thus, although there may be a greater *initial* financial incentive to participate in an adult film (amateurs can be paid up to $1,000 per film, though typically much less), longer-term profits could come through escorting from men wanting to have sex with a "porn star." An additional crossover advantage is that escorts who are recognized as adult film actors are able to charge a premium for their services (among male sex workers this premium can be hundreds of dollars more per hour and multi-hour minimums). Some websites provide separate, distinctive, listings for escorts who have appeared in adult films.

College Boys Was Unlike Many Other Agencies

Much to its benefit and chagrin, *College Boys* operated differently in contrast to other more "typical" escort agencies. Unlike traditional agencies, *College Boys* maintained a physical location where some escorts lived full-time, whereas most of its peers operate virtually as a website and dispatch center, perhaps with a physical office and maybe with an attached incall room. Second, *College Boys* was generally more permissive around terms and conditions for escorts' employment. If an escort did not want to see a client, he was usually allowed to refuse the call unless no one else could take it. Similarly, Martin was very sensitive to his escorts' own sexual interests whenever he could do so. Escorts were not often required to perform certain sexual acts, and Martin made escort's sexual boundaries very clear to clients when coordinating calls. He also demanded safer sex behavior in any appointment made through the agency.

Escorts at *College Boys* were not required to keep specified hours, though those who were available more often were generally perceived as more reliable and thus rewarded with more calls. Finally, *College Boys* did not take a cut of any tips, and it collected a smaller percentage of revenues from the second hour and any additional hours above the traditional one-hour call. This more laissez-faire approach inherent to the *College Boys* business model may have engendered loyalty among the escorts and suited Martin's style of management, even though it probably cost him some money and clients along the way.

Too Many Cooks in the Kitchen?

Both independent and agency-based escorts compete for clients' attention and possible business such that their rates can be understood through an economic analysis of supply and demand. Aggregate client demand for escort services without corresponding increases in the overall supply of escort availability (either in number of escorts or in the amount of time they can be hired) will drive up the per-hour price point. Adapting to this market, escorts will recognize they can charge a premium rate for their services due to supply scarcity. Such a model assumes a free flow of information within the marketplace, so that buyers and sellers can be aware of what is being sold and at what price. Prior to the Internet, one might have argued that such transparency was absent for male escort services; but with the Internet, clients and escorts can evaluate relative supply and demand as well as price both nationally and regionally for almost any country in the world. Prices for escorts seem to have stabilized over the past several years and are generally equivalent regardless of the country (among developed nations), something that supply-demand analyses would predict as an outcome of market transparency barring sudden shocks in service availability or customer demand (Figure 9.1).

In contrast to the traditional labor market, where women make approximately $0.77 for every $1 men make (Fitzpatrick, 2010, April 20), female escorts earn more than male escorts (Koken, Bimbi, & Parsons, 2009). This discrepancy largely represents "scarce" supply of available female escorts relative to the immense market of paying male clients, given that most men are going to be sexually interested in women. For female escorts, the escort-to-client ratio allows women the ability to charge double or even quadruple what male-for-male escorts can obtain for similar services.

Escorts must compete against each other, even if they work for the same agency. Increasing numbers of men available on the sex work market coupled with a restricted population of customers (as fewer men would be interested in sex with another man) seems to produce hourly rates for male escorts well below those of their female counterparts. At the time we wrote this book, the going hourly rate for male escorts hovered in the range of $200 to $300 in urban areas with slightly lower fees charged outside the larger metropolitan zones. This fee structure had been fairly stable for a number of years, and did not seem to be nosing upward in the recent past.

Figure 9.1.
Economic model of escort pricing based on supply and demand

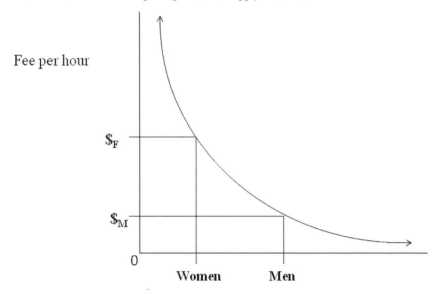

Escorts available per client

The pay gap between men and women has managed to persist across many enterprises and largely throughout history. Thus, why is it that is the supply of female escorts is limited in relative to demand, whereas there is a relative oversupply of male escorts with respect to the demand for their services? To answer these questions, one can draw from sociological, psychological, and feminist thought around human sexuality. In the United States, and throughout much of the world, social norms around female and male sexual behavior are scripted such that women are expected to be sexually conservative and restricting. Women who are perceived to be sexually active are often stigmatized as "sluts" and "whores." In contrast, men are socially scripted to act in a sexually assertive manner and, as a stereotype of the script, to desire sexual activity with a moment's notice. Because of these cultural and social expectations, heterosexual men may have a more difficult time finding available female partners. The resulting "scarcity" of sexual opportunity would be expected to increase the cost of female escort services—customer demand would outstrip supply allowing providers to charge more per encounter. Women would be discouraged from offering their sexuality to men, regardless of whether it was for pay or not. It would constrict the supply of women entering sex work relative to their population potential.

The outcome of stereotypical sexual scripts may act differently when both parties are the same sex. In essence, men seeking men may find it easier to located available sex partners. This may reduce the "need" to hire someone for sex—suppressing the demand for male escort services, except among men who either cannot find the sexual partners they desire without paying, or who do not wish to enter a more gay-identified environment (e.g., gay chatroom, bar, or bathhouse) to do so. On the supply side, some evidence suggests that escorting is more acceptable and culturally normative in gay communities (Koken et al., 2009; Parsons, Koken, & Bimbi, 2007). Thus, more men may be willing to accept pay for providing sexual services whether they actually identify themselves as escorts or not. Additional escorts in the sexual marketplace increases the escort-to-client ratio and reduces the amount escorts can reasonably charge. There are some exceptions to the traditional pay ceiling and these are extended to both female and male sex workers. These would be for instances when escorts possess some exceptional characteristic or provide an unusual service for which they can charge a premium, as we noted in the case of adult film actors.

Escorts often employ a variety of tactics to improve their business which are designed to make them more competitive and for which they may be able to charge more than the average market price. In addition to participating in adult films and advertising on multiple websites, an escort may create his own personal webpage, or he may post amateur erotic videos of himself on user-generated pornographic websites (e.g., xtube.com). In a different vein, escorts make an effort to present themselves as upper-class elite professionals in hopes of attracting a higher "class" of client. The most obvious benefit from having a wealthier client is the potential for earning repeat business or a bigger tip—with more income from fewer clients, an escort may need to work less to achieve his goals, or he can capitalize on his cachet and raise his financial sights. Moreover, escorts believe that wealthier clients will treat them better overall; they may have better manners, better hygiene, and more exquisite taste in food, drink, and entertainment.

Thus, to attract a wealthier client, an escort may improve or maintain their physical appearance by eating healthier, exercising, and having cosmetic surgery. Escorts also may vary their sexual repertoire to include more unusual activities such as sadism/masochism and bondage/domination, scenes for which they can charge more due to their relative scarcity among other escorts. More to the point, escorts may portray themselves as being in a similar economic class as their wealthier clients, whether they actually are or not, in the hope this will attract such clients to them. Though not intending for it to be used in the context of sex work, Bourdieu and Passeron (1977 [1970]) introduced the term "cultural capital" to describe non-financial social assets from which individuals may draw to augment status and economic mobility.

These include such characteristics as education, diction, dialect, social relationships and networks, and knowledge of valued cultural activities such as the arts. As presented in Chapter Four, escorts draw upon social skills when entertaining clients. Escorts appear to use these same skills to attract clients within the context of a print- or internet-based advertisements, highlighting cultural capital in the context of written online advertisement. In so doing, many men highlight their ability to carry on a conversation, indicate they are college-educated, or portray an overall sense of worldliness by noting their extensive travel, Ivy League degree, location of their residence, developed taste in fine wine and clothing, or ability to speak multiple languages.

Competition in a Virtual Marketplace

Although escorting *websites* compete against each other in terms of attracting clients' attention and escort listings, they appear to recognize the oversupplied market of available male escorts and have jumped at the opportunity to foster "competition" among escorts. For example, men4rentnow.com is one of the largest male escort websites in the United States and Europe. It has listings for escorts in more than 400 cities worldwide. The website is free for clients, reflecting their relatively scarcity, but charges escorts a monthly fee to list their advertisements—something it can afford to do given the many male escorts looking to connect with clients. Table 9.1 presents information about pricing and options escorts can expect when using the website. The base price for posting an escort ad on men4rentnow.com is $50 a month. This is a nominal fee relative to the amount of money escorts could earn in a month; escorts would easily recoup this investment with just one client. However, the website has introduced additional pricing tiers such as "Platinum" and "Premium" listings. Premium members, for $80 a month, receive "featured ads" placed ahead of Basic members and can include additional pictures. Platinum members receive even more perks, but at a higher price of $110 per month. For example, men4rentnow.com will deliver client responses and inquiries to Platinum and Premium members via text message in addition to email. Basic members only received responses via email. Text message delivery means that Platinum and Premium escorts can respond to client inquiries faster and while on the go—possibly closing a deal with a client in less time. Platinum members are also able to delete up to three client reviews per month, while Basic members can only delete one per month. This means that Platinum members have more control over preventing negative reviews from appearing within their profile. Platinum members are also able to list up to three "travel cities," Basic members can only list one. A travel city is an alternate location that an escort may visit periodically. Escort's ads appear in their home city as well as travel cities, meaning greater exposure to clients in a variety of locations. The tiered pricing

Table 9.1
Advertising and membership tiers on an escort website

Feature	Membership type		
	Platinum $110/month	Premium $80/month	Basic $50/month
Receive client responses via text message	Yes	Yes	No
Ad rotation on every page of the website	Yes	Yes	No
Ad placement	Listed before premium ads	Listed before basic ads	Listed after premium ads
Photos rotate in your ad	Yes	No	No
Number of photos in your ad	12	8	8
Number of travel cities in your ad	3	2	1
Number of reviews you can delete per month	3	2	1
Number of changes you can make to your ad	Unlimited	Unlimited	3 per month
Temporarily suspend ad	Yes	Yes	No

Note: This website was free for clients to use, and available to the public (i.e., no sign-in required). Adapted from men4rentnow.com, October 2010.

structure on men4rentnow.com is common among other well-established escorting websites.

Escorts recognize the importance of having their ads seen by potential clients given the number of competitors they face. In the summer of 2010, about 415 men were listed in the New York City section of men4rentnow.com. The first 133 ads (or the first 19 pages of ads one would have to click through) were designated as Premium and Platinum members. Other "Basic" escorts, who paid a lower price, would not have their ad appear for a client until page 20, *or beyond*. At the time we visited the site, there were 59 pages of ads for escorts in New York City alone. Thus, it would behoove an escort to pay the extra $30 or $60 for a Premium or Platinum membership to ensure his ad was among the first clients saw.

CONCLUSION

Given the breadth and complexity of the virtual marketplace for men's sexual services and how easy it has become for escorts to operate independently, it will be interesting to see how agencies like *College Boys* continue to fit into the mix. It is abundantly clear that the Internet has rapidly and dramatically changed how men hire other men for sex and companionship. These changes beg the question, "Are agencies becoming obsolete?" Only time will be able to answer that question. Nevertheless, agencies such as *College Boys* have yet managed to find a niche within the digital world, taking advantage of online cybererotica by propelling their businesses in new directions. Such adaptations are necessary in all facets of business, thus the struggles that an escort agency may face in a transitioning digital world are characteristic of the types of changes the Internet has had on other sectors of the economy.

"Brick-and-mortar" facilities have played essential historical roles in the business of sex, however, more so for female sex workers. Male sex workers still rely on agencies and hustler bars, but also seem to be paving the way for an independent market via the Internet and print advertising. Although the industry remains marginalized and highly stigmatized, sex work proliferates throughout the United States and throughout the world. Developed nations and regions with strong economies have seen a rapid transition in sex work over the Internet. These transitions have occurred in concert with diminishing street-based sex work, and other changes in technology, shifting social views about sexuality, and local laws that seem to fluctuate constantly.

Today, escorts and other sex workers have a variety of options when it comes to navigating their professions. As a result, they are faced with making complex and perhaps, deeply personal decisions with regard to how they will pursue their careers. In this chapter, we have explored some of the benefits and costs associated with navigating the market independently or in listing oneself with an agency. Ultimately, it is up to the escort to make these decisions. We have illustrated how the road sex workers take can impact them financially, legally, and socially. And, for some, their decisions can affect their physical safety.

All told, escorts exist in a competitive marketplace; their services are in demand enough to generate a good income and the balance between supply and demand plays a significant role in the going rate they can charge. In an effort to compete for clients' attention and business, escorts utilize a variety of strategies by advertising themselves, strategically and thoughtfully marketing their best assets. Escorting websites recognize this competition, and have responded in kind with priced advertising tiers from which escorts can choose. This perhaps exemplifies the strength and resilience of the business of sex, even in a rapidly-transitioning digital world.

Chapter Ten
ALL GOOD THINGS . . .

OVERVIEW

Success brings its disadvantages, unanticipated challenges that creep up from behind when everything else seems to be going well. Martin gradually grew more unsettled as his agency waxed successful: easy cash, swarms of people buzzing around him, the dizzy partying. In that sexualized environment anything seemed possible for Martin except an enduring relationship, but the frenetic activity became too much. It sucked him in too far. There were periods when he could not be found and at such times the agency suffered, and almost suffocated despite the efforts of his closest friends to keep the business going. He grew moodier and a little less reliable during that last year or two *College Boys* still operated. It was a time for us, as interested observers, to reflect upon what had been and what it all meant—we share our thoughts here in this final chapter as we discuss the agency's fitful decline. What conclusions can we reach about modern American male prostitution based on this agency's kaleidoscope of stories, emotions, and events? What does all of it say about the American Dream in a post, post-modern world?

Enter Cassandra

We had concluded the original wave of interviews and were now waiting for other, less accessible men to be available for telling their stories. Additionally, Martin also hired new men constantly. We thought about talking with several of the newer *College Boys* just as they started to escort, and then follow up with them as their involvement with the agency unfolded over time. Martin kept in touch and we told him about our ideas, but we needed to wait for funding. We emailed with him and had lunches every few weeks. Then, there was no contact at all—nothing for weeks became nothing for months. Something had gone wrong and we were concerned. Had the agency been raided? Had it folded? Finally, someone answered the phone, but it was someone else, a man we did not recognize. After identifying ourselves and explaining the project, the skeptical stranger on the other end of the line said, "Oh, that's right. Some of the guys told me about you. I'm Scott." Scott turned out to be a friend of Martin who had run a small female escort agency some time back. Martin had asked Scott to keep *College Boys* going while he was "away." You could almost hear the quotation marks in Scott's voice as he used that word.

"Away?" We asked what Martin meant, but Scott would not tell us and did not want to be interviewed or have us talk to any more of the escorts without Martin. We thanked Scott and asked him to get in touch if anything changed. We heard less and less from people at the agency. One of the escorts who contacted us a few weeks later told us that the agency had closed, that it was out of business. The former *College Boy* worried about his bills, wondering if we had any way to contact Martin for him to find some work. But Martin was nowhere to be found. Our contact told us that the other guys had drifted off and stopped working for Scott. The new manager did not have their trust, did not know the client base, and could not manage the website and phone calls. Appointments had become haphazard, and disagreements between Scott and the escorts erupted into verbal conflicts that could not be resolved. The agency had apparently come apart at the seams without Martin's personality and experience gluing it together. We thought *College Boys* was gone for good.

However, after another couple of months an email appeared using the agency's old address. Martin had returned and was reconstituting his business. The email provided a new cell phone number. It was a somewhat changed Martin who answered our call. He sounded a little older, maybe a little more sad, and more serious. Martin told us that he was trying to get more stable after letting the whirlwind carry him away—unpaid fines, intense partying, and a devastating crush on one of his straight escorts drove him "over the edge" and he had "needed time away to clear things up" both legally and personally.

During this "sabbatical," Martin met Cassandra, a woman with whom he rapidly became fast friends. Cassandra and Martin made an odd pair when you first saw them; Martin was so informal and hyperactively social contrasted with Cassandra's cooler, more analytic personality. Underneath they had a great deal in common—both former sex workers, both running escort services, and both unabashed extraverts who loved younger and relatively inaccessible men. Cassandra was around five years older and more stable than Martin, but still enjoyed a wild time and made sure she looked the part—athletic, blond curls, and tight skirts. Young men could not seem to get enough of her; Cassandra was soon dating a tall dark-haired college athlete with a quiet demeanor and very masculine personality.

Cassandra and Martin teamed up personally and professionally. Martin moved into her place, a stylish converted storefront condo with two bedrooms. Soon, he had a number of the old guys working for him and hired some new escorts which put *College Boys* back into business. Emilio and Dennis returned, the only members of Martin's old inner circle to do so. Cassandra began to expand her end as well. She brought on some additional women, repackaging her agency as *College Girls* to complement Martin's side of the shop. Their idea was to provide a full range of services for any taste clients might present. Cassandra's more business-like attitude helped to stabilize Martin whose focus mostly returned to running the agency, away from the influences and problems that had led to his hiatus. All of this went well for a couple of months, and then new problems arose after Martin and Cassandra rented an old stone row house near downtown which allowed for a spacious incall room—Martin and Cassandra were better friends than business partners. At this point, we sensed that the agency was again in trouble. The escorts did as well. Some of them began to resent Cassandra's "interference" while others took up her defense as a level-headed and direct manager, saying that Martin needed someone who was more forceful to keep him organized and out of trouble. Emilio tried to keep the peace, but with less success than before, started to drift away when he got a customer service job at the airport.

The Big Picture

Around this time, our first manuscript from the *College Boys* project was published. We started to pull together our findings to make sense of them, to share what we learned—a process that reached its apex in this book. As we leave the story of Martin, Cassandra, and their agencies in a state of uncertainty, perhaps the issues surrounding male sex work in modern North American culture can be made a bit clearer as the larger narrative in which these tales occur. And it is a story for the ages, considering that we have documentary evidence for male prostitution in the West dating back more than twenty centuries such as when Polybius (1979) complains in the second century BCE about the money young Roman nobles wasted on their "boys." A real cultural need intricately ingrained into society seems to exist for men selling sex to other men, which continues uninterrupted from that early time into our New World. What aspects of male prostitution present in today's society represent those very long-term sociohistorical trends? Which reflect more unique contextual factors woven into the prevailing Zeitgeist?

1. *Client Motivations.* We have no reason to believe that the fundamental motivations for purchasing or selling sexual and relational behaviors were any different today than in Imperial Rome or Renaissance France. The simple reason reflects the almost certain fact that human nature has not changed across the ages even if our cultures, religions, and technologies have evolved. Men purchasing an escort's time do so for several mutually compatible reasons, even if not all clients may express each of them at any one time. Consumers want to make contact with a fantasy, a locus of satisfaction and erotic desire absent from their usual lives. They are purchasing an expectation, an idea—to experience it emotionally as well as physically, to hold it concretely and to have it in their hands. The allure is powerful; it is well worth the money and always has been.

This idea may consist of relational as well as sexual elements. Relationally, the purchaser enjoys the society of a handsome and available man knowing that this person has the explicit goal of providing satisfaction. There is no risk of rejection, no hint that the escort will find someone more interesting. For the hour, night, or weekend that client will have the escort, this young man will focus on yielding the fantasy experience which led to his hire. The escort can be a temporary boyfriend, a travel companion, or a trophy to show off to friends or rivals. The client can safely flirt with him, touch his leg in a restaurant, and engage in hours of conversation. Sexually, the escort becomes the willing and cooperative partner—even when that means he is dominant, controlling, or harsh. Doing so is at the client's request and the escort subverts his own desires for those of the client, without ever letting the client know this occurs. The escort fulfills the physical, social, and emotional needs of their customer for the time contracted to do so. No reciprocation need occur from the client's end of the relationship unless that too is part of the fantasy, a script written by the client and for the client. All the escort has to do is never acknowledge any script at all, never mention that he is being compensated for his time with the customer. His job is to maintain the fantasy that he *wants* to be with the client of his own will and not for the money. He must be an actor and play his part.

No breach of etiquette enrages clients more than violation of this most basic contract with an escort. Client criticisms such as "clock watcher" or "uninterested" reflect the fact that clients do not want to remember that the escort has been hired for his time. To do so would break the spell, the desire that the escort may have come to an appointment for the money, but that once there, he stays because he enjoys the client's company. One recent negative review posted by a dissatisfied client expressed exactly this sentiment:

> I should have known from his lack of curiosity in what I wanted it wasn't going to be a good encounter. If an escort doesn't fulfill my specific requests it is very hard for me to get turned on. Perhaps he's just not into being an escort. Next time I will only hire escorts who list the things that they are into or willing to do in their profile with

much more detail; it will likely save me money and time. For me, the whole point in hiring is to be able to articulate what I want and hopefully get it. This escort seems to think the time spent together is about him only and not you unfortunately.

Escorts should always appear to enjoy themselves while talking to or having sex with clients—their experience with the client should match similar situations in their personal lives such as going out with a friend, being on a date, or just finding someone to screw at the local club based on the playbook "written" by their customer. They should focus on the client's desire, and leave their own at the door, just as an actor leaves his or her personality in the dressing room as they transform into the character their director, screenwriter, and audience expect to see. Their performance should allow clients to suspend disbelief for the time they have together, to experience a fantasy made flesh.

2. *Escort Motivations.* Playing this role earns the escort his paycheck—the chief reason he enters the job in the first place. Too often analysts examining sex work have focused on exploitation, moral degradation, or personal deviance as the normative pathways into sex work; and to be sure, those pathways do certainly exist. However, they do not appear to be the norm among the strata of sex workers which this book addresses: men choosing to enter Internet-based prostitution and escorting. One can clearly understand that a monetary motivation would not exist for persons forced into sex work against their will, and our discussion can in no way pertain to such barbaric sexual enslavement of human beings. Yet this route of entry involves no free motivation on the part of the individual. For those men entering sex work voluntarily, even if they are working on the street and in dire economic straits, income appears to be the primary motivation for selling sexual services and companionship.

We saw through our interviews and through a reading of the scientific literature from around the world that sex workers viewed their activities as a way to make money, as a job, and for some as a profession or even career. Although difficult for many outside the industry to fully accept, sex workers themselves see their trade as a means to capitalize on resources they possess in addition to or in the absence of other income-generating options. Our book also shows that male sex workers must also have the *opportunity* to learn about and become involved with the sex trade. This can happen in vivo such as when men became aware of escorting through friends working at *College Boys*. Increasingly it also occurs in virtuo, as when people encountered the agency's website by accident (as we ourselves did) and then wanted to know more about the opportunities presented by such a business.

Opportunity to enter sex work and a desire for increased income were not the only factors facilitating men's entry into escorting. A number of *psychological factors* mediated this decision for the men in our project, and likely for most other men choosing this kind of job. We found that decreased commitment to social-sexual norms represented a key element in permitting men to consider entry into escorting. If they held more traditional values, men had a much more difficult time coming into the agency, and may not have done so at all. The thought could have been a fleeting, if somewhat intriguing or disturbing, idea that would never have been acted upon. Further, potential escorts would have to be more sexually open; not just toward having sex with people they normally would not have considered, but also with respect to ceding control to the client and engaging in behaviors that might be outside one's typical repertoire. Mentoring and peer education helped men make these transitions, but it did not work for all escorts and we do not know how many men considered sex work but never quite took the plunge.

3. *Emotional and Relational Services.* We entered our study of Internet prostitution expecting it to be all about men hiring other men for sex and sex alone. Most clients clearly wanted to have sex with their rented *College Boy*, but the majority also sought an emotional or relational experience. A small group of clients requested non-sexual services as the *primary* reason for hiring an escort, more than we would have expected prior to conducting our interviews. This co-emphasis on a client's emotional as well as sexual needs as their basis for hiring escorts has emerged as one of the most surprising findings from our project, something that is appearing in the work of other researchers as well. Studies with women have found that about 40 percent of appointments for Internet-based sex workers involved no sexual activity whatsoever with this percentage dropping to 20 percent (still one in five) among street workers; men hired them to meet other needs (Venkatesh, 2010). For the men hiring women described in this study, even if they initially expressed interest in having sex, social and emotional activities assumed its place— women reported such clients expressed a high level of satisfaction nonetheless. Although the proportion of non-sexual calls was much lower in our male escort sample than in the research with women, emotional needs were integrated into most of the appointments for the men we interviewed.

Clients' often unstated desires for emotional connection and social interaction during appointments surprised inexperienced escorts; Martin and the other escorts emphasized this fact to new *College Boys* through mentorship and informal conversations. Like most outsiders to the business, new escorts believed the "myth" that men hiring escorts were only after one thing—their sex. And as you've read, like many stereotypes, there was a certain subset of clients who fit this description. Very quickly, however, new escorts at *College Boys* learned that they could do less in bed if they did more for customers socially and emotionally. They could converse with clients, listen to their troubles, get them to laugh, tell stories, and have a quiet drink or a wild time at the dance club. These activities were *just* as satisfying as sex to many of their customers, which always surprised the escorts a little bit until they thought about what sex meant to most people; what sex meant personally.

In line with much of the research on human sexuality, we posit that sexual behavior represents one particularly good and evolved means of fulfilling social and emotional needs. As a friend of ours likes to say, "Every one night stand I've had was a relationship, just a very short one!" These needs appear to be embedded in a relational context and generally fall into several motivational categories (Hill & Preston, 1996): receiving or providing nurturance, social submission or dominance, stress relief, and positive reinforcement through giving and receiving pleasure. Unconsciously, clients hired escorts for a *relational* experience which in the context of our culture finds its expression through this type of sexual behavior. Needs that could or should not be met in one's more public life perhaps would be satisfied in a more covert manner via an escort. Thus, when escorts socialized and provided support to clients, they were addressing key needs even when no sex occurred at all. If sex did occur, it would just be one other vehicle through which to satisfy a similar motivational set. Sexual and relational behaviors do not compete in the escort business; they complement one another whether or not most clients specifically request social interaction. Experienced *College Boys* had learned this fact, and used it to their advantage (by decreasing sexual activity) as well as the client's (by providing satisfaction of key needs even if via other means). Sexual behavior is relationship behavior; and it is the relational aspect of human motivation that clients satisfy when hiring an escort—their very human needs for intimacy, authority, and competence that drive the social behavior our species. Hiring a prostitute just for sex just is not enough for most people.

4. *Community.* Everyone possesses the need to belong, to feel valued, to feel like they can achieve something in the eyes of their fellows. The escorts held these same needs as well, and of course they did. Other studies discussed in this book point out the stigma faced by people working in the sexual services industry, stigma that creates a sense of isolation or, in many cases perhaps, reinforces loneliness or separation preexisting from other causes such as family strife, sexual orientation, mental health problems, and so forth. By coming together as a community, the *College Boys* agency met a variety of important needs for many of its employees. It certainly did so for Martin and his inner circle. Among those escorts relationally lacking in some way in their lives outside the agency, bonding with Martin and other escorts at *College Boys* gave them a home away from home much as a fraternity would do for young men at college. The agency provided a sense of identity, a group with whom to share stories and experiences, a clan of insiders privy to secrets, struggles, and successes that the young man would likely not share with most anyone else.

As we have argued earlier in the book, *College Boys* was a community of men who came together to satisfy the needs of its members; each person brought their own set of wants generating different levels of involvement with the agency. For many escorts this did mean a need for affiliation and approval, a sense of belonging and community. These men tended to be closest to Martin on a personal level and used the agency most for their own emotional and relational fulfillment. We believe that the more one integrated himself into the network of the agency, the less he may have been, or grown to become, tied to social connections outside it. There are too many possible reasons for this to review them all; but it could have been any number of possibilities. On one pole, men could have integrated more into the agency's relational structure based on the degree of relational satisfaction in their own lives prior to the agency. At the other extreme, working as an escort could have created emotional distance between an escort and his friends and relations. The implicit stigma and dissociation involved in his sex work may have weakened pre-existing bonds and led him to more closely affiliate among others with whom he currently had more in common. An overarching driver for the community spirit of escorts at *College Boys* may also have been reflected in the developmental age of these men as young adults or late adolescents, a time of life when one ventures out into the world. Doing so often involves joining new communities and loosening bonds with old ones—strong developmental factors which could exert a powerful influence on young men entering sex work.

5. *The Problem of Stereotypes.* Although stereotypes about sex work probably bear resemblance to its reality on some level, we would be hard pressed to find many given our experiences with the *College Boys* agency. At first, we thought we had accidentally stepped into a rather cluttered fraternity house. It was a place very similar to those that many of us may have frequented during our own college years complete with the threadbare couches, used desks, and clusters of guys talking, playing games, and watching movies (we did not stay for the other nightly activities). Looking around the room, one would not have known they had stepped into a private all-male brothel and one of the largest businesses of its type on the East Coast at that. It all just seemed so "normal" in an odd kind of way. We were waiting for the stereotypes to come down the stairs or step through the door: dirty old men, pimps in outrageous fur coats, slutty boys barely wearing a thing, emaciated teenagers looking for their next meal, or hollow-eyed heroin addicts hoping to score a hit. None of them emerged. Instead we saw a few skater guys who enjoyed video games and going out to eat pancakes, preppy college athletes, some men in their older twenties amused by the antics of younger compatriots, and normal blue-collar types who preferred a Bud Lite while watching the college football game. Everyone got along fairly well under Martin's watchful eye. And the clients looked like professional men we might see at the office or in the mall; in fact that is exactly what they were. It is what we were! Many of the escorts at *College Boys* thought

we were clients until they got to know us, participated in the interviews, and got used to our comings and goings from the agency. The lack of embodied stereotypes surprised us, even as sex researchers who wondered how many we would actually observe. Such preconceptions seem to operate so strongly and pervasively within the culture from which we come that it has been hard to leave them at the door. Through our reading and personal experiences we identified several misconceptions that many people hold about male prostitutes. We even used to believe some of these ourselves:

- Sex workers use their money only for drugs, alcohol, or partying
- Economic deprivation drives sex workers to enter prostitution
- Prostitution and escorting are the same thing
- Sex workers are psychologically and morally deviant
- Male sex workers usually have delinquent or criminal histories
- Brothel owners exploit their workers
- Male escorts usually have high-risk sexual behavior with clients
- Sex workers have little interest in conventional romantic values such as love and intimacy
- Escorting is inherently dangerous
- Clients exploit sex workers: Sex workers exploit their clients

Even today we are not sure how many of our findings and conclusions have been inappropriately skewed by unidentified and deeply ingrained biases about sex workers. Hopefully, in writing this book we will have confronted some of those obstacles to real understanding and exorcised a few from ourselves and maybe from you as well.

6. *A Safety Valve*. A basic question this book needs to address directly concerns the very existence of male prostitution itself. We have sought to do so; though will conclude our review of "the big picture" with a more direct analysis. It begins with a set of questions. If prostitution and escorting are so stigmatized then why does society "permit" them to continue? What has permitted prostitution to flourish in so many cultures around the globe and throughout the ages? Although these are general questions, they assumed particular prominence in our work with *College Boys* given that it was a male escort agency in a relatively conservative area of the state. Conceptually, there would be few areas in the United States more hostile to sexually "deviant" behavior, especially acts like prostitution that also were illegal. One might think that the authorities or anti-prostitution constituencies would try to run *College Boys* out of town. They did not; actually, quite the opposite occurred. Martin told us about arrangements with several local companies and other organizations to provide "entertainment and companionship" for their out-of-town guests. He gladly did so, believing that such contacts partially shielded *College Boys* from police scrutiny and provided the advantage of

steady referrals from the immediate area. Why would otherwise "respectable" organizations engender informal contracts with a male brothel particularly in a more socially conservative region?

We strongly believe that a response to these questions is not all that complicated or revolutionary; that it is in fact right in front of our faces. Prostitution and, in this case, male prostitution plays by society's rules. It satisfies key needs that otherwise would go unmet and could destabilize strong social norms for monogamous heterosexual marriage. Male sex work assists to preserve the stability of this system by allowing a covert safety valve for those men possessing otherwise unacceptable needs. Men can maintain the appearance of social propriety while occasionally satisfying homosexual desires outside of their primary relationships. As long as no one ever finds out about it, society is willing to turn a blind eye. The legal and social implications of discovery are so costly that clients and most sex workers have a strong motivation to keep their liaisons completely secret. Thus, we can have our cakes and eat them too: Society maintains the heterosexual and monogamous values that are so deeply rooted in its religious and cultural traditions while men not fitting neatly into that mold can express their needs in a generally satisfying, if somewhat distasteful, manner. The expense and stigma surrounding sex work insure some level of "punishment" for clients who take advantage of this safety valve—guilt or shame at violating the norms and then hiding the fact, the monetary cost of hiring escorts, fear of discovery and retribution. Such downside elements to hiring a prostitute may reduce the frequency with which it occurs, an advantage from the view of conventional society.

Furthermore, should men hiring escorts be discovered (as some always are), the "decent" people of society can objectify and castigate these individuals as depraved, immoral, and criminal. Such men can be labeled as "others" to be shunned and deployed as anti-role models to avoid. Together with forceful negative stereotypes around homosexuality and prostitution, such examples of what happens to men violating social rules could further limit utilization of male escorts as a back channel. These social sanctions could encourage men who might consider this avenue to think again and stay within the bounds of "decency." By tolerating the existence of a backdoor and heavily punishing people found to use it, the culture maintains its status quo while limiting access to alternate behavioral pathways. Perhaps, this is why we see sexual services businesses in a relatively rural conservative area like the one where *College Boys* was situated. In such places, strong negative values regarding homosexuality, as well as equally strong forces supporting traditional heterosexual marriage, create an environment in which men desiring sexual intimacy with other men would have no acceptable outlet. Instead of "allowing" these individuals to meet their needs openly, and thus establish "adverse" role models for others by challenging core social values, the culture allows a covert safety valve in the form of male prostitution.

You might ask, "If male escorting allows men to express culturally unacceptable sexual needs, why do we also see male prostitution in more sexually liberated areas such as the major East and West Coast cities of the United States?" One could reasonably argue that it is easier for men to form relationships with or just have sex with other men in such metropolitan areas. Thus, why would an escort agency or independent sex workers be needed? We suggest that gay "liberation" has made great strides, but that gay sex and gay relationships still elicit strong negative reactions from many people even in more socially "progressive" areas—strong enough where same-sex marriage is still illegal in most U.S. states and many gay men still endure discrimination, harassment, and violence even in the most permissive places. Thus, while homophobia has *decreased* it has certainly not vanished, creating an incentive for many men to follow traditional heterosexual norms in their relationships.

Even if a man were comfortable with expressing homosexual behavior and/ or identity, deeply ingrained values regarding monogamy still exert a powerful influence on how people judge each other and how we evaluate our own actions. Monogamy norms seem to operate somewhat independently from the gender of one's partner—most gays and lesbians appear to desire a sexually and emotionally exclusive relationship as much as heterosexuals do. This can be seen in the push for "same-sex marriage" which would socially legitimize gay unions as equivalent to heterosexual marriages, including in the legal and moral requirement for sexual exclusivity. Men who might prefer to have an external sexual partner outside of a primary relationship with another man (formally married or not) would still be running afoul of these strong monogamy pressures. In fact, as you have read, Martin reported the second largest category of *College Boys* clients were men in committed relationships with other men, about 20 percent of the agency's business. These typically were "out" gay men in public relationships who could probably have found other non-paid male partners with whom to have sex. Instead, they chose to hire a male escort. Why? We believe many of them did so because they were violating monogamy norms and wished this to remain secret. Finding other men in the community to connect with sexually risked their partner's discovery of the infidelity and would threaten their relationship with him. Hiring an escort substantially lowered this risk, placed the client in more control of the situation, and reduced the potential for relationship and other forms of social distress.

Male prostitution permits men to meet socially unacceptable needs without the outward social costs. Instead of being sanctioned by others for violating deeply held norms regarding sexual orientation and/or monogamy, the client pays an internal price instead. He might sanction himself via negative self-evaluations resulting in emotions of guilt or shame. He would have to pay a monetary cost to hire an escort and fulfill a fantasy or a need. For many men, it seems that this conversion of costs from the social arena to the psychological and financial represents an attractive alternative given their personal needs and situations. Instead of doing nothing, these men can pay a "price" more acceptable to them, keep the relationships that they value, and meet needs that could otherwise threaten their home life and community standing.

. . . Must Come to an End

Unlike the conflict between needs and values we discuss above, the fact of mortality cannot be bargained away nor have its costs converted into a less stressful form. No, all good things must come to an end whether that be one individual life or the families and societies in which those lives find context and meaning. *College Boys* could not escape this most basic truism any more than anything else. It was born, grew, flourished for a while, and then declined and died. Martin, at the center of his business and its essential keystone provided the impetus for each of these stages of the agency's life cycle. His actions and shortcomings killed *College Boys* as surely as his talents and boundless enthusiasm brought it to life and maturity. We end our book by closing the story of the agency, by telling you how it all ended one day in the bright early summer.

Even though the new house Martin and Cassandra rented together had spurred disagreement and sometimes argument between them, it met the needs of their agencies well and they had enough space to retreat into separate corners when they needed to do so. Martin now had about 15 men working for him. Emilio was still there and dating one of the new escorts at *College Boys*, Berto. Becky changed her membership in the *Inner Circle* and became an Advisor. She was always with Martin, his best friend and foil—something of a guardian angel who could sometimes level out his mood when he was too irritated with Cassandra for her to be of much help. Martin needed the assistance as he would cycle through phases of higher or lower stability. The business suffered a bit and he was not as successful. The men he hired were more straight, younger, and had increased histories of delinquency and antisocial behavior. Martin appeared to be going for the "bad boy" in the escorts, not that all of them were, but they were present in much greater proportion than before. Perhaps, this reflected something of his personal life—Martin's recent crushes had been with one straight guy who could be pretty rough around the edges and then another escort, a younger gay man who was struggling with legal problems and drug addiction. Because they did not return his affection in ways that he needed, Martin became somewhat sadder and a little more jaded—more cynical and sarcastic than we had seen him before. Cassandra was not at fault for starting all of the fights. The escorts worried about Martin; some tried to provide him with support when they could. Others unwittingly made the situation worse by having him party with them too much or stoking the fires of resentment with gossip and innuendo.

We began another round of interviews at the agency. Our goals were to collect data from all of the new escorts and re-interview several of the men who had been part of the project's first wave. Furthermore, we wanted to work with the *College Girls*-side of the agency. Cassandra supported our work and said that she would allow us to recruit study participants from the young women when we were ready. Because we already had the protocols and institutional approval to begin interviewing the men, we started with them. Most of our discussion occurred with the new escorts, though we were able to collect information from two of the three *College Boys* who still worked for Martin from before the agency's hiatus. None of the guys lived at the new house even though one or two of them always seemed to be around, so Martin was a little more isolated than he had been before.

Despite these concerns, Martin still retained an infectious optimism about his future and that of his agency. He was particularly excited about the business possibilities of incorporating *College Girls* into the mix so as to be able to address a wider variety of clients who might request services that an all-male agency could not provide. We fell into our old pattern of spending much of the weekend at the agency interviewing escorts or waiting to do so, observing the comings and goings throughout the day, getting to know Martin, Cassandra, and their employees better. We went out with Martin when he took escorts to appointments, talked with him about his plans for the future, and solicited feedback about our research. As ever, Martin was generous with his time and helped us a great deal.

We became aware of increased problems when Martin did not reliably return emails or phone calls. Fights with Cassandra became more intense and somewhat irrational. We could tell that she was becoming more and more frustrated with Martin's moodiness and disorganization. Several of the escorts talked to us about concerns that they had for Martin and the functioning of the agency. He seemed to be having more trouble focusing on the job of organizing all of the various appointments even though there were only about half the number of the men working for him as there were at the height of *College Boys'* operation two years prior. There were two occasions where we went down to the agency but could find no one around. One time Martin came back relatively soon, apologizing for the delay and calling the escort we had been scheduled to interview who luckily was free and could come in for our discussion. The second time Martin did not show up at all and we left.

After two more weekends for which interviews had been cancelled because Martin said he was too occupied to arrange them, we had a pair of escort participants set up for a Saturday afternoon. Early summer had come and we were going to do the taping out on the deck of the new house. There was a small garden with a grill where the escorts enjoyed socializing and appeared to feel more relaxed. We parked in the street and started to walk up to the front steps when out of the house came Tommy. He and Michael were no longer working for Martin, but had moved to a nearby city. We shouted a greeting as we had not seen him in over a year. Tommy smiled but looked worried and downcast, a very unusual demeanor for him. More unusual was his silence; we asked what was wrong. Tommy looked up. After we hugged and shook hands, Tommy said that Martin had gone.

We had just spoken with Martin the day before and begged Tommy for news. Maybe Martin was just following after some man. Maybe he just needed a break or was partying in New York for the weekend. Tommy shook his head; Cassandra told him that Martin's unpaid fines had caught up with him and that he would be gone a while. No more needed to be said. There was no talk of keeping the agency running. Without Martin to hold the fraying fabric together, *College Boys* could not survive in any form. It was done, and now done for good. All of us knew it even though none of us admitted it. We chatted briefly with Tommy for a minute and then he had to go. Our eyes shifted from his back to the front door, and then to him as we turned away and got into the car for the long return drive to campus. *College Boys* was done. We never talked to or heard from Martin again.

EPILOGUE

In the three years since we last saw Tommy on the steps of the new house, contact with the escorts has been sporadic and decreasing. At first, we heard from a few of the men who wanted to know what happened and where they could contact Martin. We told them what we could, but we really knew very little; and we had no idea how to find Martin. Cassandra offered to let us interview the women working for her side of the agency, but we chose not to do it given all that had occurred. Looking back we speculate about the wisdom of that decision, and wonder today if we made it too quickly out of shock or grief. Researchers should not get so attached to their subjects, but in these types of more anthropological projects over a number of years you do come to develop feelings for the people and begin to care about what happens to them. Maybe we needed to "cut the cord" as it were and return to a more objective and rational stance about *College Boys*. Maybe we ourselves were just done with the project after working on it for so long and the final closing of Martin's agency gave us a convenient reason to end the interviews. Did we also feel the loss of Martin and could no longer maintain that bond without him? If so, it would be a powerful testament to his personal charm and the warmth of his heart. We still miss him and wish him all the best, wherever he may be.

Of the *College Boys* themselves we know little. We talked with Tommy again about two years after the agency went under. He and Michael were still together in a house they had bought. Tommy finished college and they were working, living the American Dream. Joshua had a boyfriend and were doing well. They lived with a former client who had hired them into his business. They seemed to have a polyamorous relationship with the older man who they both seemed to adore and appreciate—all was well on their front. Reese moved out to the West Coast and we still keep in touch with him on Facebook. He is having a grand time as an attractive single man in California. His sparkle has only seemed to improve with time. We know that one of the escorts got in trouble with immigration and was deported from the United States, while another finished his biology degree and went to nursing school in another state.

We wish we knew more about everyone we interviewed. If any *College Boys* happen upon this book, know that your trust and openness is sincerely appreciated and that we thank you for sharing your lives with us. We value you, respect you, and wish you all the happiness that this roller coaster called life can provide.

"Money can't buy you love, but the rest is negotiable."–Rentboy.com manifesto

APPENDIX A

Demographic Characteristics of Agency Escorts ($N = 40$)

Characteristic	Number (%)
Age	
18–21	16 (40.0)
22–25	20 (50.0)
26–35	4 (10.0)
Education level	
Some high school	6 (15.0)
High school diploma	14 (35.0)
Current college student	5 (12.5)
Some college	5 (12.5)
2-year degree or certificate	5 (12.5)
College degree (4 years)	3 (7.5)
Graduate degree	2 (5.0)
Ethnicity	
African-American	0 (0.0)
Asian/Pacific Islander	2 (5.0)
Caucasian	30 (75.0)
Hispanic/Latino	5 (12.5)
Mixed	2 (5.0)
Other	1 (2.5)
Non-escorting employment	
None	14 (35.0)
Part-time	9 (22.5)
Full-time	17 (42.5)
Sexual orientation	
Bisexual	12 (30.0)
Heterosexual	7 (17.5)
Gay	21 (52.5)

APPENDIX B

Cast and Characters: Information about People Involved with *College Boys*

Name	Relationship with Martin*	Age	Race or Ethnicity	Sexual Identity	Education	Non-agency Employment
Martin	Self	26	Caucasian	Gay	High school diploma	None
Emilio	Advisor	18	Mixed ethnicity	Gay	2-year degree	Part-time
Andrew	Advisor	21	Caucasian	Bisexual	College student	Full-time
Tommy	Advisor	21	Caucasian	Gay	Some college	None
Nathan	Advisor	24	Caucasian	Gay	College student	Full-time
Becky	Companion	21	Caucasian	Heterosexual	High school diploma	Part-time
Nick	Companion	23	Caucasian	Bisexual	College student	Full-time
Dennis	Companion	24	Caucasian	Bisexual	High school diploma	Full-time
Michael	Companion	23	Hispanic/Latino	Bisexual	High School diploma	Full-time
Mike	Friend	23	Caucasian	Gay	2-year degree	None
Chase	Friend	18	Caucasian	Gay	High school diploma	Full-time
Zack	Friend	22	Caucasian	Bisexual	2-year degree	None
James	Associate	19	Caucasian	Gay	2-year degree	None
Marc	Associate	22	Caucasian	Bisexual	High school diploma	Full-time
Keith	Associate	23	Mixed ethnicity	Gay	Some college	Part-time
Sten	Associate	26	Other	Bisexual	Bachelor's degree	Full-time
Daniel	Associate	18	Caucasian	Gay	Some high school	None
Brian	Associate	19	Caucasian	Bisexual	High school diploma	Part-time
Rick	Associate	18	Caucasian	Gay	High school diploma	Full-time
Sergio	Associate	23	Hispanic/Latino	Gay	Bachelor's degree	Full-time
Berto	Associate	22	Hispanic/Latino	Gay	High school diploma	None
Joshua	Employee	26	Caucasian	Gay	Graduate school	Part-time

(Continued)

Name	Relationship with Martin*	Age	Race or Ethnicity	Sexual Identity	Education	Non-agency Employment
Frank	Employee	28	Caucasian	Gay	Some high school	None
Tom	Employee	29	Caucasian	Bisexual	Some college	None
Pete	Employee	20	Caucasian	Heterosexual	High school diploma	None
Jerry	Employee	23	Caucasian	Gay	High school diploma	Full-time
Mason	Employee	24	Caucasian	Gay	Some college	None
Erick	Employee	19	Caucasian	Gay	Some high school	None
Hector	Employee	23	Hispanic/Latino	Gay	2-year degree	Full-time
Ben	Employee	23	Caucasian	Heterosexual	High school diploma	Full-time
Jeff	Employee	22	Asian/Pacific Islander	Bisexual	College student	Part-time
Ethan	Employee	20	Caucasian	Gay	College student	Full-time
Ned	Employee	24	Caucasian	Heterosexual	High school diploma	None
Richard	Employee	35	Caucasian	Gay	Graduate school	Full-time
Allen	Employee	22	Caucasian	Heterosexual	High school diploma	None
John	Employee	19	Caucasian	Bisexual	High school diploma	Part-time
Tony	Employee	18	Hispanic/Latino	Heterosexual	Some high school	Part-time
Patrick	Employee	23	Caucasian	Heterosexual	High school diploma	Part-time
Wes	Employee	22	Caucasian	Bisexual	High school diploma	Full-time

Definitions of Relationships with Martin
Advisor: Part of Martin's inner circle. People he relied upon heavily.
Companion: Martin's closest friends and sources of emotional support.
Friend: People with whom Martin socialized. They enjoyed each other's company and frequently spent time together.
Associate: Escorts working with the agency who were on friendly terms with Martin, but with whom he did not spend much time.
Employee: Those individuals least socially connected to the agency.

REFERENCES

Allen, D. M. (1980). Young male prostitutes: A psychosocial study. *Archives of Sexual Behavior, 9*, 399–426.

Bailey, J. M., & Zucker, K. J. (1995). Childhood sex-typed behavior and sexual orientation: A conceptual analysis and quantitative review. *Developmental Psychology, 31*, 43–55.

Bandura, A. (1977). Self-efficacy: Toward a unifying theory of behavior change. *Psychological Review, 84*, 191–215.

Bandura, A. (1978). The self system in reciprocal determinism. *American Psychologist, 33*, 344–358.

Bimbi, D. S. (2007). Male prostitution: Pathology, paradigms, and progress in research. *Journal of Homosexuality, 53*, 7–35.

Bimbi, D. S., & Parsons, J. T. (2005). Barebacking among internet based male sex workers. *Journal of Gay and Lesbian Psychotherapy, 9*, 85–105.

Blass, T. (1984). Social psychology and personality: Toward a convergence. *Journal of Personality and Social Psychology, 47*, 1013–1027.

Bordieu, P., & Passeron, J.-C. (1977 [1970]). *Reproduction in Education, Society, and Culture* (R. Nice, Trans.). London, England: Sage.

Butts, W. M. (1947). Boy prostitutes of the metropolis. *Journal of Clinical Psychopathy, 8*, 673–681.

Cates, J. A., & Markley, J. (1992). Demographic, clinical, and personality variables associated with male prostitution by choice. *Adolescence, 27*, 695–707.

Coleman, E. (1989). The development of male prostitution activity among gay and bisexual adolescents. *Journal of Homosexuality, 17*, 131–149.

Craft, M. (1966). Boy prostitutes and their fate. *British Journal of Psychiatry, 112*, 1111–1114.

Daly, I. (2010, January 13). Exclusive: Meet America's first legal male prostitute: Former Marine "Markus" auditioned at Nevada's Shady Lady Ranch for a chance to sell his body. He got the job, but at what price?, *Details*. Retrieved from http://www.details.com/sex-relationships/sex-and-other-releases/201001/americas -first-legal-male-prostitute.

Deisher, R. W., Eisner, V., & Sulzbacher, S. I. (1969). The young male prostitute. *Pediatrics, 43,* 936–941.

Dennis, J. P. (2008). Women are victims, men make choices: The invisibility of men and boys in the global sex trade. *Gender Issues, 25,* 11–25.

Dorais, M. (2005). *Rent Boys: The World of Male Sex Workers.* Montreal, Quebec: McGill -Queen's University Press.

Dover, K. J. (1989). *Greek Homosexuality.* Cambridge, MA: Harvard University Press.

Earls, C. M., & David, H. D. (1989). A psychosocial study of male prostitution. *Archives of Sexual Behavior, 18,* 401–419.

El-Bassel, N., Schilling, R. F., Gilbert, L., Faruque, S., Irwin, K. L., & Edlin, B. R. (2000). Sex trading and psychological distress in a street-based sample of low-income urban men. *Journal of Psychoactive Drugs, 32,* 259–267.

Estep, R., Waldorf, D., & Marotta, T. (1992). Sexual behavior of male prostitutes. In Huber, J. & Schneider, B. E. (Eds.), *The Social Context of AIDS* (pp. 95–109). Newbury Park, CA: Sage.

Fitzpatrick, L. (2010, April 20). Why do women still earn less than men? Retrieved September 29, 2010, from http://www.time.com/time/nation/article/ 0,8599,1983185,00.html.

Grammer, K., Fink, B., Møller, A. P., & Thornhill, R. (2003). Darwinian aesthetics: Sexual selection and the biology of beauty. *Biological Reviews, 78,* 385–407.

Greene, J. M., Ennett, S. T., & Ringwalt, C. L. (1999). Prevalence and correlates of survival sex among runaway and homeless youth. *American Journal of Public Health, 89,* 1406–1409.

Grov, C., Bimbi, D. S., Parsons, J. T., & Nanín, J. E. (2006). Race, ethnicity, gender, and generational factors associated with the coming-out process among gay, lesbian, and bisexual individuals. *The Journal of Sex Research, 43*(2), 115–121.

Haley, N., Roy, E., Leclerc, P., Boudreau, J. F., & Boivin, J. F. (2004). HIV risk profile of male street youth involved in survival sex. *Sexual Transmission of Infections, 80,* 526–530. doi: 80/6/526 [pii] 10.1136/sti.2004.010728.

Hill, C. A., & Preston, L. K. (1996). Individual differences in the experience of sexual motivation: Theory and measurement of dispositional sexual motives. *The Journal of Sex Research, 33*(1), 27–45.

Koken, J. A., Bimbi, D. S., & Parsons, J. T. (2009). Comparing male and female escorts. In R. Weitzer (Ed.), *Sex for Sale: Prostitution, Pornography, and the Sex Industry* (2nd ed.). New York: Routledge.

Koken, J. A., Bimbi, D. S., Parsons, J. T., & Halkitis, P. N. (2004). The experience of stigma in the lives of male internet escorts. *Journal of Psychology and Human Sexuality, 16,* 13–32.

Kruglanski, A. W., Shah, J. Y., Pierro, A., & Mannetti, L. (2002). When similarity breeds content: Need for closure and the allure of homogeneous and self-resembling groups. *Journal of Personality and Social Psychology, 83,* 648–662.

Leichtentritt, R. D., & Arad, B. D. (2005). Young male street workers: Life histories and current experiences. *British Journal of Social Work,* 483–509.

Maddux, J. E., Norton, L. W., & Stoltenberg, C. D. (1986). Self-efficacy expectancy, outcome expectancy, and outcome value: Relative effects on behavioral intention. *Journal of Personality and Social Psychology, 51,* 783–789.

Mimiaga, M. J., Reisner, S. L., Tinsley, J. P., Mayer, K. H., & Safren, S. A. (2009). Street workers and internet escorts: Contextual and psychosocial factors surrounding HIV risk behavior among men who engage in sex work with other men. *Journal of Urban Health, 86,* 54–66.

Minichiello, V., Marino, R., Browne, J., Jamieson, M., Peterson, K., Reuter, B., & Robinson, K. (2000). Commercial sex between men: A prospective diary-based study. *Journal of Sex Research, 37,* 151–161.

Mischel, W., & Shoda, Y. (1995). A cognitive-affective system of personality: Reconceptualizing situations, dispositions, dynamics, and invariance in personality structure. *Psychological Review, 102,* 246–268.

Morrison, T. G., & Whitehead, B. W. (2007). "Nobody's ever going to make a fag pretty woman": Stigma awareness and the putative effects of stigma among a sample of Canadian male sex workers. *Journal of Homosexuality, 53,* 201–217.

Morse, E. V., Simon, P. M., Balson, P. M., & Osofsky, H. J. (1992). Sexual behavior patterns of customers of male street prostitutes. *Archives of Sexual Behavior, 21,* 347–357.

Morse, E. V., Simon, P. M., Baus, S. A., Balson, P. M., & Osofsky, H. J. (1992). Cofactors of substance use among male street prostitutes. *The Journal of Drug Issues, 22,* 897–994.

Morse, E. V., Simon, P. M., Osofsky, H. J., Balson, P. M., & Gaumer, H. R. (1991). The male street prostitute: A vector for transmission of HIV infection into the heterosexual world. *Social Science and Medicine, 32,* 535–539.

Nemoto, T., Iwamoto, M., Oh, H. J., Wong, S., & Nguyen, H. (2005). Risk behaviors among Asian women who work at massage parlors in San Francisco: perspectives from masseuses and owners/managers. *AIDS Education and Prevention, 17,* 444–456. doi: 10.1521/aeap.2005.17.5.444

Nemoto, T., Operario, D., Takenaka, M., Iwamoto, M., & Le, M. N. (2003). HIV risk among Asian women working at massage parlors in San Francisco. *AIDS Education and Prevention, 15,* 245–256.

Newman, P. A., Rhodes, F., & Weiss, R. E. (1998). Correlates of sex trading among drug-using men who have sex with men. *American Journal of Public Health, 94,* 1998–2003.

Padilla, M. (2007). Caribbean *Pleasure Industry: Tourism, Sexuality, and AIDS in the Dominican Republic.* Chicago, IL: University of Chicago Press.

Parker, M. (2005). Core groups and the transmission of HIV: Learning from male sex workers. *Journal of Biosocial Science, 00,* 1–15.

Parsons, J. T., Bimbi, D. S., & Halkitis, P. N. (2001). Sexual compulsivity among gay/bisexual male escorts who advertise on the Internet. *Journal of Sexual Addiction and Compulsivity, 8,* 113–123.

Parsons, J. T., Koken, J. A., & Bimbi, D. S. (2007). Looking beyond HIV: eliciting individual and community needs of male internet escorts. *Journal of Homosexuality, 53,* 219–240.

Parsons, J. T., Koken, J. A., & Bimbi, D. S. (2004). The use of the Internet by gay and bisexual male escorts: Sex workers as sex educators. *AIDS Care, 16*(8):1021–1035.

Peplau, L. A. (2003). Human sexuality: How do men and women differ? *Current Directions in Psychological Science, 12,* 37–40.

Pervin, L. A. (2001). A dynamic systems model of personality. *European Psychologist, 6,* 172–176.

Pillard, R. C. (1991). Masculinity and femininity in homosexuality: "Inversion" revisited. In J. C. Gonsiorek & J. D. Weinrich (Eds.), *Homosexuality: Research implications for public policy* (pp. 32–43). Newbury Park, CA: Sage.

Polybius (1979). *The Rise of the Roman Empire* (I. Scott-Kilvert, Trans.). New York: Penguin Classics. (Original work published in second century BCE.)

Powers, A. (2010, January 6). Male prostitution is Nevada's newest legal profession—After months of debate in the state's surprisingly squeamish brothel community, Nye County officials agree to let Shady Lady Ranch near Death Valley hire men. *Los Angeles Times*. Retrieved from http://articles.latimes.com/2010/jan/06/nation/la-na -male-prostitutes6-2010jan06.

Price, V., Scanlon, B., & Janus, M. (1984). Social characteristics of adolescent male prostitution. *Victimology, 9*, 211–221.

Pruitt, M. (2005). Online boys: Male-for-male Internet escorts. *Sociological Focus, 38*, 189–203.

Reiss, A. J. (1961). The social integration of queers and peers. *Social Problems, 9*, 102–120.

Rhiannon, T. N., & Crisp, R. J. (2010). Explaining the relationship between group identi-fication and intergroup bias following recategorization: A self-regulation theory analysis. *Group Processes and Intergroup Relations, 13*, 251–261.

Rietmeijer, C. A., Wolitski, R. J., Fishbein, M., Corby, N. H., & Cohn, D. L. (1998). Sex hustling, injection drug use, and non-gay identification by men who have sex with men: Associations with high-risk sexual behaviors and condom use. *Sexually Trans-mitted Diseases, 25*, 353–360.

Rosario, M., Schrimshaw, E. W., & Hunter, J. (2004). Ethnic/racial differences in the coming-out process of lesbian, gay, and bisexual youths: A comparison of sexual identity development over time. *Cultural Diversity and Ethnic Minority Psychology 10*(3): 215–228.

Savin-Williams, R. C. 2006. *The New Gay Teenager*. Cambridge: Harvard University Press.

Scott, J., Minichiello, V., Marino, R., Harvey, G. P., Jamieson, M., & Browne, J. (2005). Understanding the new context of the male sex work industry. *Journal of Interper-sonal Violence, 20*, 320–342.

Shaver, F. M. (2005). Sex work research: Methodological and ethical challenges. *Journal of Interpersonal Violence, 20*, 296–319.

Smith, M. D., Grov C., & Seal, D. W. (2008). Agency-based male sex work: A descriptive focus on physical, personal, and social space. *Journal of Men's Studies, 16*, 193–210.

Smith, M. D. & Seal, D. W. (2007). Sexual behavior, mental health, substance use, and HIV risk among agency-based male escorts in a small U.S. city. *International Journal of Sexual Health, 19*, 27–39.

Terry, D. J., & Hogg, M. A. (1996). Groups norms and the attitude-behavior relationship: A role for group identification. *Personality and Social Psychology Bulletin, 22*, 776–793.

Vanwesenbeeck, I. (2001). Another decade of social scientific work on sex work: A review of the research 1990–2000. *Annual Review of Sex Research, 12*, 242–300.

Venkatesh, S. (2010, September 12). Five myths about prostitution. *The Washington Post*. Retrieved September 14, 2010 from *washingtonpost.com*.

Weitzer, R. (2005). New directions in research on prostitution. *Crime, Law, and Social Change, 43*, 211–235.

INDEX

About the Authors and Series Editor

MICHAEL D. SMITH is Associate Professor of Psychology at Susquehanna University, where he divides his time between teaching, research, and university and community service. As a researcher he studies male prostitution, identity development, risk behavior, and HIV/AIDS prevention in young men. He is also a practicing clinical psychologist and a member of the American Psychological Association, Eastern Psychological Association, National Network of Rural HIV/STD Prevention Specialists, and the Society for the Scientific Study of Sexuality. He is widely published in professional journals and has made dozens of peer-reviewed presentations on issues related to public health, sex, and other issues.

CHRISTIAN GROV is Assistant Professor in the Department of Health and Nutrition Sciences at the Brooklyn College of the City University of New York, and a Faculty Affiliate with the Center for HIV/AIDS Educational Studies and Training (CHEST) in New York. His research interests center around sexual health, the Internet, and HIV/AIDS, and gay and bisexual men. The recipient of numerous fellowships and awards, he is member of the Society for the Scientific Study of Sexuality and the International Academy of Sex Research, among others. He is widely published in professional journals.

JUDY KURIANSKY, PhD, is an internationally known, licensed Clinical Psychologist and an adjunct faculty member in the Department of Clinical

Psychology at Columbia University Teachers College and in the Department of Psychiatry at Columbia University College of Physicians and Surgeons. At the United Nations, she is an NGO representative for the International Association of Applied Psychology and for the World Council for Psychotherapy, and is an executive member of the Committee of Mental Health. She is also a Visiting Professor at the Peking University Health Sciences Center, a Fellow of the American Psychological Association, cofounder of the APA Media Psychology Division, and on the board of the Peace Division and U.S. Doctors for Africa. Certified as a sex therapist by the American Association of Sex Educators and Counselors, she is a pioneer in the field of sexuality. An award-winning journalist, she hosted for years the popular "LovePhones" syndicated call-in radio show, was a feature reporter for WCBS-TV and CNBC, and still regularly comments on news and current events for television worldwide. Her wide-ranging expertise in interpersonal and international relations is evident in her books ranging from *The Complete Idiot's Guide to a Healthy Relationship* and *Sexuality Education: Past, Present and Future* to *Beyond Bullets and Bombs: Grassroots Peacebuilding between Israelis and Palestinians*. Her website is www.DrJudy.com.